What Matters Most:
Teaching for America's Future

Report of the National Commission on
Teaching & America's Future

September 1996

Contents

Appendices

Acknowledgments

The Commission wishes to express its gratitude to the many individuals and organizations who have helped make this report possible. We are grateful to those who have advised us in our work: the presenters who have shared so much of their knowledge; the advisory groups that have come together to offer support and advice; the focus groups of parents and teachers who shared their valuable insights with us; and the many who gave us feedback at Commission forums. We can hardly begin to acknowledge the invaluable contributions of so many here. We list their names in Appendices B (Commission Presentations), C (Commission Advisers), D (Research Contributors), and E (Commissioned Papers).

None of this work would have possible without the vision and guidance of our funders, the Rockefeller Foundation and Carnegie Corporation of New York. They have also extended to us a commitment and generosity that goes well beyond the financial support. We especially want to thank Marla Ucelli and Jamie Beck Jensen of the Rockefeller Foundation, and Vivien Stewart and Karin Egan of Carnegie Corporation of New York, whose support and advice were always invaluable.

Several people have also helped in various stages of assembling data and writing this report—Barnett Berry, James Harvey, Gary Sykes, Anne C. Lewis, Richard M. Ingersoll, David Monk, Eileen Sclan—and we thank them for their valuable assistance.

Preface

As you read this report, I hope you will listen to the teachers, the parents, and the children—the real people behind the studies and the numbers we present here. We did, and we were guided by what we heard.

One voice that made a tremendous impact on us was that of Evelyn Jenkins Gunn, an English teacher from Pelham, New York, who explained her passion for teaching—not why she teaches, but why she is *compelled* to teach:

> I was supposed to be a welfare statistic. . . . It is because of a teacher that I sit at this table. I remember her telling us one cold, miserable day that she could not make our clothing better; she could not provide us with food; she could not change the terrible segregated conditions under which we lived. She *could* introduce us to the world of reading, the world of books, and that is what she did.
>
> What a world! I visited Asia and Africa. I saw magnificent sunsets; I tasted exotic foods; I fell in love and danced in wonderful halls. I ran away with escaped slaves and stood beside a teenage martyred saint. I visited lakes and streams and composed lines of verse. I knew then that I wanted to help children do the same things. I wanted to weave magic. . . .

As Evelyn Jenkins Gunn understands, good teachers literally save lives. However they do it—by loving students, helping them imagine the future, and insisting that they meet high expectations and standards—the best of them are magic weavers. Many of us can remember such a teacher—one who changed our lives, so gifted that he or she transported us out of our own time and place and circumstances and jump-started the dreams and possibilities that lie within us all.

In the end, supporting the Evelyn Jenkins Gunns of this world—and, through them, all of their students—is what this Commission on Teaching & America's Future is about.

I believe the conclusions and recommendations of this report speak for themselves. Standards for students and teachers are the key to reforming American education. Access to competent teaching must become a new student right. Access to high-quality preparation, induction, and professional development must become a new teacher right. The reform movement of the last decade cannot succeed unless it attends to the improvement of teaching. If we pay attention to supporting knowledgeable teachers who work in productive schools, American education need suffer through no more dead-end reforms.

My colleagues on the Commission have been candid with each other in our discussions, and they have thought hard about what needs to be done. We hope this document launches a great debate about the critical link between improving the capacities of teachers and the future of the United States. Although each of us has distinctive ideas about what needs to be done, we are unanimous in supporting the recommendations of this report.

Finally we appreciate the hard-working staff that facilitated and supported the process of our work. Executive Director Linda Darling-Hammond's vision, expertise, and unquenchable energy provided us with a vision of the future that could be. We have been ably assisted by Associate Director Velma L. Cobb; Communications Director E. Jane Beckwith; Administrative Associate Margaret Garigan; Research Associates Marcella L. Bullmaster, Ellalinda Rustique-Forrester, and Vezuvira Kavemuii Murangi; and Senior Policy Adviser David Haselkorn. The staff, like my colleagues on the Commission, never lost sight of the fact that America's future depends on finding the best teachers, helping them develop their skills to the greatest extent, and rewarding them for their work on behalf of children and youth.

James B. Hunt Jr. (Chair)
Governor, State of North Carolina

The National Commission on Teaching & America's Future

Juanita Millender-McDonald
Congresswoman, State of California,
Washington, D.C.

Lynne Miller
Professor of Education Administration and Leadership,
University of Southern Maine, Gorham, Maine

Damon P. Moore
Teacher, Dennis Middle School, Richmond, Indiana

Annette N. Morgan
Representative, District 39, Missouri House of
Representatives, Jefferson City, Missouri

J. Richard Munro
Chairman, Executive Committee of the Board of Directors,
Time Warner Inc., New York, New York

Hugh B. Price
President & Chief Executive Officer,
National Urban League, Inc., New York, New York

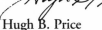

David Rockefeller Jr.
Chairman, Rockefeller Financial Services, Inc.,
New York, New York

Ted Sanders
President, Southern Illinois University, Carbondale, Illinois

Albert Shanker
President, American Federation of Teachers, Washington, D.C.

Lynn F. Stuart
Principal, Cambridgeport School, Cambridge, Massachusetts

Robert L. Wehling
Senior Vice President, The Procter & Gamble Company,
Cincinnati, Ohio

Arthur E. Wise
President, National Council for Accreditation of Teacher
Education, Washington, D.C.

Richard Wisniewski
Director, Institute for Educational Innovation,
University of Tennessee, Knoxville, Tennessee

Linda Darling-Hammond (Executive Director)
Teachers College, Columbia University, New York, New York

Executive Summary

This report offers what we believe is the single most important strategy for achieving America's educational goals: A blueprint for recruiting, preparing, and supporting excellent teachers in all of America's schools. The plan is aimed at ensuring that all communities have teachers with the knowledge and skills they need to teach so that all children can learn, and all school systems are organized to support teachers in this work. A caring, competent, and qualified teacher for every child is the most important ingredient in education reform.

The Commission's proposals are systemic in scope—not a recipe for more short-lived pilots and demonstration projects. They require a dramatic departure from the status quo—one that creates a new infrastructure for professional learning and an accountability system that ensures attention to standards for educators as well as students at every level—national, state, local school district, school, and classroom.

This Commission starts from three simple premises:

1. *What teachers know and can do is the most important influence on what students learn.*

2. *Recruiting, preparing, and retaining good teachers is the central strategy for improving our schools.*

3. *School reform cannot succeed unless it focuses on creating the conditions in which teachers can teach, and teach well.*

We propose an audacious goal for America's future. Within a decade—by the year 2006—we will provide every student in America with what should be his or her educational birthright: access to competent, caring, qualified teaching in schools organized for success. This is a challenging goal to put before the nation and its educational leaders. But if the goal is challenging and requires unprecedented effort, it does not require unprecedented new theory. Common sense suffices: American students are entitled to teachers who know their subjects, understand their students and what they need, and have developed the skills required to make learning come alive.

However, based on its two-year study, the Commission identified a number of barriers to achieving this goal. They include:
- Low expectations for student performance.
- Unenforced standards for teachers.
- Major flaws in teacher preparation.
- Painfully slipshod teacher recruitment.

- Inadequate induction for beginning teachers.
- Lack of professional development and rewards for knowledge and skill.
- Schools that are structured for failure rather than success.

We offer five major recommendations to address these concerns and accomplish our goal.

I. Get serious about standards, for both students and teachers.

- Establish professional standards boards in every state.
- Insist on accreditation for all schools of education.
- Close inadequate schools of education.
- License teachers based on demonstrated performance, including tests of subject matter knowledge, teaching knowledge, and teaching skill.
- Use National Board standards as the benchmark for accomplished teaching.

II. Reinvent teacher preparation and professional development.

- Organize teacher education and professional development programs around standards for students and teachers.
- Develop extended, graduate-level teacher-preparation programs that provide a yearlong internship in a professional development school.
- Create and fund mentoring programs for beginning teachers, along with evaluation of teaching skills.
- Create stable, high-quality sources of professional development.

III. Fix teacher recruitment and put qualified teachers in every classroom.

- Increase the ability of low-wealth districts to pay for qualified teachers, and insist that districts hire only qualified teachers.
- Redesign and streamline district hiring.
- Eliminate barriers to teacher mobility.
- Aggressively recruit high-need teachers and provide incentives for teaching in shortage areas.

- Develop high-quality pathways to teaching for a wide range of recruits.

IV. Encourage and reward teacher knowledge and skill.

- Develop a career continuum for teaching linked to assessments and compensation systems that reward knowledge and skill.
- Remove incompetent teachers.
- Set goals and enact incentives for National Board Certification in every state and district. Aim to certify 105,000 teachers in this decade, one for every school in the United States.

V. Create schools that are organized for student and teacher success.

- Flatten hierarchies and reallocate resources to send more dollars to the front lines of schools: Invest more in teachers and technology and less in nonteaching personnel.
- Provide venture capital in the form of challenge grants to schools for teacher learning linked to school improvement and rewards for team efforts that lead to improved practice and greater learning.
- Select, prepare, and retain principals who understand teaching and learning and who can lead high-performing schools.

Developing recommendations is easy. Implementing them is hard work. The first step is to recognize that these ideas must be pursued together—as an entire tapestry that is tightly interwoven. Pulling on a single thread will create a tangle rather than tangible progress. The second step is to build upon the substantial work that has been undertaken over the past decade. All across the country, successful programs for recruiting, educating, and mentoring new teachers have sprung up. Professional networks and teacher academies have been launched; many education school programs have been redesigned; higher standards for licensing teachers and accrediting education schools have been developed; and a National Board for Professional Teaching Standards is now fully established and beginning to define and reward accomplished teaching. All these endeavors, and those of many others, form the foundation of this crusade.

What Matters Most: Teaching for America's Future

When my daughter starts school, I'm hoping for a teacher who is spontaneous, someone who can follow a curriculum and yet meet the emotional and social needs of children as well. I hope for someone who has a vivid imagination and knows how to use ordinary objects to teach valuable lessons. I want my daughter to be exposed to as many cultures and ethnic groups as possible, and I want her to be academically motivated and challenged. That will take a teacher who is sensitive to the individual needs of each student. If my daughter is slow, I want a teacher who is immediately looking into that, and if she's surpassing the class, I want her to get what she needs and progress as far as she can. I want a teacher who has conflict resolution skills, who creates discipline, but not from his or her emotions. I want a teacher who uses different methods and different ways of reaching students—who can think in innovative ways and challenge the children while teaching them academically.
— Laurine Carson, a mother in Newark, New Jersey

Every year on the first day of school, parents and students await the assignment of new teachers with a mixture of eagerness and anxiety. Parents with clout often lobby to get their students into certain classes, knowing that their children's learning will depend on the quality of the curriculum and teaching they are exposed to that year. Those with means either move to affluent communities or turn to private schools in the hope of finding better teaching. Families unable to do either, but who live within reach of a "magnet" school, sometimes camp out overnight to get their students registered with some of the best teachers in the district who are working in schools that are organized to support their efforts.

These parents spend tremendous energy in search of good teaching because they know what a difference it will make to their children's future. Most of them can remember at least one outstanding teacher who made a difference in their own lives. Policymakers are just beginning to grasp what parents have always known: that teaching is the most important element of successful learning. Teaching quality will make the critical difference not only to the futures of individual children but to America's future as well.

The need for excellent teaching grows ever more pressing. On March 26, 1996, the nation's governors and President Clinton joined business leaders and educators in a National Education Summit to reaffirm their commitment to achieving higher academic standards for America's schools and students. The governors pledged to develop internationally competitive academic standards and assessments in each state within the next two years and to reallocate funds to provide the professional development, infrastructure, and new technologies needed to meet these goals. Business leaders announced their commitment to support employees' involvement in their children's education, to require evidence of academic achievement for hiring, and to make states' education standards a key factor in business location decisions. All the participants pledged to roll up their sleeves and get down to work immediately to respond to the urgent need for schools to improve so that all graduates have higher levels of skills and knowledge. Nevada Governor Bob Miller expressed the shared view: "We owe it to our children to put higher academic standards in place. If we don't, we're robbing them of their future."

This sense of urgency is well founded. There has been no previous time in history when the success, indeed the survival, of nations and people has been so tightly tied to their ability to learn.[1] Today's society has little room for those who cannot read, write, and compute proficiently; find and use resources; frame and solve problems; and continually learn new technologies, skills, and occupations. The economy of high-wage jobs for low-skilled workers is fast disappearing. In contrast to only 20 years ago, individuals who do not succeed in school have little chance of finding a job or contributing to society—and societies that do not succeed at education have little chance of success in a global economy.

Because of this, America's future depends now, as never before, on our ability to teach. If every citizen is to be prepared for a democratic society whose major product is knowledge, every teacher must know how to teach students in ways that help them reach high levels of intellectual and social competence. Every school must be organized to support powerful teaching and learning. Every school district must be able to find and keep good teachers. And every community must be focused on preparing students to become competent citizens and workers in a pluralistic, technological society.

This report offers what we believe is the single most important strategy for achieving America's educational goals: A blueprint for recruiting, preparing, and supporting excellent teachers in all of America's schools. This plan is aimed at ensuring that all communities have teachers with the knowledge and skills they need to teach so that all children can learn and that all school systems are organized to support teachers in this work. A caring, competent, and qualified teacher for every child is the most important ingredient in education reform and, we believe, the most frequently overlooked.

Furthermore, to be effective, such teachers must work in schools and school systems that are well designed to achieve their key academic mission and to support student learning. They must be focused on clear, high standards for students; organized to provide a coherent, high-quality curriculum across the grades; designed to support teachers' collective work and learning on behalf of their students; and structured to allow for ongoing parent engagement.

The most important contribution we as educators can make to the well-being of children is to enable them to deal effectively with their universe. . . . This is not, of course, a trivial task. It combines a number of concerns, ranging from teaching basic skills to readying students for the marketplace. In essence, it combines giving them the tools to analyze a situation to make an appropriate response, the self-confidence to use those tools, and the pride and motivation to use them with excellence.

— JOHN SNYDER, COMPUTER SCIENCE TEACHER, ADVANCED TECHNOLOGIES ACADEMY IN LAS VEGAS, NEVADA

We note that this challenge is accompanied by an equally great opportunity: Over the next decade we will recruit and hire more than two million teachers for America's schools. More than half the teachers who will be teaching ten years from now will be hired during the next decade. If we can focus our energies on preparing this generation of teachers with the kinds of knowledge and skills they need to succeed in helping students reach these goals, and on creating schools that use their talents well, we will have made an enormous contribution to America's future.

The Missing Link: Investment in Teachers

In 1983, *A Nation at Risk* declared our schools were drowning in a "rising tide of mediocrity."[2] Since then, hundreds of pieces of legislation have been enacted to improve them. In 1989, the nation's governors developed a set of education goals to further focus attention on the long-term work yet to be done. The goals boldly project that by the year 2000 all our students will come to school ready to learn; they will learn in safe, drug-free environments; virtually all of them will graduate with high levels of academic skills; and they will rank first in the world in mathematics and science.

Seven years later, America is still a very long way from realizing this future. Instead of all children coming to school ready to learn, more are living in poverty and without guaranteed health care than in the past.[3] Graduation rates and student achievement in most subjects have remained flat or have increased only slightly.[4] Only a small fraction of high school students can read, write, compute,

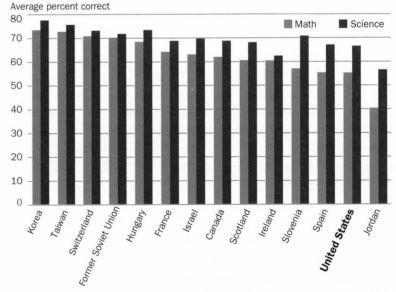

Mathematics and Science Test Scores of 13-Year-Olds
International Assessment of Educational Progress (IAEP): 1991

Average percent correct

Source: Educational Testing Service, International Assessment of Educational Progress, *Learning Mathematics and Science*. Published in *Digest of Education Statistics* 1995 (Washington, D.C., National Center for Education Statistics, 1995), pp. 432, 435

and manage scientific material at the high levels required for today's knowledge-work jobs. According to national assessments, only about 10% of U.S. 17-year-olds can draw conclusions using detailed scientific knowledge; just 7% can solve math problems with more than one step; only 7% can read and understand specialized materials; and a mere 2% can write well-developed material.[5] Meanwhile, international tests continue to show U.S. high school students ranking near the bottom in mathematics and science.[6]

This distance between our stated goals and current realities is not due to lack of effort. Many initiatives have been launched by legislators, educators, businesses, and community organizations to improve education, and many of these have had a positive effect in local communities. Nonetheless, we have reached an impasse in spreading these promising efforts to the system as a whole.

After a decade of reform, we have finally learned in hindsight what should have been clear from the start: Most schools and teachers cannot produce the kind of learning demanded by the new reforms—not because they do not want to, but because they do not know how, and the systems in which they work do not support them in doing so. Most states and school districts have not yet put in place standards and curriculum frameworks that provide clear signals about the kinds of academic learning they value. They provide few opportunities for principals and teachers to learn how to redesign their organizations and curriculum to be more effective. And most current educators were prepared years ago in programs that did not envision the kinds of challenges schools now confront and did not have access to the knowledge about teaching and learning available today.

When it comes to widespread change, we have behaved as though national, state, and district mandates could, like magic wands, transform schools. But all the directives and proclamations are simply so much fairy dust. Successful programs cannot be replicated in schools where staff lack the know-how and resources to bring them to life. Wonderful curriculum ideas fall flat in classrooms where they are not understood or supported by the broader activities of the school. And increased graduation and testing requirements only create greater failure if teachers do not know how to reach students so that they can learn.

On the whole, the school reform movement has ignored the obvious: What teachers know and can do makes the crucial difference in what children learn. And the ways school systems organize their work makes a big difference in what teachers can accomplish. New courses, tests, and curriculum reforms can be important starting points, but they are meaningless if teachers cannot use them productively. Policies can improve schools only if the people in them are armed with the knowledge, skills, and supports they need. Student learning in this country will improve only when we focus our efforts on improving teaching.

Instead of mandates and directives, our schools need agreement on purposes and support to meet new standards. Rather than proclamations, schools need policies and working environments that attract the best people to teaching, provide them superb preparation, hone their skills and commitment in the early years, and keep them in the profession by rewarding them for their knowledge, skills, and good work.

The teacher must remain the key. . . . Debates over educational policy are moot, if the primary agents of instruction are incapable of performing their functions well. No microcomputer will replace them, no television system will clone and distribute them, no scripted lessons will direct and control them, no voucher system will bypass them.

— *LEE SHULMAN,*
PROFESSOR

This Commission starts from three simple premises:

1. **What teachers know and can do is the most important influence on what students learn.**

2. **Recruiting, preparing, and retaining good teachers is the central strategy for improving our schools.**

3. **School reform cannot succeed unless it focuses on creating the conditions in which teachers can teach, and teach well.**

The Importance of Teacher Knowledge

The first premise is one that virtually every parent understands and a large body of research confirms: **What teachers know and do is the most important influence on what students learn.** Competent and caring teaching should be a student right.

Research has discovered a great deal about effective teaching and learning: We know that students learn best when new ideas are connected to what they already know and have experienced; when they are actively engaged in applying and testing their knowledge using real-world problems; when their learning is organized around clear, high goals with lots of practice in reaching them; and when they can use their own interests and strengths as springboards for learning.[7] When teachers can work together to build a coherent learning experience for students throughout the grades and within and across subject areas—one that is guided by common curriculum goals and expectations—they are able to engender greater student achievement.[8]

We also know that expert teachers use knowledge about children and their learning to fashion lessons that connect ideas to students' experiences. They create a wide variety of learning opportunities that make subject matter come alive for young people who learn in very different ways. They know how to support students' continuing development and motivation to achieve while creating incremental steps that help students progress toward more complicated ideas and performances. They know how to diagnose sources of problems in students' learning and how to identify strengths on which to build. These skills make the difference between teaching that creates learning and teaching that just marks time.[9]

Needless to say, this kind of teaching requires high levels of knowledge and skill. To be effective, teachers must know their subject matter so thoroughly that they can present it in a challenging, clear, and compelling way. They must also know how their students learn and how to make ideas accessible so that they can construct successful "teachable moments." Research confirms that teacher knowledge of subject matter, student learning, and teaching methods are all important elements of teacher effectiveness.[10]

Furthermore, studies show that teacher expertise is the most important factor in student achievement. A recent study of more than 1,000 school districts concluded that every additional dollar spent on more highly qualified teachers netted greater improvements in student achievement than did any other use of

Making the Connection: Teaching for Real Learning

Hector Ibarra's middle-school science students are not yet researchers at Cal Tech or graduate students at MIT, but they already are scientists in the making. They identify and monitor the levels of radon, carbon dioxide, and electromagnetic radiation. They investigate the efficiency of water and energy fixtures. They measure the flow rates of sink aerators, retrofit water-consuming toilet tanks, and compare the energy used by incandescent and fluorescent light bulbs. They design, build, and race miniature solar cars.

"My approach to teaching builds upon the natural curiosity that is an integral part of all children," says Hector, who teaches earth and life sciences at West Branch Middle School in West Branch, Iowa. He develops hands-on environmental projects that guide students through their own discoveries and allow for real-life applications. All of his experiments are written in a question format requiring students to form a hypothesis, develop a procedure, collect and analyze data, and arrive at conclusions.

Hector's assignments encourage his students to go beyond the walls of their school. In a research project he designed with two public utility companies and a private management firm, the entire student body of West Branch Middle School measured and compared the efficiency of water and energy fixtures in their homes. The project won a host of awards, including one from the Environmental Protection Agency. According to EPA Administrator William Rice, the students' work "saved the community an estimated 40,000 gallons of water a week and helped reduce emissions of sulfur dioxide, carbon monoxide, and nitrogen dioxide through the use of energy-saving practices and devices."

Hector exposes his students to the cutting edge of scientific research and keeps himself there as well. Like his mother, an elementary teacher in his native Mexico who gave birth to him in the one-room schoolhouse where she taught, Ibarra lives education. Maybe that explains why, even with a full teaching load, Hector Ibarra is still going to school, at work on his doctorate in science education.

*   *   *

What are bubble blowers, tiny trucks, and a mini-merry-go-round doing in a precalculus classroom? They are helping Frank Vanzant bring complex mathematical concepts to life for his high school students at Tullahoma High School in Tullahoma, Tennessee. Having come to math education from a career in electrical engineering, Vanzant understands the importance of students' developing an appreciation for math in the real world.

The measure of his success in his trigonometry, precalculus, and Advanced Placement calculus courses can be seen in his students' achievements. More than half of Frank's students earn scores at the "exceptionally well-qualified" level on the AP tests in calculus, as compared with about 17% nationally. Students like Genetta Gibson, who went on to major in engineering at Tennessee Tech, are living testimony to his influence. "I just loved him as a teacher," says Genetta. "He really cared whether or not we all understood what he was teaching."

Frank's commitment to his work runs deep. "I know of no other profession that can be as rewarding as teaching," he avers. "A teacher's influence on his students and society can never be fully observed or measured."

Behind Frank Vanzant's problem-solving drive and can-do spirit lies the reflective, questioning, philosophical nature that is indispensable in some measure to all educators. "I believe," he says, "that teachers should constantly evaluate and adjust their methods in the classroom to better meet the needs of the students and society. The most effective teachers are those who also view themselves as professional students. Teaching demands not only leading students toward developing a desire to learn, but also maintaining that desire in oneself."

Adapted from the Milken Family Foundation, *The Impact of the Educator* (Santa Monica, Calif.: The Milken Family Foundation), pp. 10, 74. Copyright © 1995 by the Milken Family Foundation. Reprinted with permission.

Demand for K-12 Classroom Teachers
Projected through 2005

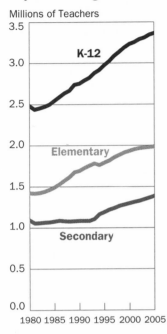

Source: U.S. Department of Education, *Projections of Education Statistics to 2005* (Washington, D.C.: National Center for Education Statistics, 1995), p. 72

school resources.[11] Another study, comparing high-achieving and low-achieving elementary schools with similar student characteristics, found that differences in teacher qualifications accounted for more than 90% of the variation in student achievement in reading and mathematics.[12]

At a time when all students must meet higher standards for learning, access to good teaching is a necessity, not a privilege to be left to chance. And competent teaching depends on educators who deeply understand subject matter and how to teach in ways that motivate children and help them learn. Like doctors, engineers, and other professionals, teachers must have access to high-quality education and career-long opportunities to update their skills if they are to do their jobs well. In addition, quality controls must work to ensure that those who cannot teach effectively do not enter or stay in the profession.

The Need to Prepare and Keep Good Teachers

The second premise is also one that policymakers are just now beginning to comprehend: **Recruiting, preparing, and retaining good teachers is the central strategy for improving our schools.** In the next decade, the United States will need to hire more than two million teachers to handle huge enrollment increases, replace an aging teacher workforce ready to retire, and respond to the chronic attrition of new teachers that plagues American schools. Although some of these will be former teachers returning to the field, most will be newly prepared during this time, and the quality of their preparation will, to a large extent, influence the quality of teaching our schools provide.

By 1998, America's schools will enroll more children, 52 million, than they have ever enrolled before, even at the height of the baby boom. Schools already report shortages of qualified teachers in subjects like mathematics, physics, chemistry, and bilingual and special education. High-poverty urban and rural schools face persistent hurdles in hiring the teachers they need, and across the nation there is a critical need for many more teachers who reflect the racial and cultural mix of students in schools. Yet many school districts do little to recruit teachers or to keep good ones in the profession. They treat teachers like easily replaceable, interchangeable cogs in a wheel, meeting most of their personnel needs with last-minute scrambles to put warm bodies in classrooms.

In addition, current reforms have created new expectations for teachers that most have not been prepared to meet. To help diverse learners master much more challenging content, teachers must go far beyond dispensing information, giving a test, and assigning a grade. They must themselves know more about the foundations of subject areas, and they must understand how students think as well as what they know in order to create experiences that produce learning. Moreover, as students with a wider range of learning needs enter and stay in school—a growing number whose first language is not English, many others with learning differences, and others with learning disabilities—teachers need access to the growing knowledge that exists about how to teach these learners effectively. More teacher education programs are preparing teachers well for these new demands, but they are still too few and far between.

Clearly, the nation's teacher recruitment and development challenges are daunting. At the same time, these formidable challenges offer equally compelling opportunities. With major changes occurring in the teaching force while reforms are beginning to take root, the possibilities for recruiting and educating teachers well from the start are greater than they have ever been. With dedication, determination, and clarity of vision, our society can use this opportunity to develop a diverse, well-prepared, and culturally responsive teaching force that can serve as a foundation for the schools needed to maintain a prosperous and just society.

The Imperative to Create Schools That Support Learning

The third premise is one that people inside schools understand, but those outside may not: **School reform cannot succeed unless it focuses on creating the conditions in which teachers can teach, and teach well.**

Although many recent reforms are beginning to make a difference, most schools are still not structured to support high-quality teaching: Teachers do not have enough sustained time with their students each day and over the years to come to know them well and to tackle difficult kinds of learning with them; neither do they have time with their colleagues to work on improving what they do.

Inconsistent expectations for students and unequal financial and material resources are also major problems. A haphazard hodgepodge of policies has left schools without clear, compelling standards connected to the means to achieve them. Consequently, educators in different communities—and even in classrooms within the same building—often teach toward very different ends, with little help in building a powerful, cumulative learning experience for their students. Meanwhile, supports for teaching challenging subject matter—intellectually rigorous curriculum materials, laboratories, and computers—are absent from many schools.

Successful schools have found that they need to create communities that work toward shared standards, where students are well known both personally and academically, where parents are involved as partners, and where a variety of teaching approaches are used. Research concludes that much higher levels of achievement are found in smaller schools and units within schools where teachers know students and their families well, and where they can reinforce one another's efforts.[13] By developing common curriculum goals and working in teams, teachers can support high performance for their students.

In addition, like restructuring businesses, schools that have found ways to educate all students well have done so by providing ongoing learning for teachers and staff. They couple greater authority for classroom teachers and a greater press for achievement with the professional learning needed to give educators the tools they need to succeed with students.

The Bottom Line . . .

The bottom line is that there is just no way to create good schools without good teachers. Those who have worked to improve education over the last decade have learned that school reform cannot be "teacher-proofed." Success in any aspect of reform—whether creating standards, developing more challenging curriculum and assessments, implementing school-based management, or inventing new model schools and programs—depends on highly skilled teachers working in supportive schools that engender collaboration with families and communities.

No top-down mandate can replace the insights and skills teachers need to manage complex classrooms and address the different needs of individual students, whatever their age. No textbook, packaged curriculum, or testing system can discern what students already know or create the rich array of experiences they need to move ahead.

Exhortations to improve students' "higher order" thinking abilities accomplish little without able teachers who know how to support challenging learning. Concerns about "at-risk" children—those who drop out, tune out, and fall behind—cannot be addressed without teachers who know how to teach students who come to school with different learning needs, home situations, and beliefs about what education can mean for them. There is no silver bullet in education. When all is said and done, if students are to be well taught, it will be done by knowledgeable and well-supported teachers.

The High Stakes Involved: The Nature of America's Future

At issue in this discussion are very high stakes. The education challenge facing the United States is not that its schools are not as good as they once were. As some of their severest critics concede, they are better in many ways than they have ever been, having raised graduation rates and basic literacy for a much more inclusive group of students throughout this century.[14] The problem is that our complex, technological society requires that schools now help the vast majority of young people reach levels of skill and competence once thought within the reach of only a very few.

As recently as 1950, most people held blue-collar jobs in factories or businesses that involved fairly simple tasks, planned and organized by others. Schools stressed similar kinds of routine work for most students. The kind of teaching needed for these skills was not complicated. Teachers could manage by following workbooks and texts even if they did not have deep knowledge of subject matter or a command of varied teaching methods. If students did not succeed in school, it was not a major problem. Most did not even need to graduate from high school to make a good living in the manufacturing era.

But by the early 1990s, most assembly-line manufacturing jobs had disappeared from the United States. Blue-collar workers will comprise only about 10% of the workforce by the year 2000.[15] The "knowledge work" jobs that are replacing them require people to plan and organize much of their own work, manage teams, and use high levels of technical know-how. These new skills require an education that teaches students to frame their own problems, organize themselves, and persevere in complex projects rather than passively filling in worksheets. They demand mastery of advanced subject area content, research, and thinking skills formerly taught only to students thought to be headed for the best colleges. And they require classrooms in which students learn to work together successfully in teams rather than alone at their seats.

Tens of thousands of people not educated for these demands have been unable to make a successful transition into the new economy. A growing underclass and a threatened middle class include disadvantaged young people who live in high-poverty communities as well as working-class youth and adults whose levels of education and skills were sufficient for the jobs of the past but not for those of today and tomorrow. Those who succeed and those who fail are increasingly divided by their opportunities to learn.

In this knowledge-based society, the United States urgently needs to reaffirm a consensus about the role and purposes of public education in a democracy—and the prime importance of learning in meeting those purposes. The challenge extends far beyond preparing students for the world of work. It includes building an American future that is just and humane as well as productive, that is as socially vibrant and civil in its pluralism as it is competitive.

Today, Americans watch in dismay as the nation is split between wealth and poverty; as communities are divided by race and class; and as the backbone of our national life, the great American middle class, is left wondering about the future of its children when financial markets boom with every new corporate "downsizing." The central concepts that define America, ideas about justice, tolerance, and opportunity, are being battered.

In this environment, education must attend not simply to the nation's material well-being, but to its human core as well—to the intellectual and

The Core of Teaching

At the very core of teaching is the task of helping students make connections between what they already understand and the new concepts, information, or skills [we want them to learn]. Scientists of the human mind tell us we can remember very few totally separate items at once, and all learning is a process of somehow associating new information with old. So this is my job as a teacher: to help students make connections. And to do that, I need to have a pretty good picture of what their understandings are—or I need a way to probe those understandings.

At any moment, I have to decide whether to present information or stand back and let a student discover it. I have to know when and how to encourage, compel, accept, judge, nurture, admonish, humor, provoke, and inspire 30 individuals. Now if I am teaching your son or daughter, you undoubtedly hope that I understand your child well enough to make those decisions—so often spontaneous ones—wisely. And if I really understand your kid, if I can see into his soul a bit, or if I can figure out how his mind works when he's wrestling with a particular concept or skill, or if I can find a way to make him passionately interested in what I teach, I just might be able to inspire him to real heights. But if I don't understand, I can damage your child. I can turn him off, or set him back, or crush his feelings, or stifle his opportunities.

If I as one teacher fail to reach, nurture, and inspire your son or daughter, it's probably not the end of the world; a child can probably recover from this single experience. But if entire educational systems repeatedly misjudge or work ineffectively with certain children . . . we have a problem of national dimensions.

— CYNTHIA ELLWOOD, TEACHER, MILWAUKEE, WISCONSIN

Source: Cynthia Ellwood, "Preparing Teachers for Education in a Diverse World," *Rethinking Schools: An Agenda for Social Change*, edited by David Levine, et al. (New York: The New Press, 1995), pp. 246-247.

political values that long ago established America's moral claim on the admiration and envy of the world: the impulses toward innovation and entrepreneurship; toward cooperation and altruism; and toward action, creativity, and community. America's schools have always been the primary social agents to take on the task of blending the world's many into a nation of one.

We must reclaim the soul of America. And to do so, we need an education system that helps people to forge shared values, to understand and respect other perspectives, to learn and work at high levels of competence, to take risks and persevere against the odds, to work comfortably with people from diverse backgrounds, and to continue to learn throughout life.

All Americans have a critical interest in building this kind of education system. For example,

- Low levels of literacy are highly correlated with welfare dependency and incarceration—and their high costs.[16]

- More than half the adult prison population has levels of literacy below those required by the labor market.[17]

- Nearly 40% of adjudicated juvenile delinquents have learning disabilities that were overlooked and went untreated in school.[18]

- By the year 2010 there will be only three workers for every Social Security recipient, as compared with 16 in 1950. If all these future workers are not capable and productive, the older generation's retirement security and our social compact will be in grave danger.[19]

We cannot afford the continued expansion of prison populations, public assistance programs, and unemployment. Where we should be investing at the front end in education programs, preschool rolls, and job training, we are spending money at the back end on state penitentiaries, welfare rolls, and unemployment checks. Our failure to invest in adequate education and job chances means that a shrinking share of American citizens must generate the tax base that supports the rest of the nation—the young, the old, the ill, and those who are not now productive. We need to expand the number of people who can contribute to the nation's economy rather than those who must be supported from it. It is clear that if we do not invest in schools that can create adequate life chances for all of our young people, the results will be disastrous for both individuals and the nation.

Beyond these statistics and pressing concerns lies a sobering human reality—many of the nation's children are in deep trouble. Over the last generation, American families and communities have changed profoundly. We lead advanced nations in rates of childhood poverty, homelessness, and mortality rates for those under age 25, and we lag in rates of children enrolled in preschool education. Most children live in a single-parent household at some time while they are growing up. Many parents are hurried and harried as they try to earn enough to support their families and attend to their children's needs with fewer community supports to help them. Many children arrive at school hungry, unvaccinated, and frightened because the plagues of modern life—crime and violence, drug and alcohol abuse, lack of adequate health care—rage on unabated. Teachers are well aware that today's students lead much more stressful lives than did students of a generation ago. But despite the dedication of their staffs, most schools are organized as though none of this had happened.

At the same time, our schools are more diverse and rapidly becoming more so. More students, including those with a variety of special needs, enter and stay in school longer than ever before. In addition, by the year 2010, at least a third of all children in this country will be members of groups currently considered "minorities." Big-city schools are already educating a new generation of immigrants from Eastern Europe, Central America, Asia, and Africa, one that rivals in size the great immigrations of the 19th and early 20th centuries.

This nation has always drawn its strength and its unique character from its diverse peoples—those who began here and those brought here under duress as well as those who have come seeking haven, carrying little more than hope, a willingness to work for a new future, and a dream of a better life for their children. America's schools have always been the major vehicle for developing the skills and the shared ideals that make the American dream possible. Today more than ever, as the nation catapults into an era demanding high levels of knowledge and skill from all its citizens, its success in embracing and enhancing the talents of these new and previously unincluded members will determine much of its future. Schools need partners in this work, including high-quality systems of preschool education and health care to which all children have access, and community supports that help families build a safe and healthy family life.

In short, to meet the needs of the 21st century, schools must successfully teach many more students from much more diverse backgrounds. And they must help them master more challenging content many times more effectively than they have ever done before. This means that teachers must understand students and their many pathways to learning as deeply as they comprehend subjects and teaching methods. It means that teachers need to understand how students of different language backgrounds and cultures can be supported in learning academic content and how those with a range of approaches to learning can be met with a variety of teaching strategies. It also means that schools must reorganize themselves to enable more intensive kinds of learning, supported by close, personal relationships as well as new technologies.

This point is critical: It is not just that educational demands are increasing, but that the very nature of learning is changing. Students must do more than learn new facts or cover more chapters; they must learn to integrate and apply their knowledge in more complex ways to more difficult problems. This means that teachers must accomplish very different things that require them to work in new ways. Consequently, the nature of their preparation and the settings in which they teach must change substantially as well.

[Emma Belle Sweet] taught me many things, and especially geography, in that large sixth-grade class in the old Fourth Ward School in Albuquerque, now long since destroyed by fire. But nothing could be so important to me and of such enduring quality as her simple, human act of figuratively leading me gently by the hand to a sense of self-respect, dignity, and worth.

— RALPH BUNCHE,
NOBEL PEACE PRIZE WINNER

The Right to a Qualified Teacher

In the face of our nation's needs, the impediments to good teaching are formidable. It is now time to address openly what is only tacitly acknowledged when educators answer questions about their occupation with the response, "I'm just a teacher." Despite glimmers of hope created by recent reforms, teaching continues to be treated as low-status work, much as it was 80 years ago when teaching positions were among the few available to women and minorities. In the United States, teaching has long been viewed as little more than a combination of glorified baby-sitting and high-level clerical work. Although progress has been made in recent years, teachers in many school districts are still underpaid, micromanaged, and treated as semiskilled workers.

Many states and districts have spent more energy trying to develop regulations intended to prevent poor teaching than trying to prepare top-flight teachers. Below-market wages produce chronic shortages of qualified teachers in fields like mathematics and science. Standards for entry into teaching are inconsistent and frequently unenforced. Teacher preparation is often inadequate, whether for the second-grade teacher—often expected to be a jack-of-all-trades with little in-depth subject matter knowledge—or for the eleventh-grade chemistry teacher, prepared with little in-depth teaching knowledge for the challenges posed by higher standards, changing technologies, and a more diverse student body.

By the standards of other professions and of teacher education in other countries, U.S. teacher education has historically been thin, uneven, and poorly financed. Although some schools of education provide high-quality preparation, others are treated as "cash cows" by their universities, bringing in revenues that are spent on the education of doctors, lawyers, and accountants rather than on their own students. As a result, teachers do not always have adequate disciplinary preparation in the fields they teach or adequate knowledge and supervised practice to enable them to use effective teaching strategies.

Moreover, teacher recruitment is ad hoc; hiring and tenure decisions are often disconnected from any clear vision of quality teaching; beginning teacher mentoring and professional development for experienced teachers are the first things eliminated in budget cuts. Working in isolation with few chances to update their skills, teachers are deprived of knowledge that would allow them to succeed at much higher levels. Meanwhile, most education dollars are spent on staff and activities other than classroom teaching.

But our schools' most closely held secret amounts to a great national shame: Without telling parents they are doing so, many districts hire unqualified people as "teachers" and assign them full responsibility for children. More than 12% of all newly hired "teachers" enter without any training at all, and another 14% enter without having fully met state standards.[20] Although no state will allow a person to fix plumbing, guard swimming pools, style hair, write wills, design a building, or practice medicine without completing training and passing an examination, more than 40 states allow school districts to hire teachers on emergency licenses who have not met these basic require-

Qualifications of Newly Hired Teachers, 1990-91

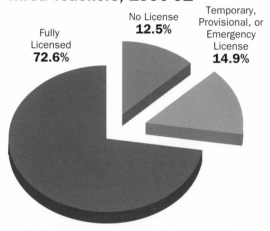

Fully Licensed **72.6%**

No License **12.5%**

Temporary, Provisional, or Emergency License **14.9%**

Source: U.S. Department of Education, Schools and Staffing Survey, 1990-91. Unpublished tabulations, National Data Resource Center, 1993

Percentage of Public School Teachers with a State License and a Major in Their Main Teaching Assignment Field: 1990-91

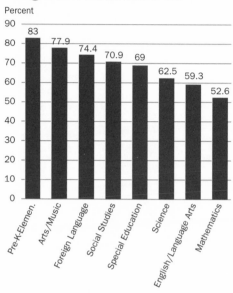

Percent

Field	Percent
Pre-K-Elemen.	83
Arts/Music	77.9
Foreign Language	74.4
Social Studies	70.9
Special Education	69
Science	62.5
English/Language Arts	59.3
Mathematics	52.6

Source: U.S. Department of Education, Schools and Staffing Survey, 1990-91, Published in Marilyn M. McMillen, Sharon A. Bobbitt, and Hilda F. Lynch, *Teacher Training, Certification, and Assignment in Public Schools*: 1990-91 (paper presented at annual meeting of the American Educational Research Association, New Orleans, LA, April 1994)

ments. States pay more attention to the qualifications of veterinarians treating the nation's cats and dogs than to those of teachers educating the nation's children and youth.

In many states, standards are simply waived whenever school districts want to hire teachers who cannot make the grade. Sometimes this is a function of genuine shortages in fields of short supply. Often, however, it occurs due to short-sighted hiring procedures, administrative convenience, efforts to save on teacher costs in favor of more "important" areas, and plain old-fashioned patronage. Although hundreds of studies have shown that fully prepared teachers are more effective than those who are unqualified, the practice of hiring untrained teachers continues.[21]

Will Rogers once quipped that "you can't teach what you don't know any more than you can come back from where you ain't been." His common-sense advice has been lost on many school districts. Consider:

- In recent years, more than 50,000 people who lack the training required for their jobs have entered teaching annually on emergency or substandard licenses.[22]

- Nearly one-fourth (23%) of all secondary teachers do not have even a college minor in their main teaching field. This is true for more than 30% of mathematics teachers.[23]

- Among teachers who teach a second subject, 36% are unlicensed in the field and 50% lack a minor.[24]

Qualifications of Secondary School Mathematics and Science Teachers

By school racial composition

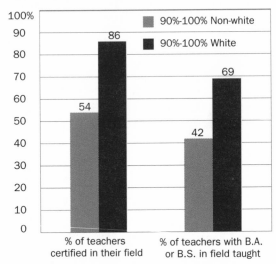

Legend:
- 90%-100% Non-white
- 90%-100% White

% of teachers certified in their field: 54 (Non-white), 86 (White)
% of teachers with B.A. or B.S. in field taught: 42 (Non-white), 69 (White)

Source: Jeannie Oakes, *Multiplying Inequalities: The Effects of Race, Social Class, and Tracking on Opportunities to Learn Mathematics and Science* (Santa Monica, Calif.: RAND Corporation, 1990), p. 61

Qualifications of High School Teachers

By school poverty level

% of teachers without at least a minor in the field they teach

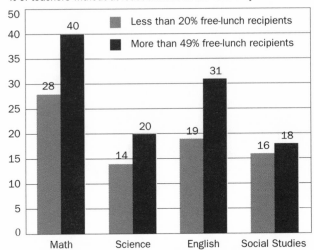

Legend:
- Less than 20% free-lunch recipients
- More than 49% free-lunch recipients

Math: 28, 40
Science: 14, 20
English: 19, 31
Social Studies: 16, 18

Source: U.S. Department of Education, Schools and Staffing Survey, School and Teacher Questionnaires, 1990-91, Published in *Teacher Supply, Teacher Qualifications, and Teacher Turnover: 1990-91* (Washington, D.C.: National Center for Education Statistics, 1995), p. 26

- 56% percent of high school students taking physical science are taught by out-of-field teachers, as are 27% of those taking mathematics and 21% of those taking English.[25] The proportions are much higher in high-poverty schools and in lower track classes.

- In schools with the highest minority enrollments, students have less than a 50% chance of getting a science or mathematics teacher who holds a license and a degree in the field he or she teaches.[26]

In the nation's poorest schools, where hiring is most lax and teacher turnover is constant, the results are disastrous. Thousands of children are taught throughout their school careers by a parade of teachers without preparation in the fields they teach, inexperienced beginners with little training and no mentoring, and short-term substitutes trying to cope with constant staff disruptions.[27] It is more surprising that some of these children manage to learn than that so many fail to do so.

Unequal resources and inadequate investments in teacher recruitment are major problems. Other industrialized countries fund their schools equally and make sure there are qualified teachers for all of them by underwriting teacher preparation and salaries. However, teachers in the United States must go into substantial debt to become prepared for a field that in most states pays less than any other occupation requiring a college degree.

Meanwhile, teachers' salaries, like all other education expenditures, vary

Teacher Salaries Around the World

Upper Secondary Teacher Salaries

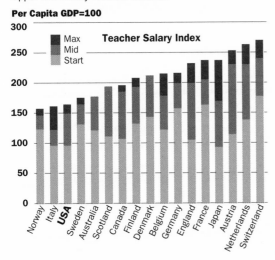

Per Capita GDP=100

Teacher Salary Index

Legend: Max / Mid / Start

(Countries, left to right: Norway, Italy, USA, Sweden, Australia, Scotland, Canada, Finland, Denmark, Belgium, Germany, England, France, Japan, Austria, Netherlands, Switzerland)

Source: F. Howard Nelson and Timothy O'Brien, *How U.S. Teachers Measure Up Internationally: A Comparative Study of Teacher Pay, Training, and Conditions of Service* (Washington, D.C.: American Federation of Teachers, 1993), p. 99

Comparisons of Earnings by Occupation

Average annual earnings in the previous year, 1991

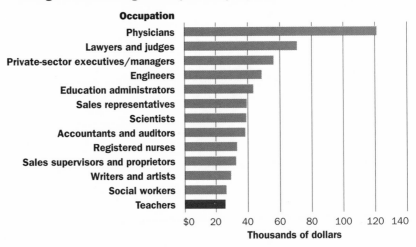

Occupation

Physicians, Lawyers and judges, Private-sector executives/managers, Engineers, Education administrators, Sales representatives, Scientists, Accountants and auditors, Registered nurses, Sales supervisors and proprietors, Writers and artists, Social workers, Teachers

Thousands of dollars

Source: U.S. Department of Education, National Adult Literacy Survey, 1992. Published in the *Condition of Education 1995* (Washington, D.C.: National Center for Education Statistics, 1995), p. 161

greatly among districts and states. For example, average salaries in 1991 ranged from $20,354 in South Dakota to $43,326 in Connecticut,[28] with salaries in affluent suburban districts much higher than those in cities or rural communities within the same area. Because rich schools spend as much as ten times what poor schools do,[29] they can recruit the most highly educated and experienced teachers. Benefiting from recent reforms, many of the new teachers in these wealthy districts are better prepared than ever before. The result is a bimodal teaching force in which some teachers are increasingly expert and others are wholly unprepared. For every newly hired teacher without training, there is another who enters with a master's degree from a rigorous teacher education program.

This situation is not necessary or inevitable. While the hiring of unprepared teachers is a long-standing tradition in the United States, the practice was almost eliminated during the 1970s with scholarships and loans for college students preparing to teach, Urban Teacher Corps initiatives, and Master of Arts in Teaching (MAT) programs, coupled with wage increases. However, the cancellation of most of these recruitment incentives in the 1980s led to renewed shortages when student enrollments started to climb once again, especially in cities. Between 1987 and 1991, the proportion of well-qualified new teachers in public schools—those entering teaching with a college major or minor and a license in their fields—actually declined from about 74% to 67%.[30]

For all these reasons, the quality of teaching in the United States varies dramatically across classrooms and communities. Some children benefit from high-quality curriculum taught by able and committed teachers who understand their subjects and how to teach so that their students excel. Others trudge through uninspired texts and workbooks with little intellectual challenge, taught by teachers who know little about their subjects and even less about how children learn. And while some schools are using the most up-to-date knowledge about how to teach successfully, a surprising number actually require teachers to use strategies that research has found to be ineffective.[31] We can do better. And we must.

We know how to prepare teachers to teach well. All around the country, successful programs for recruiting, educating, and mentoring new teachers have been launched. Professional networks and teacher academies have sprung up. Many education schools have been redesigned; stronger standards for teacher licensing and accreditation of education schools have been developed; and a new National Board for Professional Teaching Standards has begun to define and recognize accomplished teaching.

However, we have been much more skillful at inventing programs than at creating policies for making these good ideas widespread. Current efforts are isolat-

Covering the Curriculum . . .

Visiting a fourth-grade class, I was greeted by the teacher. "Welcome to our class," she said. "I'm on page 307 of the math text, exactly where I'm supposed to be according to board guidelines."

There was not much going on—two students were asleep, several were looking out the window, a few were reading their math books. I discovered later that virtually every student in the class was failing math. But this teacher was doing her job, moving through the set curriculum, dutifully delivering the material, passing out the grades. If the students did not learn math, that was not her responsibility.

. . . Or Teaching for Understanding?

Sandra McLain's Writing to Read room bustles with 18 first-grade children conducting experiments, writing on computers, illustrating, and reading. In one corner of the room, a group of first-grade students is working on a lab experiment investigating traits of plants. Students are classifying, sorting, and measuring as they finish up a three-week unit focused on seeds, stems, and leaves. Above them is a poster board displaying vegetables and their traits, with categories they developed that reveal a great deal of what they are learning. These students wear visors with the word "scientist" inscribed on top.

Other students are writing about what they are learning. Those students wear visors with the word "author" inscribed on top. Sandra deftly reads and critiques Constance's work, and says, "You just about have a science book written." Constance joyously responds with a "YES!" Another student rushes up to Sandra showing her an essay. A student comes up to me wearing yet another visor, this one with "illustrator" on top, showing me his picture that went along with his essay about his science experiment. In other corners of the room, a child is sitting on a bean bag reading while next to him another child "meets an author" on audiotape. Across the room there are three computers where students brush up on phonemes. "The more they write, the more they learn," Sandra explains.

Adapted from: William Ayers, "The Shifting Ground of Curriculum Thought and Everyday Practice," *Theory Into Practice* 31 (Summer 1992): 259; and Barnett Berry, "School Restructuring and Teacher Power: The Case of Keels Elementary," in Ann Lieberman (ed.), *The Work of Restructuring Schools: Building from the Ground Up* (New York: Teachers College Press, 1995).

ed and piecemeal. Moreover, they are layered onto a system that resists investments in high-quality teaching—a system that does little to help teachers acquire greater knowledge and skill, rewards teachers for leaving the classroom, and tolerates extraordinary inequalities in students' and teachers' opportunities to learn.

There is a better way. In most European and Asian countries, teachers are highly respected, well compensated, and better prepared. They receive much more extensive training in content and pedagogy before they enter teaching, and they have much more regularly scheduled time for ongoing learning and work with their colleagues. In addition, they work in school settings that are structured so that they can focus on teaching and come to know their students well. These nations do not spend more on education, but they invest more in teaching than in bureaucracy, hiring many fewer nonteaching staff and many more teachers who take on greater responsibility with greater supports. Like progressive firms, they work to get things right from the start. Rather than spend money on add-ons and band-aid programs to compensate for the failures of teaching, they spend their education resources on what matters most: well-trained teachers who work intensively with students and with other teachers to improve teaching and learning. And they get better results.

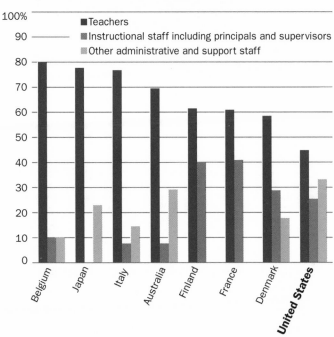

Comparisons of Educational Staff By Function

Legend:
- ■ Teachers
- ■ Instructional staff including principals and supervisors
- ■ Other administrative and support staff

(Bar chart with countries: Belgium, Japan, Italy, Australia, Finland, France, Denmark, United States; y-axis 0–100%)

Source: Organization for Economic Cooperation and Development (OECD), *Education at a Glance: OECD Indicators* (Paris: OECD, 1995), table p31, pp. 176-177

Students in some states in the United States perform as well as those in top-ranked countries, while other states' students rank with countries at the bottom. The best and worst performers are distinguished in part by the attention they pay to teacher quality. Top-ranked states like North Dakota, Minnesota, and

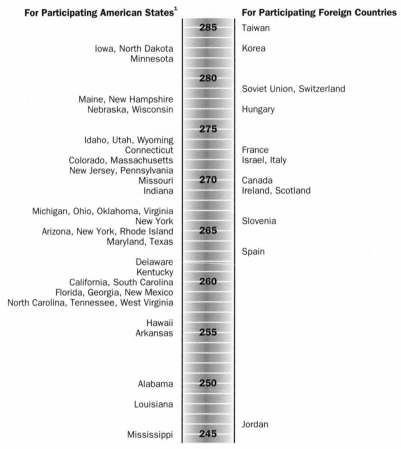

Average Mathematics Proficiency Scores for 13-Year-Olds (in Other Countries): 1991 or 1992

For Participating American States[1]		For Participating Foreign Countries
	285	Taiwan
Iowa, North Dakota Minnesota		Korea
	280	
		Soviet Union, Switzerland
Maine, New Hampshire Nebraska, Wisconsin		Hungary
	275	
Idaho, Utah, Wyoming Connecticut		France
Colorado, Massachusetts		Israel, Italy
New Jersey, Pennsylvania		
Missouri	**270**	Canada
Indiana		Ireland, Scotland
Michigan, Ohio, Oklahoma, Virginia		
New York		Slovenia
Arizona, New York, Rhode Island	**265**	
Maryland, Texas		
		Spain
Delaware		
Kentucky		
California, South Carolina	**260**	
Florida, Georgia, New Mexico		
North Carolina, Tennessee, West Virginia		
Hawaii		
Arkansas	**255**	
Alabama	**250**	
Louisiana		
		Jordan
Mississippi	**245**	

Notes:
1. The states of Alaska, Illinois, Kansas, Montana, Nevada, Oregon, South Dakota, Vermont, and Washington did not participate. The District of Columbia is not displayed.

Mathematics Proficiency has a range from 0 to to 500 with:
Level 250 = Numerical operations and beginning problem solving
Level 300 = Moderately complex procedures and reasoning

Source: U.S. Department of Education, *Education in the States and Nations* (Washington, D.C.: National Center for Education Statistics, 1993), pp. 56-57. Published in David C. Berliner and Bruce J. Biddle, *The Manufactured Crisis: Myths, Fraud, and the Attack on Americas Public Schools* (Reading, MA: Addison-Wesley, 1995), p. 61

Iowa all have professional standards boards that have enacted high standards for teacher preparation and licensing. They have virtually eliminated the practice of hiring unqualified teachers. Those at the bottom, however, still hire very large numbers of untrained teachers each year—9% of newly hired teachers in Alabama and Mississippi and 23% in Louisiana were unlicensed in 1991—and their students' learning suffers for it.[32]

Hence this Commission's sense of urgency. Our society can no longer accept the hit-or-miss hiring, sink-or-swim induction, trial-and-error teaching, and take-it-or-leave-it professional development it has tolerated in the past. The time has come to put teachers and teaching at the top of the nation's education reform agenda.

Our Goal for America's Future . . .

We propose an audacious goal for America's future. Within a decade—by the year 2006—we will provide every student in America with what should be his or her educational birthright: access to competent, caring, qualified teaching. No more hiring unqualified teachers on the sly. No more nods to teacher education programs that fail to prepare teachers adequately. No more ignoring the problems of teachers who do not teach well. Children are compelled by law to attend school, and most states promise them a thorough and efficient education. In the face of these state mandates, students have a right to benefit from the knowledge and skill possessed by qualified teachers.

This is a challenging goal to put before the nation and its educational leaders. But if the goal is challenging and requires unprecedented effort, it does not require unprecedented new theory. Common sense suffices: American students are entitled to teachers who know their subjects, understand their students and what they need, and have developed the skills required to make learning come alive.

We need to create a rising tide of excellence in our nation's classrooms if our children are going to succeed. This report describes a set of building blocks for doing so:

- **Standards for student learning** that allow teachers and parents to organize their efforts in a common direction;

- **Standards for teaching** that define what teachers must know to help their students succeed;

- **High-quality preparation and professional development** that help teachers develop the skills they need;

- **Aggressive recruitment** of able teachers in high-need fields;

- **Rewards for teacher knowledge and skill**; and

- **Schools organized for student and teacher learning** in the ways they staff, schedule, and finance their work.

We believe all these issues must be tackled together, rather than handpicked to deal only with the easiest ones. Anything less will shortchange our children and compromise the American future.

A Better Way: Faye Freeman's Class

Faye Freeman's third-grade class bubbles with energy and purpose. As the day begins, children enter smiling and cluster around her desk to find out what lies ahead. The day's work plan is on the board, right above a row of inviting children's books on the chalk tray. The 26 students from this small urban community in New Rochelle, New York, reflect a typical American classroom in 1996 and a full range of learning needs: Their homes range from housing projects and small bungalows to elegant colonials. About one-third are African American or Latino; two of the children speak languages other than English at home; another two receive special education services part of each day.

These distinctions are meaningless here, however. The class hums like a well-rehearsed orchestra as students move to their places in the middle of the room for meeting time. To prepare for a story-writing assignment, they brainstorm ideas about how to make their group work productive. Freeman skillfully guides the discussion and writes their ideas on the board: "Everyone should share." "Cooperate and work together." "Sometimes we have to compromise." "Respect everyone's ideas."

She reminds them to make a web of their ideas so that they can figure out how to put them in order. The children hurry back to their desks, clustered together in groups of four to six, and begin work immediately. "You have to get everyone's ideas," one tiny girl reminds a young boy at her table. Everyone is hard at work, heads leaning toward one another as they offer and record ideas. Some run to the bookshelf for dictionaries and other books that provide the research they need. In the middle of one web, a group has written "The terrible storm." "First it started drizzling," the recorder has noted. "What happens next?" a visitor asks. "We don't know!" the recorder exclaims, as though that should be obvious. "Then it started to pour!" her tablemate offers. They are off and writing.

Faye moves from one group to the next, checking, questioning, prodding, hugging, nudging. The students need little help. They are already seasoned writers. They write every day in every area of the curriculum—explaining their math problems; recording their steps in constructing dams, levers, and pulleys; researching countries and historical figures; expressing their ideas in poetry and stories. These assignments help students develop both the clarity of their thinking and their writing skills. It is no wonder that this class scores at the top of the district each year on the district's writing assessment. "If you come in this room, you have to work," one child notes proudly.

All kinds of parents request Faye Freeman, and all kinds of students thrive in her class—both those who struggle to learn and those who soar. The elements of good teaching are readily apparent: lots of interesting work; plenty of opportunities to practice and succeed; clear expectations and structure, blended with opportunities to imagine and create. New ideas are introduced through connections to children's lives and experiences, then taken much further with careful scaffolding of new concepts. Cooperative and individual tasks are skillfully managed to build on students' strengths and address their needs. The rich curriculum always demands active intellectual effort. "She teaches us to think even when we don't have to!" exclaims one student.

Like other great teachers, Faye Freeman's career is that of a learner. Her mother taught four generations of students in a one-room K-8 schoolhouse ("the colored school," Faye notes) in a little town in North Carolina. Faye's undergraduate degree from Suffolk University in Boston and master's degree from Bank Street College of Education in New York were pivotal, she believes, in helping her attend to children's thinking as a basis for shaping teaching. "It made me a better teacher. . . . I really need to know what the students are thinking." She is now in a doctoral program at Columbia University's Teachers College because "I was getting burned out, but what I really needed was to go back to school . . . I wanted to grow; I wanted to learn."

Faye's path mirrors that of other excellent teachers who have developed their skills more or less on their own by reading, attending workshops, and sending themselves off to school for new insights into teaching. Whatever they learn they immediately turn to the benefit of their students. They will tell you, as Faye does, that the dollars they invest in their own studies are as essential to their students' success as the dollars they continually spend for classroom materials and supplies.

Many teachers like Faye Freeman entered teaching several decades ago when it was one of only a few professional careers available to women and people of color. Although she is often urged to go into administration, Faye's heart is in the classroom where she can see her students grow and achieve. Generations of parents and students are grateful that it is.

Dimensions of the Challenge

In a truly rational society, the best of us would be teachers, and the rest would have to settle for something less.

— *Lee Iacocca*

The public reveals an understanding of the importance of teaching that is not yet apparent in the pronouncements of experts and officials. In a recent Gallup poll, the great majority of voters identified the quality of public education as the most important issue for the 1996 presidential campaign.[33] When asked, "What is the most important thing public schools need in order to help students learn?" the top response, by a large margin, is "good teachers."[34]

Americans understand that teachers are the key to improving education, and they put their faith in teachers to do so. When asked, "Whom do you trust to make decisions about schools?" parents (67%) and teachers (64%) are runaway favorites—far outdistancing education experts (47%), business leaders (29%), elected officials (28%), and Washington bureaucrats (14%).[35]

However, based on its two-year study, the Commission is convinced that seven unresolved issues present formidable barriers to enacting the agenda the public says it wants. These barriers define the dimensions of the challenge facing American schools and teachers. They are:

1. **Low expectations for student performance.**
2. **Unenforced standards for teachers.**
3. **Major flaws in teacher preparation.**
4. **Painfully slipshod teacher recruitment.**
5. **Inadequate induction for beginning teachers.**
6. **Lack of professional development and rewards for knowledge and skill.**
7. **Schools that are structured for failure rather than success.**

Low Expectations for Student Performance

Throughout this century, little academic achievement has been expected of most students, who were presumed to be preparing for low-skilled jobs. Schools have rationed challenging curriculum—the kind that requires independent thinking, writing, planning, and performance—to the 10% to 20% of students who were thought to be headed for intellectual pursuits. While the economy and society now demand this kind of curriculum for virtually all students, teaching in many classrooms still features the anemic texts, "chalk and talk" lectures, and fill-in-the-blanks workbooks of an earlier age. These strategies will not enable students to acquire the new basics they need: the abilities to understand and use complex materials, communicate incisively, plan and organize their own work, solve mathematical and scientific problems, create ideas and products, and use new technologies in all of these pursuits.

Standards that reflect these imperatives for student learning are largely absent in our nation today. This is not well understood, however, because American students are at once overtested and underassessed. The widespread use of standardized tests creates the illusion that learning is regularly evaluated. Although current tests do measure some things, they generally are not directly related to the school curriculum and ignore many important kinds of learning. Unlike tests in other countries, which are usually essay, oral, and performance examinations tied to a common curriculum, multiple-choice tests of basic skills that predominate in the United States tend to represent low-level skills and provide little useful information for teaching.[36] Similarly, school textbooks and guides rarely reflect a powerful, coherent concept of curriculum. The standards they implicitly represent are out of synch with our needs and provide little useful leverage for reform. In addition, many schools, colleges, and employers find the current evidence about student learning is not compelling enough to make judgments about what students know and can do.

This situation is changing, although slowly. Since 1989, when President Bush and the nation's governors—under the leadership of Bill Clinton, then governor of Arkansas—developed the National Education Goals, educators have made a concerted push to develop demanding, "world-class" curriculum standards in key areas, including mathematics, science, English, history, geography, civics, and the arts. These standards are being used in many states to develop new curriculum frameworks that help clarify what students must learn to be successful in today's world, along with assessments that reflect the real-world tasks students should accomplish to meet the standards.

This process should be supported and accelerated so that high-quality, professionally informed curriculum guidance is widely available to help teachers organize their teaching and build on the work of their predecessors. For students, new curriculum and assessments need to support challenging academic coursework from elementary school to high school and higher standards for graduation that better reflect the demands of today's society. Assessments of performance should provide richer information about learning throughout the grades and evaluations at the end of high school that are relevant to the decisions of colleges and employers. In addition to all the efforts teachers must make to teach to new standards, students will need to work hard to meet them. To have a reason to do this, they must know that their work counts in determining school placements, graduation, access to good jobs, and admission to higher education. Schools that are explicit about the achievements that are expected of students can provide clarity for students and leverage for teachers in the long process of developing proficient performance.

This Commission is convinced that common agreement on what students should know and be able to do is long overdue. Without publicly established

A good teacher is someone who tries to understand students as individuals at all times, who has solid lessons for us but brings in his or her own personal experiences to make it more interesting. You don't know how much you are learning until you get home and start thinking about it. My English teacher, for example, gets us involved in literature and handles the classroom so that everyone participates. She knows her subject. She must have read every book plus some!

— DAMON BANKS,
STUDENT, JAMES ISLAND HIGH SCHOOL,
CHARLESTON, SOUTH CAROLINA

standards for content and performance grounded in high expectations for learning, we will continue what we have now—an unacknowledged national curriculum, predicated on low expectations, unaligned with our needs, and developed without public oversight by publishers and testmakers.

We are confident that, although difficult, the effort to develop standards will ultimately bear fruit, to the benefit of our students, our schools, our teachers, and our future. Much of this confidence rests on the general public's common sense and support for higher student achievement. Recent polls show that more than 80% of parents and the public favor high academic stan-

Standards for Learning

Curriculum standards in Long Beach, California, used to be lists of topics, long ones taken mostly from the teachers' guides to textbooks. There was no need to refer to them often because if teachers just followed the text, they were meeting the district requirements. No one questioned where they came from, and few actually cared. Yet, this community, affectionately known as "Iowa by the Sea" because of Midwestern immigrants who settled here generations ago, is undergoing major change. Another wave of immigrants from all over the world is requiring teachers to reexamine their skills, just as the more challenging expectations conveyed in California's curriculum frameworks and national professional standards are causing them to reassess the content they teach.

New content standards have become a tool to address these changes. The standards now in use in Long Beach are hot items that seem to pop up everywhere but on a shelf. Developed by groups of teachers and administrators over many months, they draw upon nationally developed standards, state curriculum frameworks, and local expertise. Once the standards in core subject areas had been reviewed by teachers, revised, and adopted, they became the basis for selection

of textbooks instead of the other way around. They provide a basis for discussing education. Parents of preschoolers, for example, receive pamphlets about reading and math standards. Family curriculum nights plunge parents into doing projects related to standards.

The new standards cover the basics and also emphasize understanding and applications of skills. The previous curriculum guide for algebra merely listed more than 50 topics without asking students to demonstrate mastery of what they learned. The new algebra standards emphasize such tasks as analyzing, investigating, applying, describing, and visualizing real-world problems.

Tougher standards for students required totally different approaches to professional development. Teachers realized they needed new knowledge of content and methods to teach to higher standards. Gradually, teacher learning activities are being organized around the new standards with an emphasis upon using student work as the basis for discussions of teaching and learning.

Raising content standards for students ultimately will affect everything from teacher preparation programs to state assessment policies. For Marshall Middle School principal Karen DeVries, it

began with a yearlong effort to enable teachers to examine the standards and relate them to their instruction. Each month in department meetings, Marshall teachers go over their assignments, explain how they relate to specific standards, and submit student work to illustrate the linkages. Before the new standards, teachers "sort of did their own thing," explains science department chair Thomas Ibarra, and students often repeated lab experiments and units from one year to the next. "Organizing around the content standards has been a non-threatening way to get coordination into the curriculum," he says. Not only is science instruction now more focused, but new teachers can look at the documentation system and know immediately what students have been doing.

After just a few months of organizing professional development around standards, DeVries believes the content standards are "intruding on the traditional isolation of teachers" and encouraging teachers to talk about student work. They are beginning to exchange ideas about what is a high performance standard. By sharing their work, she says, "teachers also are sharing what most motivates kids, what really helps improve their learning."

dards and clear guidelines for curriculum. They also want schools that offer support for student learning—schools that are engaging and humane, that make learning interesting and enjoyable for students, and that teach the values that underlie democratic living: honesty, respect for others, and equal opportunity.[37]

We see standards in the same way—as an organizing framework that provides one crucial component for greater student learning. Standards that outline a core curriculum entitlement, along with assessments that reflect the demands of 21st century life, can help schools focus their energies. The essential companion to this effort, then, is the investment in teacher and school capacities that makes possible the kinds of teaching parents want and all students need.

Unenforced Standards for Teachers

Setting standards is like building a pyramid: Each layer depends on the strengths of the others. Students will not be able to achieve higher standards of learning unless teachers are prepared to teach in new ways and schools are prepared to support high-quality teaching. Higher standards for students must ultimately mean higher standards for teachers and schools. Otherwise, the end result of the standards movement will be more clearly documented failure rather than higher levels of overall achievement.

Teaching in ways that help diverse learners master challenging content is much more complex than teaching for rote recall or low-level basic skills. Enabling students to write and speak effectively, to solve novel problems, and to design and conduct independent research requires paying attention to *learning*, not just to "covering the curriculum." It means engaging students in activities that help them *become* writers, scientists, mathematicians, and historians, in addition to learning *about* these topics. It means figuring out *how* children are learning and what they actually *understand* and can *do* in order to plan what to try next. It means understanding how children develop and knowing many different strategies for helping them learn.

Teachers who know how to do these things make a substantial difference in what children learn. Furthermore, a large body of evidence shows that the preparation teachers receive influences their ability to teach in these ways.[38] However, many teachers do not receive the kind of preparation they need, and few standards are in force that distinguish those who know how to teach successfully from those who do not.

Most parents and members of the public assume that teachers, like other professionals, are educated in similar ways, so that they acquire common knowledge and meet common standards before they are admitted to practice. You would be correct if you assumed that any doctor you chose had studied anatomy, physiology, pathology, and much more, and that any lawyer you selected had learned the basics of torts, contracts, and criminal and civil law. Both also will have passed a rigorous test of their knowledge and ability to apply it. You would be incorrect much of the time, however, if you assumed that any teacher to whom your child was assigned had a degree in his or her

A lot of times we don't expect enough of the students. That to me is lack of respect. To me, *expect* is *respect*. In other words, if you don't expect something of someone, they'll be satisfied with less. I think that's been done with women and minorities throughout the years. And they'll never see that next plateau. So I think you have to make it fairly rigorous. If they don't get it, just sit down and roll up your sleeves and *be* with them. It seems to work.

— W. DEAN EASTMAN,
SOCIAL STUDIES TEACHER,
BEVERLY HIGH SCHOOL, BEVERLY, MASSACHUSETTS

The one thing that I will always remember about Mrs. James is that she WAS history. She knew everything. You could have put her in the shoes and dress of any person in history and she would have been them, because she knew it so well. . . . It's knowing the subject so well, being passionate about it, and wanting to teach it to *these* students [that makes the difference]. Mrs. James loves us— she tells us that every day—and she loves U.S. history, so she's passionate about the subject, she's done all of her homework, and she wants to be there.

— LYNNE DAVIS,
HIGH SCHOOL SENIOR

subject; had studied child development, learning, and teaching methods; and had passed tests of teaching knowledge and skill. In fact, well under 75% of teachers meet this standard.[39]

Because of haphazard policies and back-door hiring, many people who teach have had no training at all, and those who do go through schools of education receive very different preparation. Some states require a degree in the discipline to be taught, extensive education coursework, and practice teaching, and a master's degree for a continuing license. Others require less than a college minor in a subject area, a few weeks of student teaching, and a couple of methods courses.

Because most states do not require schools of education to be accredited,[40] only about 500 of the nation's 1,200 education schools have met common professional standards. States, meanwhile, routinely approve all of their teacher education programs, including those that lack qualified faculty and are out of touch with new knowledge about teaching. There often are political incentives to do so, since these programs provide extra revenue to fund other departments and schools.[41] Then, rather than requiring candidates to pass common performance standards, states ask schools of education to recommend their own students for a license. Thus, a weak school of education that could not itself receive accreditation is asked to recommend for a license candidates who also have not met professional standards.

While states recently have begun to require some form of testing for a teaching license, most are little more than multiple-choice tests of basic skills and general knowledge, widely criticized by educators and experts as woefully inadequate to measure teaching skill.[42] Furthermore, in many states the cutoff scores are so low there is no effective standard for entry. Although these tests may be better than nothing, they fall short of what is needed to adequately sort those who can teach from those who cannot, and to send a clear signal to schools of education about what teachers need to know and be able to do.

Finally, until recently, teaching has not had a body of accomplished teachers charged with setting standards for professional practice like those that govern other professions. The bottom line is that, across the country, there has been no foundation of common expectations for what teachers must know before children are entrusted to their care.

When people seek help from doctors, lawyers, accountants, or architects, they rely on the unseen work of a three-legged stool supporting professional competence: accreditation, licensing, and certification. In most professions, candidates must graduate from an accredited professional school that provides up-to-date knowledge and effective training experiences in order to sit for state licensing examinations that test their knowledge and skill. These tests ensure that candidates have acquired the knowledge they need to practice responsibly.

In addition, many professions offer examinations leading to recognition for advanced levels of skill—such as certification for public accountants who earn a CPA; board certification for doctors in areas like surgery, pediatrics, or oncology; or registration for architects. This recognition takes extra years of study and prac-

The Three-Legged Stool of Teacher Quality

The three-legged stool of quality assurance—teacher education program accreditation, initial teacher licensing, and advanced professional certification—is becoming more sturdy as a continuum of standards has been developed to guide teacher learning across the career. When these standards have been enacted in policy, teacher preparation and professional development should be focused on a set of shared knowledge, skills, and commitments.

Accreditation: A rigorous new set of standards for teacher preparation programs has been developed by the National Council for Accreditation of Teacher Education (NCATE). NCATE-accredited institutions must show how they prepare teachers to teach to the student standards developed by professional associations such as the National Council of Teachers of Mathematics, one of NCATE's 30 professional organization members. They also must show how they prepare teachers to meet new licensing standards (see below) regarding content knowledge and skill in curriculum planning, assessment, classroom management, teaching strategies for diverse learners, and collaboration with parents and colleagues. To date, about 500 of 1,200 teacher education programs have received professional accreditation through NCATE.

Licensing: Under the auspices of the Council of Chief State School Officers, a consortium of more than 30 states and professional organizations has formed the Interstate New Teacher Assessment and Support Consortium (INTASC). This consortium has created a set of performance standards for beginning teacher licensing and is developing new examinations that measure these standards. The new examinations draw upon the pace-setting work of the National Board for Professional Teaching Standards (see below) and evaluate teaching in terms of how well teachers can plan and teach for understanding, connect their lessons to students' prior knowledge and experiences, help students who are not initially successful, analyze the results of their practice on student learning, and adjust it accordingly. If new teachers can do these things, they will be prepared to teach for the new student standards that are emerging and to develop the more advanced skills of a Board-Certified teacher.

Certification: The National Board for Professional Teaching Standards was instituted in 1987 to establish rigorous standards and assessments for certifying accomplished teaching. A majority of the Board's 63 members are outstanding classroom teachers; the remaining members include school board members, governors, legislators, administrators, and teacher educators. Expert, veteran teachers who participate in the Board's assessments complete a year-long portfolio that illustrates their teaching through lesson plans, samples of student work over time, videotapes, and analyses of their teaching. They also take tests of content knowledge and pedagogical knowledge that tap their ability to create and evaluate curriculum materials and teaching situations. The Board's standards are being used by some school districts to guide ongoing professional development and evaluation as well as certification of accomplished practice.

The Commission recommends that this framework be used to guide education policy across the states so that every teacher prepares at an NCATE-accredited institution, demonstrates teaching competence as defined by INTASC standards for initial licensing, and pursues accomplished practice as defined by the National Board for Professional Teaching Standards.

Teacher Quality

Teacher Education Accreditation (NCATE)

Initial Licensing (INTASC)

Advanced Certification (NBPTS)

tice and is based on rigorous performance tests that measure the highest standards of competence. Those who have met these standards are then allowed to do certain kinds of work that others cannot. The standards are also used to ensure that professional schools incorporate new knowledge into their courses and to guide professional development and evaluation throughout the career. Thus, these advanced standards act as an engine that pulls along the knowledge base of the entire profession.

This three-legged stool finally exists for teaching as well. High-quality, coherent standards for accreditation, licensing, and advanced certification now exist and could become a powerful lever for change.

- A National Board for Professional Teaching Standards (hereafter referred to as the National Board) was established in 1987 to define standards for advanced certification of accomplished veteran teachers. The National Board began offering assessments in 1994 and had certified 374 teachers as of June 1996. In some districts these teachers receive extra pay and qualify to become mentors or lead teachers. A number of districts are incorporating the National Board's standards into ongoing professional development and evaluation for teachers.

What's Important about Standards: A Teacher's View

When I was asked by the National Board for Professional Teaching Standards to serve on a committee to write the Early Adolescence/English Language Arts Standards, I was concerned about the sensibility and feasibility of such a daunting task. Standards for all language arts teachers? Impossible, I thought. No one could reach consensus. Nor should they, I believed. However, I agreed to attend the first meeting for a number of reasons: to listen in on the conversation, to see what it was we each valued, and to see if the National Board was serious about giving teachers voice. If they weren't, I would resign. I decided to stay.

I stayed, too, because during the three years that it took us to describe what accomplished teachers know and are able to do, I learned that the journey was far more important than the final destination. The discussion, sometimes arguments, around the table always sent me back to my classroom a better teacher. The endeavor of creating standards allowed me to participate in a professional conversation with other educators. We are seldom given the time for such conversations in our own schools. I left those meetings questioning what I do, why I do what I do, and how well I do those things.

In a scene from *Stuart Little,* Stuart volunteers to fill in as a substitute teacher. He asks the students, "How many of you know what's important?" The standards document is an attempt to answer *what is important* that language arts teachers know and are able to do. It is a draft of our best thinking at the moment. It is a guide, meant to be a living, breathing, evolving document that allows for flexibility, diversity, and growth.

We need the finest language arts teachers to stay in the classroom so they can help students become the most articulate readers, writers, and speakers they can be. Perhaps this certification process will keep teachers intellectually challenged and learning for life. Perhaps [it] will teach all educators, and others outside the profession, that continually questioning and searching for what is important is more valuable than having all of the answers.

— *LINDA RIEF, MIDDLE SCHOOL TEACHER, DURHAM, NEW HAMPSHIRE*

Adapted from Linda Reif, "Message from the Editors," *Voices from the Middle* 2, no. 4 (November 1995): 1. Copyright © 1995 by the National Council of Teachers of English. Reprinted with permission.

- A consortium of more than 30 states and professional associations—the Interstate New Teacher Assessment and Support Consortium (INTASC)—has begun to develop National Board-compatible licensing standards and performance examinations for beginning teachers as they enter the profession.

- The National Council for Accreditation of Teacher Education (NCATE) has developed a rigorous set of standards linked to those of the National Board and INTASC to hold schools of education and their programs accountable.

Here, as with standards for students, the profession is on the cusp of serious reform. These standards, however, have yet to be embedded in most state and district policies where they could influence who enters and remains in classrooms, how they are prepared, and how they teach. The critical issue for improving the caliber of teaching is creating a viable system for using standards to guide teacher learning and create accountability.

Major Flaws in Teacher Preparation

Much has changed in the world around schools: Students, family life, the economy, expectations for learning, and the job of teaching are all different than they once were. However, the ways in which teachers prepare for their work are, in most places, still very much unchanged from two or three decades ago.

For new teachers, improving standards begins with teacher preparation. Prospective teachers learn just as other students do: by studying, practicing, and reflecting; by collaborating with others; by looking closely at students and their work; and by sharing what they see. For prospective teachers, this kind of learning cannot occur in college classrooms divorced from schools or in schools divorced from current research.

Yet, until recently, most teacher education programs taught theory separately from application. Teachers were taught to teach in lecture halls from texts and teachers who frequently had not themselves ever practiced what they were teaching. Students' courses on subject matter were disconnected from their courses on teaching methods, which were in turn disconnected from their courses on learning and development. They often encountered entirely different ideas in their student teaching, which made up a tiny taste of practice added on, without connections, to the end of their coursework. When they entered their own classrooms, they could remember and apply little of what they had learned by reading in isolation from practice. Thus, they reverted to what they knew best: the way they themselves had been taught. Breaking this cycle requires educating teachers in partnerships with schools that are becoming exemplars of what is possible rather than mired in what has been.

Long-standing problems with traditional teacher education programs have been widely documented in recent years.[43] Difficulties include:

- **Inadequate Time.** The confines of a four-year undergraduate degree make it hard to learn subject matter, child development, learning theory, and effective teaching strategies. Elementary preparation is considered weak in subject matter; secondary preparation, in knowledge of learning and learners.

- **Fragmentation.** Key elements of teacher learning are disconnected from each other. Coursework is separate from practice teaching; professional skills are segmented into separate courses; faculties in the arts and sciences are insulated from education professors. Would-be teachers are left to their own devices to put it all together.

- **Uninspired Teaching Methods.** For prospective teachers to learn active, hands-on and minds-on teaching, they must have experienced it for themselves. But traditional lecture and recitation still dominates in much of higher education, where faculty do not practice what they preach.

- **Superficial Curriculum.** "Once over lightly" describes the curriculum. Traditional programs focus on subject matter methods and a smattering of educational psychology. Candidates do not learn deeply about how to understand and handle real problems of practice.

- **Traditional Views of Schooling.** Because of pressures to prepare candidates for schools as they are, most prospective teachers learn to work in isolation, rather than in teams, and to master chalkboards and textbooks instead of computers and CD-ROMs.

The absence of powerful teacher education is particularly problematic at a time when the nature of teaching needs to change—and when those entering may never themselves have experienced the kind of challenging instruction they are expected to offer. It is difficult to improve practice if new teachers teach as they were taught and if the way they were taught is not what we want. As one analyst explains:

> [The] improvement of practice problem . . . [is] very serious. We are caught in a vicious circle of mediocre practice modeled after mediocre practice, of trivialized knowlege begetting more trivialized knowledge. Unless we find a way out of this circle, we will continue re-creating generations of teachers who re-create generations of students who are not prepared for the technological society we are becoming.[44]

Both in the United States and abroad, many efforts are under way to deal with these challenges. Countries like Germany, Luxembourg, and Belgium have long had systems in which teachers earn an undergraduate degree in a discipline (sometimes two) and then pursue two to three more years of graduate-level education studies that include an intensive teaching internship in schools. Examinations of subject matter and teaching knowledge occur throughout this process. Since the 1980s, reforms in France, Japan, Taiwan, and elsewhere have begun to follow suit: encouraging or requiring teacher education at the graduate level and adding yearlong internships in which teachers combine coursework and on-the-job practice under careful supervision by veteran teachers.

In the United States, about 300 colleges have created graduate-level teacher education programs that allow for more extended clinical training. These efforts have focused on transforming curriculum to address the demands of teaching for greater understanding and teaching a more diverse student population, and

Learning to Teach in Germany, France, and Japan

Teacher education in the former West Germany has long been considered an international flagship. As one report noted of the system's rigorous standards and training, "In Germany, those who can, teach." Prospective teachers get degrees in two subjects, write a thesis, and pass a series of essay and oral exams before they undertake pedagogical training. Two years of teaching preparation include teaching seminars combined with classroom experience— first observing and then, after four to six weeks, beginning to practice in a classroom with a mentor teacher. Over the two years of internship, college and school-based supervisors observe and grade at least 25 lessons. At the end of this period, candidates prepare, teach, and evaluate a series of lessons, prepare a curriculum analysis, and undergo another set of exams before, finally, they are ready to teach.

In 1989, France undertook a sweeping overhaul of teacher education, motivated by a conviction that both elementary and secondary teachers needed to understand subject matter disciplines and pedagogy more fully if their students were ultimately to succeed at more challenging kinds of learning. Now,

after completing an undergraduate degree, would-be teachers apply for a highly selective two-year graduate program in a new University Institute for the Preparation of Teachers. There they learn about teaching methods, curriculum design, learning theory, and child development while they conduct research and practice teaching in affiliated schools. Teachers are supported in their studies by government stipends, and they receive a salary in their final year of training, during which they take on a teaching position under supervision, much as a doctor does in a residency.

Japan also launched major reforms of teacher education in 1989. The changes place more emphasis on graduate-level teacher education and add an intensive one-year internship to university training in education. After passing a highly competitive teacher appointment examination, beginning teachers are assigned to a school where they work with a master teacher who is released from his or her classroom to advise and counsel interns. Master teachers observe each intern's class weekly and give the intern the opportunity to observe the classes of other teachers. These observations are especially helpful to beginning teach-

ers like Kenji Yamota, who observed that "only after I try what I observe do I begin to think." First-year novices also participate in retreats, seminars, training sessions, and 60 days of in-school professional development on topics such as classroom management, computer use, teaching strategies, and counseling methods.

Kenji also values what he learns informally from his colleagues. Each teacher has a desk in a shared staff room, and the desks are grouped to promote interaction. New teachers are placed next to veterans in their grade level. Every morning teachers hold a brief meeting in the staff room and return later in the day to work and relax. Once a week, they share an extended block of time for demonstrations, lesson planning, and other joint work. Learning to teach is considered a lifelong task that is well-supported throughout the career.

Sources: John Holyoake, "Initial Teacher Training: The French View," *Journal of Education for Teaching* 19 (1993): 215-226; Nancy Sato and Milbrey W. McLaughlin, "Context Matters: Teaching in Japan and in the United States," *Phi Delta Kappan* 66 (1992): 359-366; Nobuo K. Shimahara and Akira Sakai, *Learning to Teach in Two Cultures: Japan and the United States* (New York: Garland Publishing, 1995); and T. Waldrop, "Before You Lead a German Class, You Really Must Know Your Stuff," *Newsweek* 118 (December 1991): 62-93.

on integrating theory and practice by creating new professional development school (PDS) partnerships with schools that exhibit state-of-the-art practice. Professional development schools serve as sites for student teaching and internships for preservice teachers where practice can be linked to coursework. They also create long-term relationships that allow university and school faculties to work out common programs of teacher preparation and ongoing professional development.

These new programs and partnerships have the potential to reinvent teacher education just as the development of extended medical education and the creation of teaching hospitals transformed medical education following the advice of the Flexner Report in 1910.[45] But they are fragile, as many exist on soft money and as exceptions to current policies, and the preponderance of teacher education practice has not yet changed. Thus far, only a few states, such as Minnesota and Ohio, have taken steps to actively support substantially restructured training for teachers that would include extended internships or residencies in professional development schools.

Slipshod Recruitment

Many problems that undermine the creation of a strong teaching force are the product of mismanaged, uncoordinated systems that create snafus and inefficiencies at every possible turn. There is no way to comprehend what a hopelessly wasteful system of teacher preparation and recruitment we have in place without some understanding of how new teachers are prepared, hired, and introduced to the profession. All along the way, systems passively receive those who come to them rather than aggressively recruiting those who should apply; then they treat promising candidates with abandon, losing many along the way.

The first sieve is the pathway through traditional undergraduate teacher education, which many candidates enter not because they are committed to teaching but because getting a teaching credential seems like good job insurance. According to one estimate, of 600 students who enter a large four-year teacher education program early in their college years, only 180 complete the program and only about 72 actually get placed in teaching jobs. Of these, only about 30 or 40 remain in the profession several years later.[46] National data indicate an overall attrition rate of about 75% along the pipeline from the beginning of undergraduate teacher education through about the third year in teaching: About 60% of those who start out in undergraduate teacher education programs complete them; of these, about 60% enter teaching in the next year; of these, about 70% stay for more than three years.[47] Although graduate programs are more successful at placing and keeping recruits in teaching, they are still the exception to the rule.

Then there is the tortuous process of landing a teaching job. Especially in large districts, public school hiring practices are a case study of systems so consumed with procedures and paperwork that they forget what they are trying to do. A RAND Corporation study found that many districts do not hire the best-

The Cincinnati Initiative for Teacher Education (CITE)

"What better way to prepare for your first year of teaching? Classroom management is stressed all through school by the professors, but no matter what people tell you, you just have to *do* it. Had I been a first-year teacher at a school without this support, I would have been lost."

— *Prospective teacher Janet Barnes during her fifth-year teaching internship at Shroder Paideia Middle School, a CITE professional practice school*

Janet Barnes's experience as a graduate student intern in Debbie Liberi's eighth-grade science class was entirely different than the one her mentor had had entering teaching many years earlier. In addition to the fact that Janet is learning in a collaborative team setting in a professional practice school, Liberi recalls that "eighteen years ago I was unique among my peers because I had mentors within the building as a first-year teacher. But many of my contemporaries quit after a year or two. . . . This, I think, is a much better setup."

Janet's experience is an outgrowth of the efforts of a group of faculty from the University of Cincinnati and the Cincinnati public schools who sat down one afternoon in 1987 to figure out how to "redo" teacher education. Their goal: to define what makes an effective teacher and to design a process that would prepare such teachers. Their conclusion: The standard model of preparation would need major overhaul to provide graduates with much more than a bit of subject matter knowledge and the hint of an educational philosophy. To ensure that teachers would be prepared to teach diverse students for understanding, they created a new program that includes:

- *Two degrees, two majors.* Teachers receive a bachelor's degree in their discipline as well as a bachelor's degree in education to ensure a solid intellectual grasp of both.

- *A fifth-year internship.* A full-year internship combines half-time teaching responsibility with coordinated seminars under the joint supervision of campus- and school-based faculty.

- *Professional practice schools.* A group of professional practice schools with a shared vision work with the university to provide the settings for students' fieldwork assignments and internship placements.

Students conduct observations, fieldwork, and tutoring in professional practice schools beginning in their second year. During the fifth year, they are assigned and paid as half-time "intern" teachers working with experienced lead teachers in professional teams. The teams include other teachers, school-based university faculty, and fellow interns, who usually number six or eight to a building.

Hays Elementary School principal Mary Martin sees many benefits to this approach:

I see it as a vehicle for getting new strategies and ideas into the building, which will be shared with Hays teachers, who have much to share in turn with the interns. The ultimate good, of course, is that we're helping Cincinnati public schools to pull in better-trained, qualified teachers, with more realistic outlooks on the total educational picture.

Teacher union president Tom Mooney adds that CITE makes "teacher training a clinical, field-based, reality-centered experience . . . and brings practicing teachers and education faculty into new working relationships." Superintendent Michael Brandt concurs that CITE's internship gives prospective teachers "exposure to real life in the classroom before they are launched on their own." As a growing number of CITE graduates are hired, the result for the district is "better trained teachers and better educated students," Brandt says.

Adapted from the Cincinnati Initiative for Teacher Education, "Interns: Successful Collaboration Is Paying Off," *Initiatives: Newsletter of the Cincinnati Initiative for Teacher Education* 5 (Spring 1995). Copyright © 1995 by the Cincinnati Initiative for Teacher Education. Reprinted with permission.

qualified applicants for teaching positions because their own procedures keep them from doing so. Critical problems include uncoordinated recruitment, cumbersome screening processes that create bottlenecks, unprofessional treatment of applicants, hiring decisions delayed until the school year starts, teacher assignment and transfer policies, and obstacles to teacher mobility such as salary caps for veteran teachers, lack of licensing reciprocity among states, and the inability to transfer pension benefits from state to state.[48]

In large districts, logistics can overwhelm everything else. It may take until midsummer for principals to confirm vacancies or for school district officials to hear of them. Teachers who are retiring often delay notifying the principal or district of their plans. Where transferring teachers must be placed before new teachers can be hired, the entire hiring process is delayed. Lacking funds to computerize their systems, many central offices still keep candidate data in file folders that are frequently misplaced and that prevent applicants from being considered for more than one vacancy at a time. In the Information Age, it is sometimes the case that central offices cannot find out about vacancies, principals are left in the dark about applicants, and candidates cannot get any information at all.

Before its recent overhaul, Fairfax County, Virginia, found that its largely unautomated 64-step process added delays and reduced its ability to hire the best-qualified candidates.[49] In gargantuan districts like New York City, Los Angeles, and Chicago, thousands of qualified candidates who want to teach have had to take jobs elsewhere because they encountered unending problems in the system's procedures and could not even get interviews until the school year had already started.

Districts in states and cities that do not have a timely budget process also suffer from the fact that they may not know how many candidates they can hire until late summer. Budget battles have caused many cities to dismiss hundreds of teachers each spring, only to scramble to rehire them in the fall when many have gone on to other jobs. Wild pendulum swings from layoffs to hundreds of unfilled vacancies are a way of life in many such districts.

Finally, studies have found that some districts hire unqualified teachers for reasons other than shortages, including occasional out-and-out patronage; a desire to save money on salaries by hiring low-cost recruits over those that are better qualified; and beliefs that more-qualified teachers are more likely to leave and less likely to take orders.[50] When these and other new teachers leave in frustration because they are underprepared for teaching and undersupported by the current induction practices, the hiring scramble begins all over again.

Much of the problem of teacher supply is a problem of distribution that could be solved with more thoughtful and coherent policies. While there are shortages of qualified candidates in particular fields (e.g., mathematics and science) and particular locations (primarily inner city and rural), the nation each year produces more new teachers than it needs. While some school districts cannot find the applicants they need, others have long waiting lists of qualified teachers eager for work. Some states routinely export their surplus teachers; others scramble to import them. Thousands of teachers fail to make the transition

Swimming Upstream in New York City: What Does It Take to Get Hired?

"It was the most insensitive, discouraging, incomprehensible process I have ever experienced," says Lori Chajet of her yearlong quest to get a teaching job in New York City. It was only because she was extraordinarily persevering that Chajet, a Brown University graduate with a master's in education from Teachers College, Columbia University, survived the bureaucratic obstacle course that defeated many others.

Despite the fact that New York has continuing high demand for teachers and frequent shortages, well-prepared teachers are discouraged from applying for jobs. Chajet was advised to start the process of getting a file number even before she started her preparation program. Then followed countless attempts to speak to someone at the New York City Board of Education by phone, waiting weeks just to receive the wrong forms, and several hourlong train trips to Brooklyn to hand-deliver documents. Just getting a file number required five different processes—initial check-in and registration, fingerprinting, a physical checkup, a transcript review, and an oral interview—some requiring separate processing fees payable only by individual postal money orders.

This experience was shared by most recruits studied by New York's Education Priorities Panel, which recommended after its two-year study that the city hiring system be scrapped. "I had to file the same exact papers four times," reported one teacher. "They'd send me letters that something wasn't right and I'd have to go back in person." Another reported, "I've had my fingerprints taken five times and paid for it each time. What do they do with those records? I took the TPD [Temporary Per Diem] test for regular

education and special education. I took the NTE [National Teachers Examination] and passed all three parts. I took all my education credits." What does it take to be a teacher? The panel found that fewer than 10% of the city's new teachers actually made it through the certification process in one piece.

Chajet persevered through similar travails—including the inexplicable return, after three months, of her unprocessed application for a license—only to find that she would not even know what vacancies were available until late August. "I was stunned. I couldn't believe that this was the process that they expected all beginning teachers to go through—a whole summer of not knowing to just start teaching in a whole new environment as the kids arrive. How could I spend the summer planning and preparing without knowing who and where I'd be teaching?"

By this time Chajet, an Ivy League graduate with a master's degree, felt that her chances of teaching were as good as the next person on the street. Finally, after a long roller coaster of a summer, she landed a job from a school that she had visited earlier in the spring—though not without additional paperwork and trips to the Board of Education and the local district office to become officially hired. She recalls one of these visits when after waiting in line she was told, "I'm sorry, you're just not important enough right now." Chajet feels much more appreciated now that she is a full-time teacher, but notes that the daily demands of classroom teaching are nothing compared with the frustrations of New York City's hiring process.

Not everyone is able to endure. When Harvard graduate Tracy Seckler,

also armed with a master's degree in teaching from Columbia, sent out dozens of letters and résumés to New York City schools in April, she found that she would have to wait until after Labor Day to even learn of vacancies. Determined to teach, she felt she had to look elsewhere. Outside the bureaucratic entanglements of New York City, she found personalized treatment, well-organized early hiring procedures, and attention to teacher quality in affluent suburban Scarsdale, New York. "While I was getting busy phone signals from the New York City Board of Education," Seckler recalls, "Scarsdale's personnel office was calling me with different possibilities for scheduling an interview." She was impressed that teachers, parents, and principals participated in her interview, and that she was asked insightful questions about teaching and her philosophy of education rather than about course credits and money orders.

Of her move to Scarsdale, Seckler says, "I never intended to teach anyplace other than New York, but the possibility of beginning teaching with no opportunity to visit the school, see the kids, or talk with the teachers began to look completely unappealing." In May, while Chajet was still waiting in line at the New York City Board of Education, Seckler was offered and accepted a job teaching kindergarten for the following year. By June she was meeting with her future students and colleagues and planning with excitement for her first class of students.

from the places they were prepared to the places where the jobs are due to lack of information about where to apply, lack of reciprocity in licensing between states, and ridiculously cumbersome application procedures.

Second, districts frequently ignore existing entry standards in hiring, either because they do not believe existing standards are meaningful or because the pressure to put a teacher—any teacher—in the classroom is overpowering, especially as Labor Day approaches and many districts finally get around to hiring. Faced with the option of classrooms full of students and no teachers or unqualified "teachers" in classrooms, some districts choose unqualified teachers without a second's hesitation.

Another option—creating more proactive and streamlined recruitment and hiring systems—is frequently not considered. As a result, funds are wasted on the training of many who do not enter or stay in teaching; many would-be teachers cannot find jobs while unqualified entrants are hired; and many teachers are placed outside the subject areas in which they were prepared.

Some problems, however, are national in scope and require special attention: There is no coordinated system for helping colleges decide how many teachers in which fields should be prepared or where they will be needed. Neither is there regular support of the kind long provided in medicine to recruit teachers for high-need fields and locations.[51] Critical areas like mathematics and science have long had shortages of qualified teachers that were only temporarily solved by federal recruitment incentives during the post-Sputnik years. Currently, more than 40% of math teachers and 30% of science teachers are not fully qualified

Slipshod Recruitment

Sabrina Vaught was shocked by what she learned about teacher hiring in her first teaching stint. Sabrina entered Teach for America (TFA) after a year of teaching high school English in Korea. She had hoped to teach high school in a high-need area, but was placed in a Louisiana elementary school. Sabrina was appalled to learn, after the fact, that the TFA interviewer had decided she should not teach high school because of her "petite frame and high-pitched voice" and that the district personnel director selected her to teach kindergarten "because I looked from my picture like I would be a good kindergarten teacher."

Vaught was troubled about going into

an elementary classroom after only a few weeks of training. But, she says, "I'd promised to do this. I was still under the impression that there was a classroom of kids that wasn't going to have a teacher and they were waiting for me, and if I didn't go they would have subs that would change every two days."

Within two months, Sabrina had decided to leave teaching and enter a school of education. "I had a lot of kids who were frustrated and I was frustrated because I wanted to help them and didn't have the training to do that." A car accident clinched her decision. Before leaving, however, she met an experienced certified teacher whom she learned had initially applied for her job.

Sabrina was amazed by what she found. "Here we were supposed to be teaching in shortage areas, and this woman had ten years of teaching experience in elementary education. Of course she was going to cost several thousand dollars more a year so they didn't hire her. She went to teach in [the all-white] private school," while Sabrina was hired to teach in the nearly all-black public school. When Sabrina left, her principal hired a certified replacement that afternoon. "That was troubling to me, too," Sabrina confessed, "because then I thought, 'What was I doing?'" She had never imagined that "teacher shortages are defined by money, rather than by lack of qualified people."

for their assignments.[52] Studies show that unqualified teachers produce lower levels of learning for their students,[53] and that, compared with other nations, United States students are less well taught in science and mathematics throughout the grades.[54] In addition, many schools cannot offer advanced courses in these fields because they lack teachers who can teach them.

Well-prepared urban teachers and teachers of color are in short supply as well. While nearly one-third of today's students are members of minority groups, the number of teachers of color declined sharply during the 1980s and has only recently climbed to 13% of the teaching force.[55] With the exception of candidates of color, most would-be teachers hope to return to the suburbs and small towns where they grew up. They do not plan to teach in central cities, even though that is where most jobs are.[56] Little is being done to counteract these trends. Since the successful federal recruitment programs of the 1970s ended, only a few states have created supports in the form of scholarships or loans to prepare teachers for high-need areas and fields.

Simply streamlining and rationalizing the processes of teacher recruitment, hiring, and induction, as some states and districts have done, would go a long way toward putting qualified teachers in every classroom. In addition, investing once again in the targeted recruitment and preparation of teachers for high-need fields and locations is a national need. It should also be stressed that large pools of potential midcareer teacher entrants are available, and highly successful programs have been created in many colleges for preparing them to teach. What we need now is the energy and imagination to exploit, on a nationwide scale, the reservoirs of talent that could be turned to teaching from downsizing corporations, military and government retirees, recent graduates, and teacher aides already in the schools.

New Teachers Sink or Swim

Of all of education's self-inflicted wounds, the continued tolerance for extraordinary turnover among new teachers is among the most remarkable. Chronic, high rates of teacher replacement—particularly for teachers in the first two or three years of their careers and particularly in urban school districts—increase the pressure on teacher recruitment and initial placement systems incessantly. This pressure is particularly severe during times of high demand like the one we are now entering, because beginning teachers will be hired in ever greater numbers, and unless conditions change, they will leave much more rapidly than older teachers do.

Turnover in the first few years is particularly high because new teachers are typically given the most challenging teaching assignments and left to sink or swim with little or no support. They are often placed in the most disadvantaged schools and assigned the most difficult-to-teach students, with the greatest number of class preparations (many of them outside their field of expertise) and a slew of extracurricular duties. With no mentoring or support for these teachers, it is little wonder that so many give up before they have really learned to teach. Alone in their classrooms, without access to colleagues for problem solving or role modeling, discouragement can easily set in.

In the past, people thought that whatever teachers needed to know could be acquired quickly and prior to entering a classroom. Once a teacher received a license to teach, he or she was considered ready for practice, in need of no more help. Early in the nation's educational history there may have been some justification for this belief; today there is none. The weight of accumulated evidence clearly shows that traditional sink-or-swim induction contributes to high attrition and to lower levels of teacher effectiveness.[57]

The kinds of supervised internships or residencies regularly provided for new entrants in other professions—architects, psychologists, nurses, doctors, engineers—are rare in teaching, but they have proven to be quite effective where they exist. Beginning teachers who receive mentoring focus on student learning much sooner; they become more effective as teachers because they are learning from guided practice rather than trial-and-error; and they leave teaching at much lower rates.[58] A study of California teachers found that the combination of high-quality, university-based teacher education followed by first-year mentoring produced teachers who were substantially more effective than those who received either university-based training or first-year mentoring alone.[59]

Many other countries have highly developed mentoring and induction programs following teacher education to help novice teachers in their first years on the job. States like Connecticut and districts like Toledo, Cincinnati, Columbus, Rochester, and Seattle have developed programs to support new teachers, often in partnership with unions and universities. The best of these efforts involve beginners in yearlong internships at "professional development schools" before they are hired, at which point they are assigned to an experienced mentor who works intensively with them during their first year of teaching.

Although some states have created programs for new teacher induction, few have maintained the commitment required. With a few exceptions, initiatives during the 1980s focused on evaluation and failed to fund mentoring.[60] Others provided mentoring that reached only a few eligible teachers or withered as funds evaporated. Again, the problem is not that we don't know how to support beginning teachers; it is that we have not yet developed the commitment to do so routinely.

Lack of Supports or Rewards for Knowledge and Skill

In addition to the lack of support for beginning teachers, most U.S. school districts invest little in ongoing professional development for experienced teachers and spend much of these limited resources on unproductive practices. Estimates of professional development support range from only 1% to 3% of district operating budgets, even when the costs of staff time are factored in.[61] Even the most generous estimates, however, are paltry compared with the expenditures invested in employee development in leading corporations and in other countries' schools.[62]

In addition, district staff development is still characterized by one-shot workshops that have very little effect on practice, rather than more effective approaches that are linked to concrete problems of practice and built into teachers' ongoing work with their colleagues. These workshops tend to offer ideas for classroom management or teaching that are not tied to specific subject areas or problems of practice, that do not offer follow-up help for implementation, and that are replaced at the next workshop with another idea—the new "flavor of the month"—offering little continuity in building practice. These offerings often bear little relation to what teachers want to study. Two-thirds of teachers report that they have no say in what or how they learn on the job.[63] As one New York teacher commented of his frustration with his district's top-down approach to managing staff development: "They're offering me stress reduction workshops when I need to learn how to help students meet these new standards. My stress comes from not having the tools to help my students succeed!"

Most U.S. teachers have almost no regular time to consult together or learn about new teaching strategies, unlike their peers in many European and Asian countries where teachers have substantial time to plan and study with one another. In Germany, Japan, and China, for example, teachers spend between 15 and 20 hours per week working with colleagues on developing curriculum, counseling students, and pursuing their own learning. They regularly visit and observe other schools and classrooms, attend seminars provided by university faculty and other teachers, conduct group research projects, and participate in teacher-led study groups.[64]

Teachers in these countries generally share a work room in which they spend breaks throughout the day and meet regularly to work on curriculum, assessment, and school management together. Japanese and Chinese teachers offer demonstration lessons to each other, discussing the nuances of specific concepts, how they might be presented, what kinds of questions students might have, and what kinds of questions teachers should ask to elicit student interest.[65] Researchers have noted that class lessons in these countries are extraordinarily well crafted because of teachers' systematic efforts to work together to perfect their practice.[66] German teachers hold "curriculum conferences" within the school to develop materials and look at student work. They also work together on committees examining curriculum, assessment, and other schoolwide matters.[67] The result is a rich environment for continuous learning about teaching and the needs of students.

Instead of these ongoing learning opportunities, U.S. teachers get a few brief workshops offering packaged prescriptions from outside consultants on "in-service days" that contribute little to deepening their subject knowledge or teaching skills. Difficult problems of teaching and learning—"How can I explain quadratic equations?" "Why doesn't Ellen understand what she reads?"—are never discussed in these contexts. While teachers are being asked to engage their own students in active learning, problem solving, and inquiry, they rarely experience this kind of learning themselves. As one longtime student of staff development notes of current practice:

A good deal of what passes for "professional development" in schools is a joke—one that we'd laugh at if we weren't trying to keep from crying.

I appreciate staff development, but sometimes it doesn't seem well planned. For example, we have designated work days without students, but along comes a consultant with an instructional game that we already know, but we have to spend time learning it again. We feel stressed because there are things we need to get done, but we won't have time.

— ALVAREZ ANDERSON,
FRENCH TEACHER, C. E. MURRAY HIGH SCHOOL,
GREELEYVILLE, SOUTH CAROLINA

Historical View of Teacher Development

Professional knowledge is developed by "experts" who hand it down to teachers.

Teachers work alone implementing required procedures.

It's everything that a learning environment shouldn't be: radically under-resourced, brief, not sustained, designed for 'one-size-fits-all,' imposed rather than owned, lacking intellectual coherence, treated as a special add-on event rather than as part of a natural process, and trapped in the constraints of the bureaucratic system we have come to call "school." In short, it's pedagogically naive, a demeaning exercise that often leaves its participants more cynical and no more knowledgeable, skilled, or committed than before.[68]

As we describe later, more productive strategies have begun to emerge in some school districts where teachers are involved in ongoing networks and partnerships that reflect their teaching concerns. Teacher networks allow teachers in many school districts to work with one another over time on issues of subject matter teaching. School-to-school networks help educators work together on schoolwide change. School-university partnerships provide forums for study groups and school-based research on issues of immediate concern. Teacher academies provide sites for shared problem solving, exchanges of teaching ideas, and intensive institutes. Engaging in new teacher assessments provides teachers with another vehicle for deepening their learning.

Unlike old approaches that see professional development as delivering simple recipes to teachers working in isolation, these new approaches connect teachers to one another through in-school teams and cross-school professional communities that tackle problems of practice over time. Though different in

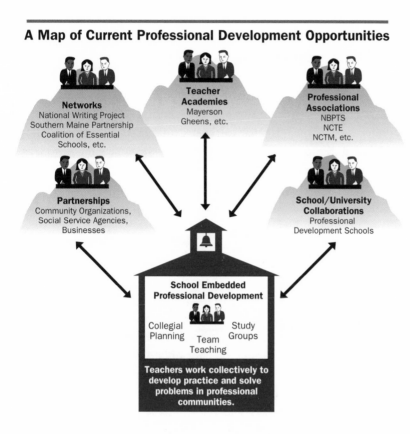

A Map of Current Professional Development Opportunities

Networks
National Writing Project
Southern Maine Partnership
Coalition of Essential
Schools, etc.

Teacher Academies
Mayerson
Gheens, etc.

Professional Associations
NBPTS
NCTE
NCTM, etc.

Partnerships
Community Organizations,
Social Service Agencies,
Businesses

School/University Collaborations
Professional
Development Schools

School Embedded Professional Development

Collegial Planning   Study Groups
Team Teaching

Teachers work collectively to develop practice and solve problems in professional communities.

some respects, all of these approaches share certain features. They are:

- Connected to teachers' work with their students;

- Linked to concrete tasks of teaching;

- Organized around problem solving;

- Informed by research;

- Sustained over time by ongoing conversations and coaching.[69]

Over and over again, teachers attest to the usefulness of these kinds of opportunities for transforming their teaching—and to their scarcity in most school settings. Great teachers who are lucky enough to be in places where such opportunities are offered find ways to take advantage of them, usually on their own time and money. But most teachers have little access to this kind of learning, and few incentives to seek it out.

If great teaching is to spread beyond a few pockets of excellence, schools need to think systematically about how to encourage and reward it. As Phillip Schlechty, the president of the Center for Leadership in School Reform, has observed, in most schools the only reward is the lack of punishment. Current incentives in education do not acknowledge outstanding teaching, support teachers in taking on the most challenging work, or reward greater knowledge and skill.

There are many ways in which greater knowledge is demeaned in teaching. Novices who enter without preparation are paid at the same levels as those who enter with highly developed skills. Mediocre teachers receive the same rewards as outstanding ones. And unlicensed "teachers" are placed on the same salary schedule as teachers licensed in two or more subjects.

Within teaching, there is a flat career structure that places a low ceiling on lifetime earnings. Entering novices take on exactly the same kind of work as 30-year veterans, with little differentiation based on expertise. All of these incentives maintain a status quo in which ability has little currency, and highly capable people are as likely to be discouraged from entering teaching as they are encouraged to enter and remain.

Current incentives only haphazardly reward learning aimed at better teaching. Monetary incentives take the form of salary increases tied to graduate course-taking, which rewards seat time, not greater effectiveness. Great teachers have few incentives to stay in the profession. In the vast majority of districts, the greatest status accrues to those who work farthest away from children: The only way to advance is to leave the classroom for an administrative job or a specialist position. These jobs not only pull talent out of the classroom where students could benefit directly; they contribute to a proliferation of nonteaching staff that ultimately reduces funds that could buy smaller classes and more teachers.

One tribute to the shortsightedness of the existing system is that it recognizes experience with easier work instead of rewarding senior teachers for tackling difficult learning problems. This has been necessary because there are so few other incentives in the system to retain good teachers. As teachers gain experience, they can look forward to teaching in more affluent schools, working with easier schedules, and dealing with "better" classes. Teachers are rarely given concrete incentives to apply their expertise to the most challenging learning problems or to major system needs.

These problems of career structure and compensation need to be tackled in concert. Only bare-bones improvements in teacher compensation systems can be anticipated unless they are connected more directly to teaching expertise, thus garnering greater public support as well as greater school productivity. Development of a much richer, deeper, broader concept of a true *career* in teaching must be accompanied by incentives for teachers to grow and diversify their skills in ways that help students reach high standards of achievement.

Schools Structured for Failure Instead of Success

One of the management truisms of the 1990s holds that every organization is perfectly organized to produce the results that it gets. Nowhere in American life is this more true than in our schools. On some unconscious level schools tolerate student failure because they mistake it for a commitment to higher standards. Designed to support a very limited kind of learning and a very particular kind of learner, schools only rarely hold themselves responsible for the success of every student. And most are structured in ways that make it impossible for them to do so.

Today's schools are organized in ways that support neither student nor teacher learning well. Like the turn-of-the-century industries they were modeled after—most of which are now redesigning themselves—current school structures were designed to mimic factories that used semiskilled workers to do discrete pieces of work in a mass production assembly line. Thus, teachers' work is divided up and handled individually; students pass by in large groups, conveyor belt-style, to be stamped with a lesson before they move on to the next stop. As bureaucracies have grown from this structure, traditional schools have come to suffer from three major flaws:

1. They use time nonproductively, passing students off from teacher to teacher for short periods of learning, thus making it difficult for them to learn intellectually challenging material or to be well known by school staff.

2. They use staff nonproductively, assigning work in disconnected ways, isolating teachers from one another, and allocating too many people to jobs outside of classrooms. This undermines collective goal setting and problem solving, prevents knowledge sharing, and makes it difficult for anyone to take responsibility for student learning.

3. They use money nonproductively, allocating far too many resources to nonteaching functions and staff. This allocation of resources then makes it difficult to provide teachers with the time and supports they need to do high-quality work.

In addition, information technologies that could enable alternative uses of staff and time are not yet readily available in schools, and few staff are prepared to use them in ways that could optimize teaching and learning for both students and teachers. New technologies could dramatically reshape how schools operate, but most have not yet imagined how technology could empower teachers to teach more effectively as well as to transform administrative tasks, communication with parents, and continuing professional development.

Current structures and traditions make it difficult for schools to create the three conditions that research has consistently found to be the most powerful determinants of both student academic achievement and safe, positive environments:

1. Teacher expertise, including opportunities for ongoing learning;

2. Common, challenging curriculum requirements; and

3. Small school units and classes that are organized to allow teachers to know their students well over time.[70]

The combination of these elements of productive schooling is relatively rare in American school systems. First of all, teachers are generally isolated, working alone rather than in teams, with little or no shared planning time, and pursuing disconnected agendas without a set of common curriculum goals to guide them. This makes it difficult for teachers to share expertise or to get their teaching to "add up" in a cumulative way. Lower-grade teachers have almost no time to share ideas with colleagues. Upper-grade teachers do not share students, so they cannot integrate their work, evaluate student progress, or solve student problems together. Teachers meet infrequently together and have few communication vehicles such as electronic networking to allow them to share information or work more closely together.

Second, teaching and other services are fragmented. Unlike schools in many other countries where teachers often stay with their students for multiple years and multiple subjects, American schools typically pass students off to different teachers for each grade and subject, as well as to other staff for counseling and special programs. Just as teachers begin to know their students reasonably well, they must pass them on to someone else who must start all over again trying to figure out how they learn.

In contrast, Japanese teachers stay with their students for at least two years. As one principal explains, "The first year you look and listen; then in the second year the real learning can begin."[71] German teachers keep the same students for two to four years through tenth grade. A principal who, like most European school heads, also teaches, explains:

Teaching and Technology: Current Barriers

A recent report of the Office of Technology Assessment reveals how far the nation's schools are from becoming technologically supported workplaces for students and teachers:

While schools had 5.8 million computers in 1995 (about one for every nine students), fewer than half of teachers use computers regularly for instruction. Only 19% of classes in English, 7% in math, and 3% in social studies use computers.

Most school computers are already outmoded. In 1994, 85% of the equipment installed in schools could not handle multimedia uses or connect to outside resources. Only 3% of schoolrooms have access to on-line databases.

Sixty percent of instructional areas in schools have no telephone lines, and 87% do not have access to fiber optics or cable. Only one teacher in eight has a telephone in class and fewer than 1% have access to voice mail.

Both access to and use of information technologies are heavily skewed toward higher-income schools. Schools attended by low-income students have fewer computers and are half as likely to have access to the Internet.

Although 18 states now require some technology preparation for a teaching license, only 10% of new teachers in 1994 felt they were prepared to integrate new technologies into their instruction. Fewer than half of experienced teachers had participated in professional development on the uses of new technologies.

Beyond issues of access to adequate hardware, software, and communications links are other barriers to the effective use of technologies in schools: the absence of a vision for technology use that takes into account new curricular and other possibilities; the lack of training and ongoing support for curriculum integration; and the lack of teaching time to experiment with new technologies, share experiences with other teachers, plan lessons using technology, and attend technology courses or meetings.

Source: Office of Technology Assessment (OTA), *Teachers and Technology: Making the Connection* (Washington, D.C.: U.S. Congress, 1995). Adapted from the *OTA Report Summary,* April 1995.

We don't lose several weeks each September learning a new set of names, teaching the basic rules to a new set of students, and figuring out exactly what they learned the previous year; and we don't lose weeks at the end of the year packing students back up. Most importantly, teachers and students get to know each other—teachers get to know how each student learns, and students know which teachers they can go to for various kinds of help. The importance of this is incalculable.[72]

In addition, because teachers serve as counselors, they know their students from a personal as well as an academic perspective. And because they work in teams, they can help each other solve problems related to individual students and to teaching. These arrangements turn out to be much more effective for learning—especially the intensive learning demanded by high standards—than the assembly-line strategies used by U.S. schools.

In addition, traditional school structures use time badly. School courses and time blocks assume that all students in a group will learn at the same pace—an assumption long known to be inaccurate. Flexible schedules, extended learning blocks, and technology aids that would allow teachers to vary the resources they use with different students are rare. Typical time blocks for learning—the usual 42-minute periods or shorter blocks for elementary school subjects—are too short for the kinds of tasks needed to develop high levels of performance: extended discussion, sustained project work, writing, research, or experimentation. Students rush from one class to another, barely getting settled and engaged in serious work before they must jump up en masse to run to the next class. Teachers have almost no time to plan together, build well-crafted lessons, or consult with one another about problems of practice. The teacher's job is defined as meeting with large groups of students virtually all day. All of the other functions of the school are assumed by other people—supervisors and specialists—who are supposed to plan, augment, and coordinate the work of teachers, as well as attend to the proliferation of reporting requirements bureaucracies generate.

Finally, there are far too many people on the sidelines. The overspecialization of American schools has led to a wide array of services for students that are administered by different people in separate divisions reporting to other people who must then coordinate their tasks and manage extensive paperwork. In a typical school system, there is one staff member for every nine children, but fewer than half of them are classroom teachers. Consequently, class sizes average 24 and can reach well over 30.[73] Although nonteaching staff work hard, their work is structured in ways that do not support student learning well. When a dozen different people with large caseloads are supposed to treat different parts of the student, both accountability and effectiveness are reduced. No one has deep knowledge of the students' needs or clear responsibility for solving problems. In addition, this form of organization creates a huge need for coordination, which drains resources from classrooms into offices around the periphery of teaching.

What all of this adds up to is an unanticipated design flaw. Although more and more adults are working in schools, fewer and fewer are actually in the classroom.

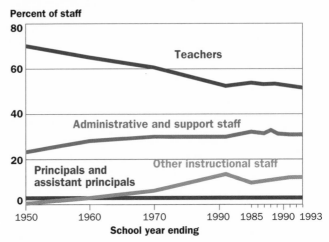

Type of Staff Employed by Public Schools In full-time equivalents

Percent of staff

Teachers

Administrative and support staff

Other instructional staff

Principals and assistant principals

School year ending
(1950, 1960, 1970, 1990, 1985, 1990, 1993)

Note: Plotted points in each chart include school years ending: 1950, 1960, 1970, 1981, 1985-1991, 1993.

Source: U.S. Department of Education, National Center for Education Statistics, Statistics of State School Systems, Common Core of Data. Published in *The Condition of Education* 1993 (Washington, D.C.: National Center for Education Statistics, 1993), pp. 148, 149 and *The Digest of Education Statistics*, 1995, p.89

Indeed, the proportion of professional staff classified as teachers has declined consistently over the years, from more than 70% in 1950 to 52% in 1993. Of these, more than 10% are specialists not engaged in classroom teaching.[74]

During this period, the number of nonteaching staff increased by more than 40%[75] as schools grew in size and added many more administrative and support staff; school problems were increasingly treated with special categorical programs; and top-down reforms created larger bureaucracies. According to a U.S. Department of Labor study, more than 21% of elementary and secondary school employees in 1986 were administrators and their support staff; another 21% were engaged in services like maintenance and transportation; and 58% were engaged in teaching and professional specialties, including counseling, testing, and librarianship.[76] About three-quarters of this last category (roughly 43.5% of the total) were classroom teachers. In short, for every four classroom teachers, there are nearly six other school employees in the United States.

By contrast, teaching staff in other countries make up 60% to 80% of public education employees (see table 1).[77] Rather than hiring lots of nonteachers who plan and manage the work of teachers, these countries hire more teachers and give them time to plan and manage their work together—and hence to become ever smarter about what they do. In a recent eight-nation study, the United States had by far the lowest ratio of core teaching staff to other professional staff (less than 1:1), well behind the leader, Belgium, at 4:1.

The organizational assumptions that led to this way of managing work are now being abandoned in high-performance businesses that are flattening hierarchies, organizing work so it is done in teams rather than by isolated workers, and investing in more highly skilled employees who can take on a wider array of roles

Table 1: International Comparison of Instructional and Other Staff, By Country

Country	Percent of Staff Who Are:			Ratio of teachers and principals to other staff
	Teachers	Instructional staff including principals	Other administrative and support staff	
Belgium	80.0%	10%	10.0%	4.0 : 1
Japan	77.4%	—	22.6%	3.4 : 1
Italy	76.4%	7.3%	14.5%	3.5 : 1
Australia	69.1%	7.1%	28.6%	1.9 : 1
Finland	60.8%	39.2%	—	1.55 : 1
France	60.0%	40.0%	—	1.5 : 1
Denmark	57.9%	28.1%	15.8%	1.3 : 1
U.S.	43.6%	24.2%	33.9%	0.75 : 1

Source: Organization for Economic Cooperation and Development (OECD), *Education at a Glance: OECD Indicators* (Paris: OECD, 1995), in *Using What We Have To Get the Schools We Need: A Productivity Focus for American Education* (New York: The Consortium on Productivity in the Schools, 1995), p. 44

and responsibilities and who have access to technologies that allow them to work more efficiently. Schools that have restructured their work in these ways have been able to provide more time for teachers to work together *and* more time for students to work closely with teachers around more clearly defined learning goals.[78]

Like the "learning organizations" that management expert Peter Senge writes about,[79] these schools continually improve what they do because they create teams that develop a common sense of organizational goals and shared ideas about how things work. As people work together to analyze what's working and to solve problems, they develop the ability to see how the whole and its parts interact with each other to create today's reality and tomorrow's possibilities.

While U.S. teachers typically report that they do not have the time and resources to do their work, that they have too few opportunities to interact with colleagues and little influence on school policies and practices, teachers in restructuring school environments feel differently. A recent survey of teachers regarding the effects of recent school reforms[80] found that those in restructuring schools with site-based management were much more likely to report they were engaged in important educational changes, such as more rigorous graduation standards, performance-based assessment practices, emphasis on in-depth understanding rather than superficial content coverage, cooperative learning, and making connections between classroom practices and students' home experiences.

In addition, these teachers were much more likely to report that their schools were providing more structured time for them to plan and work with each other on professional matters, enabling them to observe and coach each other in the classroom, work in teams, and meet with students and parents.

Because of these changes, teachers in reforming schools felt they had more opportunity to adapt their instruction to the needs of their students and to invent more effective methods, rather than being constrained by district routines or outmoded methods. They were more optimistic about principal-teacher relationships, working conditions for teachers, the educational performance of students, the professional status of teachers, and their own job satisfaction. They were significantly more likely to report themselves very satisfied with their career as a teacher and to see teachers as the agents of reform rather than as the targets of reform.[81]

Moving Ahead

These seven barriers—low performance expectations for students; unenforced standards for teachers; major flaws in teacher preparation programs; the practice of leaving new teachers to flounder in their first year; the lack of serious professional development for teachers; few rewards for knowledge and skill; and poorly organized schools—are the major challenges that must be addressed. But the nation's efforts to address them are continually sidetracked by a set of myths that divert the public's attention from putting teaching at the top of the nation's education reform agenda.

Fatal Distractions: Five Myths about Teaching

I t is quite clear that the challenges confounding teacher improvement are long-standing and complex. There are no "silver bullet" answers that will fix them tomorrow. They require thoughtful, coherent, long-range solutions. Yet even successful efforts to deal with these problems have made little headway against a persistent set of beliefs that substitute bromides and platitudes for the hard work required to improve teaching.

The Commission thinks of these beliefs as myths, but they are so powerful that they amount to fatal distractions diverting attention from the need for reform. Like any myth, these are contested perceptions: There is some truth in them, along with much that is not true. Like any myth, they have a life of their own that does not reflect changing times and realities. Like any myth, they can be used to hamper or accelerate positive change. It is time to confront these perennial myths, so that they can give way to more productive foundations for moving forward. Among them, five stand out:

Myth #1: Anyone can teach.

Myth #2: Teacher preparation is not much use.

Myth #3: Teachers don't work hard enough.

Myth #4: Tenure is the problem.

Myth #5: Unions block reform.

Myth #1: Anyone Can Teach

Sometimes this myth is expressed with the old bromide: "Those who can, do. Those who can't, teach." A twist on this sentiment is the view that "teachers are born and not made." However stated, this attitude is as widespread as it is distasteful and cannot be ignored.

The idea that anyone can teach is nonsense—as any parent organizing a child's birthday party or chaperoning a high school dance can attest. Being responsible for a room full of children or adolescents for even a few hours can be one of the most difficult, frustrating assignments of adult life, even if the goal is merely survival rather than productive learning.

Most college graduates can recall brilliant professors who knew a great deal about their fields—but could not explain what they knew to their students. Most people have also experienced the book-bound lectures of teachers who did not themselves understand their material—or their students—and were barely a chapter ahead of the class. And many parents suspect that some teachers manage ineptly, because their children report being confused or intimidated by some teachers, but not others.

Literally hundreds of studies confirm that the best teachers know their subjects deeply, understand how people learn, and have mastered a range of teaching methods.[82] These findings hold true for high school fields ranging from mathematics and science to vocational education, as well as for early childhood and elementary education. Better prepared teachers are strikingly more effective in developing higher-order thinking skills and in meeting the needs of diverse students through different learning approaches.[83]

In short, the belief that anyone can teach—or the view that teaching skills cannot be taught—is misguided and dangerous. Anyone can teach? Students everywhere know better—and so should educators and policymakers.

Myth #2: Formal Teacher Preparation Is Not Much Use

This myth is pernicious because it describes what many veteran teachers remember about their teacher education courses of 20 years ago as well as what some members of the public think about how one learns to teach. There are two beliefs lurking beneath this myth. One is that teacher education programs are hopelessly poor and better avoided—perhaps even a disincentive for smart people to enter teaching. The other is that teaching is best learned, to the extent it can be learned at all, by trial-and-error on the job. A large body of evidence contradicts both of these beliefs, but they linger on.

Even given the shortcomings of some teacher education programs, studies over the last 30 years consistently show that fully prepared teachers are more highly rated and more effective with students than those whose background lacks one or more of the elements of formal teacher education—subject matter preparation, knowledge about teaching and learning, and guided clinical experience.[84] In addition, the profession has worked to redesign teacher preparation programs over the last decade. Many colleges of education are integrating new standards for students and teachers into the curriculum, incorporating new knowledge, and creating extended internships. Older teachers' memories of teacher education programs are less relevant to today's reality with every passing year.

Furthermore, talented recruits are entering schools of education in record numbers. Due to recent reforms, both standards and interest have been steadily rising. By 1991, graduates of teacher education programs had higher levels of academic achievement than most college graduates, reversing the trends of the early 1980s.[85] The only entering teachers with lower than average college achievement were those who entered on emergency licenses without teacher preparation.[86] A number of major state universities have developed five-year programs of teacher education, created professional development school partnerships, and made other changes that have dramatically strengthened teacher preparation. Top state universities in Wisconsin, Michigan, Tennessee, Virginia, Kansas, Ohio, New Hampshire, Texas, and Florida are among them. They are joined by graduate-level Master of Arts in Teaching (MAT) programs at Columbia, Harvard, Stanford, and many others in training tens of thousands of talented candidates across the country, and they have more top-flight applicants than they can accept.

As for the second half of the myth, many high-quality alternative pathways into teaching have proved effective in preparing nontraditional entrants—midcareer recruits and retirees from business and the military—to enter and succeed at teaching. The Commission endorses these programs. The most successful offer a streamlined, carefully constructed curriculum that integrates courses on learning theory, development, teaching methods, and subject matter knowledge with an intensively supervised internship prior to entry.[87] Because they are tailored to the specific needs of recruits and are undertaken in partnership with nearby schools, they can concentrate preparation within a 9- to 12-month program and provide the additional mentoring that really prepares candidates to teach.

In contrast to these well-designed nontraditional routes, programs offering a few weeks of summer training before new hires are thrown into the classroom are not an adequate answer. These kinds of programs, developed by a few states and school districts as well as outside vendors, have proven to be even lower in quality than the programs they aim to replace. Studies of such efforts consistently reveal severe shortcomings: Recruits are dissatisfied with their training; they have greater difficulties planning curriculum, teaching, managing the classroom, and diagnosing students' learning needs. Principals and other teachers typically rate them lower on key teaching skills, and they leave teaching at higher-than-average rates. Most important, their students learn less, especially in areas like reading and writing, which are critical to later school success.[88]

If this Commission's recommendations are accepted, there will be no more shoddy education programs. Equally important, there will be no more resources wasted on quick-fix solutions masquerading as real answers to complex problems.

Myth #3: Teachers Don't Work Hard Enough

Skeptics and cynics are always with us, and their first question is, how hard can it be to work 180 days a year, with half the afternoon free? And if teachers' salaries are lower than those of other college graduates, isn't that because the job is so easy? In fact, because teachers' visible schedules mirror those of students it is easy to believe that teachers enjoy an undemanding life. But the truth is American teachers work very hard—typically 50 to 55 hours per week and most days over their vacations.[89]

The job of an American high school teacher, described here, requires enormous hard work along with creativity and skill:

<u>WANTED</u>

College graduate with academic major (master's degree preferred). Excellent communication/leadership skills required. Challenging opportunity to serve 150 clients daily on a tight schedule, developing up to five different products each day to meet individual needs, while adhering to multiple product specifications. Adaptability helpful, since suppliers cannot always deliver goods on time, incumbent must arrange for own support services, and customers rarely know what they want. Ideal candidate will enjoy working in isolation from colleagues. This diversified position allows employee to exercise typing, clerical, law enforcement, and social work skills between assignments and after hours. Typical work week: 50 hours. Special nature of the work precludes amenities such as telephones or computers, but work has many intrinsic rewards. Starting salary $24,661, rising to $36,495 after only 15 years.

Because American teachers have little time during the school day for planning, locating materials, talking with parents, meeting individually with students, consulting with one another, or grading papers, they do all of these things after school hours, typically well into the evenings, on weekends, and during "vacations." As one teacher explained to us,

> People think we work six hours a day but I'm still there till five or even seven. They think we get the summer off, but I'm taking courses or planning for next year. . . . We don't have part-time jobs.

Despite a shorter school year, no nation requires teachers to teach a greater number of hours per day and year than the United States. American teachers teach more than 1,000 hours per year, far more than teachers in other industrialized countries, who teach between 600 and 800 hours per year, depending on the grade level.[90] In most European and Asian countries, teachers spend between 17 and 20 hours of a 40- to 45-hour work week in their classrooms with students. The remaining time is spent at school planning and working with colleagues, as well as parents and students.[91]

In contrast, most U.S. elementary school teachers have three or fewer hours for preparation each week (only 8.3 minutes for every hour in the classroom), and secondary teachers generally have five preparation periods per week (thirteen minutes per hour of classroom instruction).[92] Most teachers spend at least 10 to 15 hours each week outside school preparing lessons and grading homework and papers. This time is spent in isolation, in contrast to the in-school time of teachers in other countries, which is spent primarily in collaborative planning and learning.

U.S. teachers don't work hard? Teachers overseas report they could not succeed in the conditions under which American teachers work.[93]

Myth #4: Tenure Is the Problem

Teachers, like everyone else in an era of corporate downsizing, value job security. However, there is in fact no such thing as lifetime "tenure" in public schools. What public school teachers receive after three years on probation is a presumption in their favor that they will be rehired for one-year terms unless cause for not hiring them can be demonstrated.

For many years, the "tenure" offered after probation was expected to compensate for lower wages and poor working conditions in schools. Tenure began as a response to arbitrary dismissals of qualified teachers when school boards wanted to offer positions to friends and relatives; when they fired senior teachers to save money by hiring inexperienced replacements; or when board members forgot that schools are nonpartisan and went after teachers on grounds of politics or personal belief.

No one can doubt that these protections continue to be needed today. Scarcely a month goes by that major newspapers do not report at least one scandal regarding the award of school contracts or positions. Good teachers with experience still need and deserve a presumption of employment when budget cuts loom. And as ever-present debates about curriculum underline—Is evolution scientifically valid or simply a plausible alternative to creationism?—the substance of learning is always a potential source of political mischief.

In these situations and others, teachers deserve some protections. They are entitled to employment security that protects them from potential manipulation or corruption and from zealots of the Left or Right intent on imposing their personal views of the world through the classroom.

However, to support tenure is not to advocate job security for incompetents. Tenure for teachers makes sense only when offers of continued employment are based on evidence of competence. This is where the system sometimes breaks down. When reemployment is *pro forma*, an important quality assurance mechanism is undermined. Several local teachers unions, affiliates of both the American Federation of Teachers and the National Education Association, convinced that incompetent teachers harm the entire profession, have taken steps with their school boards to evaluate and assist teachers and counsel poor ones out of the profession, both during probation and after it ends. Some boards and unions have also taken the leadership to find ways to recognize and reward good teachers for their knowledge, skills, and performance. We believe that both kinds of initiatives—those that improve or remove poor teachers and that recognize good ones—are essential, and our recommendations endorse these approaches.

Myth #5: Unions Block Reform

School boards and policymakers have sometimes been quick to accuse educational unions and professional organizations of being a major cause of our current school problems. Teacher organizations are condemned for being too political, too concerned with the bread-and-butter issues of salaries, and too bureaucratic and inflexible to respond to reform initiatives and challenges. They have been characterized as obstructionists in our quest for better schools. That perspective is partially a result of the history of collective bargaining between the members of such organizations and their employers, in many states a history of struggle that has included divisive strikes.

Bargaining in the traditional mode has pitted unions and school management against each other and has not fostered collaborative relationships. It has occasionally established a division between practitioners and policymakers, perpetuated mistrust among stakeholder groups, and resulted in overly cumbersome contractual requirements. Unintentionally, collective bargaining agreements have sometimes established or continued conditions that are inimical to change. As contracts have evolved within school bureaucracies and have mirrored the systems in which they are embedded, many have come to include rules that are restrictive during a time of reform. The same is true of many federal, state, and local regulations, whose roots in old systems and procedures can be frustrating when changes are sought. Roadblocks to reform that are a product of the system we have developed exist on all sides.

But what is sometimes mistaken for protection of the status quo is often reasoned caution about untested educational fads that teachers fear may impede the education of children or weaken our fundamental commitment to free public schools. Although it doesn't make nightly news, teacher groups have often been at the forefront of the movement to improve schools and enact greater quality assurances in teaching. A number of recent research studies have documented how reforms have been initiated, embraced, and strengthened by teacher associations in communities across the country, ranging from Wells, Maine, and Miami, Florida; to Hammond, Indiana, and Louisville, Kentucky; to Bellevue, Washington, and Cerritos, California.[94]

As school boards and teacher unions have become aware of public reactions to their conflict and of threats to public education, they have moderated their disagreements and emphasized cooperative work on such issues as school improvement initiatives; changes in teacher education programs; and greater quality assurance from entry and tenure to advanced certification. In a growing number of places, progressive school boards, superintendents, and teacher associations are inventing new ways of managing schools through negotiated responsibility for school improvement and shared accountability for student learning. They are creating partnerships for the redesign of schools and seeking to ensure that only competent, caring people enter and remain in teaching.

Teacher organizations for the 21st century have improved student learning at the heart of their mission. Through their collective voice, teacher unions have argued for better preparation, the hiring of qualified teachers, and better conditions in schools because they know that gains on these fronts are gains for students. They have begun to push for greater professionalism and to challenge the status quo within their own ranks. Although there is a need to build more secure bridges between unions and school boards, recent efforts point the way to a new era in which teacher organizations and local policymakers join forces on behalf of student advocacy and professional accountability.

Beyond the Myths: An Action Agenda for Change

Each of these distractions has deflected our efforts from the serious work of reform. It is time to move beyond them to create an agenda for change that incorporates what works. There is little mystery involved here. Preparing teachers for the 21st century is difficult, but there are plenty of examples that it is possible. We know what to do. We know a great deal about what it takes to be a good teacher; we know what teachers need to know in order to succeed; and we know how to prepare teachers so they can be successful.

The good news is that reforms stimulated by policymakers and the profession have encouraged major changes across the country—in teacher preparation; standards for accreditation, licensing, and certification; improved salaries and more aggressive recruitment; induction of beginning teachers; and greater accountability for teacher quality. These changes are evidence of a deepening commitment to professionalism in teaching.

The bad news is that these efforts are not the norm in education—nor are they systematically incorporated into the education system. What we find, instead, is a promising innovation here, a new practice there, but only rarely are they connected to each other. At the same time, the relentless need for teachers means that many states and districts continue to ignore entry standards for teachers, quietly reneging on their obligations to students and the rhetorical commitments they have made to parents.

What is required is a great national crusade united behind the proposition that competent teaching is a new student right. We must understand that if this nation is to prepare all of its children for the challenges of the 21st century, teaching must be able to recruit and retain able, well-prepared teachers for *all* classrooms. These entrants must be equipped with the knowledge, skills, and dispositions that will enable them to succeed with *all* students. And, *all* of their workplaces must offer them the support they need to develop and grow as professionals in a lifelong career.

The recommendations that follow are banners behind which the crusade's supporters can rally.

A Better Way: Teaching for Tomorrow . . . Today

Envisioning how new goals can be reached is the first step to achieving them. Many of the recommendations of this Commission already exist in some places. This scenario—a real story—illustrates how new conditions for teaching and new careers for teachers can come alive.

Ask middle school teacher Bonnie Dorschel to describe the ideal teaching and learning environment and she responds, without hesitation, "We have it." The reason for her enthusiasm is clearly not a function of fancy facilities or affluent surroundings. The cluster of rooms she shares with her interdisciplinary teaching team within Douglass Middle School in Rochester, New York, is make-do. Her students in this special program are, purposely, more than ordinarily diverse. And she teaches an extra period a day while managing additional responsibilities as one of Rochester's lead teachers responsible for mentoring first-year teachers.

What is it that keeps this 30-year veteran of teaching energized and committed to teaching when she considered leaving the profession just a few years ago? There are at least three answers to this question: Bonnie's work with other colleagues in creating a successful new program for urban students, her recent successful efforts to pursue National Board Certification, and her work as a lead teacher in Rochester's career continuum—a role that allows her to share her talents with beginning teachers and others who want or need assistance in learning to teach.

Bonnie is a member of a ten-teacher team, FIRST CLASS, which began in 1990 as an alternative within the traditionally organized, 1,300-student Douglass Middle School. The idea first flickered when a few teachers became excited about field studies as a way of engaging young adolescents; it grew as they conducted their own research. The more they discovered about adolescent development and learning, the more inappropriate traditional teaching and organization seemed.

Although the whole school was not ready to make changes, the team received permission to organize a program for 150 students within the larger school. FIRST CLASS is designed to be a supportive environment for their students—so city-wise and vulnerable to failure—to work together "toward individual and collective success in a climate of diversity, peacemaking, and academic rigor." Says Bonnie, "We want to make a change in the kids' lives. None of us wants to give up on them."

Their successes are already tangible: In FIRST CLASS, all of the students have passed the school district's writing/literacy tests for the past two years and suspensions are lower than in the rest of the building. Parents like the frequent contacts and the grading system, which emphasizes effort and growth in four areas: engagement, collaboration, independence and self-direction, and performance (quality of work). The team sees substantial growth in their students over time—in their ability to make decisions, work with adults, and facilitate their own learning.

Teaching Diverse Learners to New Standards

At the beginning of the school day, Bonnie team teaches with math teacher Pina Buonomo. Their teaching is based on standards gleaned from the work of national standard-setting groups. Math literacy classes are interdisciplinary and focused on helping students master complex goals like communicating mathematically, solving problems, reasoning, inventing, constructing meaning, and making connections. In this untracked, cross-grade class of 28 students, Bonnie and Pina focus on potential, not labels. A visitor cannot tell which students might be identified as gifted, average, or learning disabled. The teachers know their students well enough, however, to determine how best to organize cooperative learning and who should tutor whom. Their discussions about adolescent development, as well as weekly meetings about individual students' progress and problems, are bolstered by having the students as "family" for three years.

"They know us and we know them really well," says Bonnie. " But best of all, they are comfortable about talking to adults when they leave here, and that's a good thing to be able to do in high school."

In her account of teaching and learning for a portfolio submitted to the National Board for Professional Teaching Standards, Bonnie describes one student's interactions with others and with her, illustrating how knowing a student well influences instructional decisions:

"The leader alternates from being a positive role model and a peer mediator to instigator of conflict between her peers. . . . I have asked her to help with B and to model leadership qualities, and some days she is wonderful; other days she is unwilling to cooperate. We talk, and our relationship is generally positive, but I need to remember that although she looks much older, there is a little girl inside.

I remember that when I frequently observe her sucking her thumb. Her writing skills are poor, but she expresses herself verbally very well. She is very funny, and we appreciate each other's sense of humor. I want to respect her need to sit near her friends but will make it clear that group work must be done. I often join their group or ask them to use the tape recorder while they are working. It seems to work."

Teaming with another teacher is a boon for Bonnie, who did so even before FIRST CLASS started. Not only is it a better way to organize class time and deal with individual needs and problems, but when teachers know each other's priorities and values, "we can work together for the kids more easily."

She and Pina agree, for example, "that you can't go head to head with adolescents." Built into the FIRST CLASS program is conflict resolution training for all students and teachers. This is part of the Friday block sessions that deal with personal concerns and choices as well as progress on academic goals.

Community connections are a favorite aspect of FIRST CLASS for Bonnie. Students select community agencies to work with each year—the children's hospital, a mission for the homeless, or perhaps a shelter for battered women and their children. The teachers in FIRST CLASS are moving toward requiring community service for eighth-grade graduation because, says Bonnie, it is a way for young people "to see the connectedness of our lives." Bonnie also integrates studies of Rochester's sister cities—in Mali, France, or Germany, for example—into the curriculum. This also introduces FIRST CLASS students to

foreign languages.

Later in the day, about a dozen students gather in Bonnie's classroom around a long, wide table that takes up most of the room surrounded by cabinets and student work. Other students are just finishing up projects at the seven computers against one wall or at the table where their bookmaking work had been spread. "I use technology in all the things I do in reading," Bonnie explains, including creating books, problem solving, and predicting outcomes. She combines reading strategies and computer applications adroitly, fostering collaboration among her students. She is available in her mini-computer lab whenever anyone needs her—before or after school, during lunch, and when teachers and students come in to work together. She also conducts workshops throughout the district and provides support to other teachers within Douglass Middle School.

The small group settles down for recreational reading. Bonnie and her colleagues think of literacy in its most exciting sense, an ability to enjoy speaking, listening, writing, and reading. Her students draw from drama, poetry, shared novels, Shakespeare, and their own book publishing to learn what literacy means. Journal-keeping by teachers and students is a common element in all of the classes.

The recreational reading group is now almost finished with a Civil War novel, *War Comes to Willy Freeman*, and is discussing the personal aspects of slavery and freedom. Bonnie chooses recreational reading books frequently because she knows most of her students do not read on their own at home. "Few people do," she notes candidly.

She asks the group respectfully, "Is there anyone who doesn't want to read today?" Finding them all ready, she leads a discussion, constantly urging her students to put themselves in the shoes of the novel's protagonist, Willy: "Remember, she is only 14, she has no one to turn to, no one knows she is free. What would you do? Go back? Keep running?" The students discuss all of Willy's options, debating and defending their own choices. They agree to finish the book at home and to be ready to talk about the ending at the next class.

A Collective Vision for Redesigning School

To Bonnie, it is important to see students investing in their own learning. And it is essential "that I am surrounded by people who want that." Generated by the desire to act on shared beliefs about teaching, FIRST CLASS fosters collaboration and respect among adults as well as students. Every teacher in FIRST CLASS teaches a multidisciplinary project group, a math and literacy class, and a psychology class. The team has a specialist in each subject area who serves as a resource for both students and teachers. Team members take on the hyphenated role of teacher-counselor. Each team member works with a small group of students in homeroom and again in the psychology block to help students succeed and make viable choices.

Special education teachers are part of the team, helping provide strategies for students with learning disabilities, such as using precise language when explaining or asking questions. Nancy Sundberg, a special education teacher, is the team's chief researcher, constantly searching for information about the ideas and projects they undertake.

The teachers develop curriculum together, basing science and social studies content on a cycle of themes that engage students in projects during their three years in the program. The theme of "Local Connections: Rochester and New York State," for example, involves study of habitats and ecosystems, international sister cities, "Rochistory," and the underground railroad. Bonnie chooses field studies directly tied to the themes. In the French language and culture project, for example, art studies focused on the Impressionists, so she took students to the Lilac Festival and to the Impressionist room at the art gallery for a painting class. Each unit finishes with an exhibition where students are both teachers and learners, using written, artistic, taped, and oral presentations to describe their work.

Collaboration and Professional Development

While certain times are set aside during the week to discuss students and logistics, teachers talk together all the time. Bonnie's huge table is often a center of operations and discussion, the mini-computer lab against the wall a place for teachers and students to zero in on projects whenever no classes are taking place. The teachers are quick to praise each other, but they acknowledge that consensus building gets rough at times. Some teachers are tidy; some can only work in chaos. Their efforts to develop student assessment needed support. Were they to depend only on their own experience and knowledge, the team members might be unable to continually enrich their vision. Part of their collaboration, however, has been

to pursue opportunities for professional growth that support their goals.

For example, Bonnie and the others participate in Performance Assessment Collaboratives in Education, a five-year national project to explore the use of portfolios in urban classrooms that supports the teachers' desire to find alternatives to traditional assessments. They are also part of New Standards, a project to benchmark standards and assessments to world-class levels. This helps them focus on student work to evaluate their own success as well as that of students. The attributes of accomplished teaching, as expressed in the assessments of the National Board for Professional Teaching Standards, guide their professional practice.

This last activity stems from the leadership of the Rochester Teachers Association in supporting the National Board. Three teachers (half of all those certified in New York on the first round), came from FIRST CLASS. Bonnie and the others who passed certification helped each other with materials and videotaping, then negotiated released time for the next group of Rochester teachers who applied for certification.

The National Board process, says Bonnie, "forced me to look more closely at my work and made me more comfortable with asking students for their input on my teaching. They really like to be involved." She also relishes the collaboration that team teaching, PACE, and the other professional activities require. "I don't see myself alone anymore," she says. "I learn from first-year teachers, from the most gifted and experienced teachers. We spend a lot of time watching and learning."

Union vice president Tom Gillett,

formerly a high school English teacher, asked to become part of FIRST CLASS in order to qualify as an applicant for National Board certification. He has stayed at FIRST CLASS as one of those who became certified not only because of the support the program gives to students, but also because of the process the team goes through. "People are here for the same reason," he says, "even though they don't all think the same way." Learning from one another and supporting students is the goal, and it permeates all that the team does.

Serving the Profession through Lead Teaching

It is afternoon now, and Bonnie has moved on to another of her responsibilities—that of a mentor teacher for Rochester's Career in Teaching (CIT) program. The program provides mentoring for all beginning teachers and for veteran teachers having difficulty. Lead teachers are selected for their expertise in teaching via a rigorous process of evaluation. These teachers provide intensive assistance and advise a panel of administrators and teachers on contract renewal for those with whom they work.

These evaluations support a career ladder with steps in compensation for moving from an initial internship (supervised by a lead teacher) to "residency," to professional teacher status, and then to lead-teaching status later in the career. The CIT program has also established new approaches for ongoing teacher evaluation relying on the standards and portfolio processes modeled on that of the National Board for Professional Teaching Standards. In structuring their professional development and gathering evidence about their teaching, teachers include evidence about student learning as well as input from colleagues, students, and parents.

Bonnie is visiting with Gretchen Breon and Joan Labrosa, who have neighboring classrooms on the top floor of a spanking new middle school. Joan spent almost a decade in a career at Kodak before deciding to go back to graduate school to prepare for teaching. Gretchen came from a career in recreation. No amount of experience, however, could have fully prepared them for the first year of teaching. Bonnie's mentoring has been a lifeline.

Bonnie visits them and two other new teachers every week, as well as one tenured teacher who has asked to be observed by a mentor. On this day, Bonnie sits at the back of Gretchen's classroom to follow the behavior of three students who have been giving the teacher extra trouble. She notes whom they talk to, what draws their interest, what distracts them, then discusses her observations after the class and gives some suggestions. "You need to decide," she tells Gretchen, "if you want your students to talk while taking notes. If you do and want them to finish, too, then perhaps you could use a timer." These important tips, small and large, are what help beginning teachers master the innumerable complexities of teaching.

"Bonnie not only finds materials for me and informs me about contractual details, but she is so reassuring," says Gretchen. "Some days are just terrible, but she's there to put me back together again. We talk about the problems, and then she says, 'Now, let's move on.'" Bonnie notes that the most important tool with those she mentors is trust.

"They have to know that it is OK to make mistakes, that I'm the one to make mistakes in front of." Knowing that Bonnie is certified by the National Board is especially important to Gretchen. It affirms that Bonnie "is a good role model for me."

Bonnie is an advocate, but she also is an evaluator. Under the CIT program, mentors assess the potential of beginning teachers and make recommendations about their probationary status. It is Bonnie's responsibility to encourage those she is mentoring in, or out, or to another level of teaching. She accepts this awesome task because "we don't want people in teaching who can't do good things for children." Under the CIT program, about 8% of Rochester's beginning teachers are not renewed for a second year of teaching.

Personal Values, Professional Life

When Bonnie Dorschel began teaching many years ago in a safe suburb of Rochester, she had only traditional notions of a career and of teaching and learning. Children sat in rows, teachers taught in years that rarely changed from September through May. But she was bored. Bonnie chose to move to Rochester, ultimately teaching at all levels, including some college-level classes. While raising three children, she obtained a master's degree in urban education and state certification in reading, English, and administration. Courses did not count as much as the opportunities she found to enjoy and explore new people and ideas, whether in a sister city in France, a Korean cultural camp, or a local classroom using technology to expand students' knowledge.

Bonnie is well aware of the changes

in the city where she and her family have chosen to live and work. When she started teaching, "seventh-graders were not getting pregnant, parents were home when you called." She would never have thought it necessary to call a student in the mornings to get her up (as she did with one child whose parents left very early for work). Nor would she have thought it important to read the police blotter of the local weekly to know what's going on in the lives of kids at home.

Despite her enthusiasm for teaching in an urban classroom, Bonnie felt hemmed in by policies and practices she did not feel were appropriate for her students. She thought about "closing the door on teaching," but then the FIRST CLASS team began to form and the Career in Teaching program empowered her to make a real contribution to the quality of the profession. For the first time, she felt she had a say in the policies and supports needed for teachers and students.

Bonnie sees herself as an uncompromising optimist, a view that is revealed as much in her conversations with colleagues as it is with students. "I have fun meeting the challenges of working with kids over time," she says. "And most of what I learn comes from the excellence around me. I'm pleased with the changes we are making." Most of all, Bonnie is grateful to be working with people "who push their limits. . . . All of us are just a work in progress."

Recommendations: An Action Agenda for Change

As various panaceas have been advanced in the last decade to solve the problems of learning in America, education reform has moved in fits and starts. Indeed, the "reform *du jour*" has become a problem in its own right in American schools because teachers have learned to ride out the latest fad on the well-founded assumption that it too will pass.

Reform can succeed only if it is broad and comprehensive, attacking many problems simultaneously. But it cannot succeed at all unless the conditions of teaching and teacher development change. Indeed, when this Commission's recommendations are put into place, educators will find that they end the waves of reform that crash over American schools without effect because our schools will have developed the capacity to continually renew and improve themselves.

Our proposals provide a vision and a blueprint for the development of a teaching profession for the 21st century that can make good on our nation's goals for education. They are systemic in scope—not a recipe for more short-lived pilots and demonstration projects. They require a dramatic departure from the status quo—one that creates a new infrastructure for professional learning and an accountability system that ensures attention to standards for educators as well as students at every level—national, state, local school district, school, and classroom.

If the press for higher educational standards has taught us anything, it is that congruence matters: If the actions of federal and state governments do not support the work of local school districts, and if those of school districts do not support the work of schools, very little of worth can be accomplished. What goes on in classrooms between teachers and students may be the core of education, but it is profoundly shaped by what parents and principals do and by what superintendents, school boards, and legislatures decide. When various parts of the system are working against one another, the enterprise lurches around like a carriage pulled by horses running off in different directions.

Congruence and commonality of effort in a decentralized system require that we prepare people—both educators and policymakers—to manage that system in a way that is guided by shared commitments and knowledge. Without that common knowledge base to inform practice, there can be no guideposts for responsible decision making.

What we are proposing is a set of steps to ensure the common base of knowledge and commitments upon which a truly democratic system of education can be built. We are urging a complete overhaul in the systems of teacher preparation and professional development in this country to ensure that they reflect and act upon the most current available knowledge and practice. This redesign should create a continuum of teacher learning based on compatible standards that operate from recruitment and preservice education through licensing, hiring, and induction into the profession, to advanced certification and ongoing professional development.

We also propose a comprehensive set of changes in school organization and management that will provide the conditions in which teachers can use their knowledge much more productively to support student learning. And finally, we recommend a set of measures for making sure that only those who are competent to teach or to lead schools are allowed to enter or to continue in the profession—a starting point for creating professional accountability.

For the first time, a broad-based group of policymakers and educators—including those who will have to take courageous steps to put these recommendations in place—have put forth this sweeping agenda for change and pledged to take the steps needed to implement it. We understand that these proposals are not easy to undertake and that the self-interest of various constituencies will be shaken in the process of bringing them to life. However, we believe that this comprehensive set of reforms is absolutely essential to guarantee every child a caring, competent, and qualified teacher . . . and to guarantee America a just and prosperous future.

We challenge the nation to embrace a set of turning points that will put us on the path to serious, successful, long-term improvements in teaching and learning for America. By the year 2006,

- All children will be taught by teachers who have the knowledge, skills, and commitments to teach children well.

- All teacher education programs will meet professional standards, or they will be closed.

- All teachers will have access to high-quality professional development and regular time for collegial work and planning.

- Both teachers and principals will be hired and retained based on their ability to meet professional standards of practice.

- Teachers' salaries will be based on their knowledge and skills.

- Quality teaching will be the central investment of schools. Most education dollars will be spent on classroom teaching.

We offer five recommendations to accomplish these goals:

I.   Get serious about standards for both students and teachers.

II. Reinvent teacher preparation and professional development.

III. Fix teacher recruitment and put qualified teachers in every classroom.

IV. Encourage and reward teacher knowledge and skill.

V.   Create schools that are organized for student and teacher success.

These recommendations are interrelated. Standards for students affect expectations of teachers and the organization of schools. Standards for teachers affect their preparation, their induction into teaching, and their continuing development as well as the roles they are capable of assuming. Experienced teachers, as well as novices and candidates, benefit from exposure to professional development schools. Changes in school structures affect everything else. However, for the sake of clarity, we treat these issues separately below. At the close, we describe how they should come together.

I. Get serious about standards for both students and teachers.

WE RECOMMEND: *renewing the national promise to bring every American child up to world-class standards in core academic areas.*

WE RECOMMEND: *developing and enforcing rigorous standards for teacher preparation, initial licensing, and continuing development.*

Standards for Students

The country needs to continue its work on standards defining what young people should know and be able to do. These should reflect the demands of today's society and support more challenging academic coursework and higher standards for graduation. Like those in other countries and like the much-applauded work of the National Council of Teachers of Mathematics in the United States, the standards really should be frameworks for curriculum, expressed in slim notebooks that outline a core of expectations toward which all students should strive, not a telephone book incorporating every topic under the sun. Such frameworks should be clear about common knowledge and skills while allowing for local adaptations that bring ideas to life for students in different communities and enable students to develop different interests and specialties beyond the core, especially as they move through high school. The standards and frameworks should be a central subject of ongoing conversations with parents and community members so that all those whose efforts must be mobilized on behalf of students understand what they are working toward.

States should continue to work on incorporating these standards into curriculum frameworks and assessments that provide rich information about actual student performance, enabling teachers and parents to understand what children can do and how to support their ongoing learning. In the effort to advance standards, implementation must go well beyond the platitude that "all children can learn." All children are human; by definition all of them can learn.

Using Student Standards to Develop Teaching Practice

In two local middle schools, the mathematics teachers have been worrying about a new state performance assessment to be given in eighth grade. Last year, when the test was piloted at their school, test scores plummeted. These teachers are anxious to understand better what it is that students need to know to do well on the new assessment. Two teachers volunteer to organize material from the pilot test, such as students' portfolios, and the scoring sheets. The teachers also have their student records. Each teacher gets a packet of portfolios, scoring sheets, and a few other records for ten students from across classes.

In preparation for the first meeting, they pore over the assessment but feel that they do not adequately understand either what the tasks are asking or the ways in which students' work was scored. They decide to engage in one of the tasks themselves. They complete the task and analyze it closely for what it covers mathematically and what kinds of things one needs to know and be able to do in order to do it. They then turn to looking at their students' performances and begin to see more about the different ways in which the students interpreted and approached the task. Over the course of several meetings, they repeat this cycle with different tasks. Doing the tasks is actually kind of fun, and they find that they are much better able to "see" the students' work and thinking after they have climbed inside of the tasks themselves.

Later in the year they develop a list of the kinds of understandings that the assessment seems to tap and the kinds of problems they saw in students' work. This raises a host of questions for them about how to help students do better and where to seek resources for their own learning. One of the teachers proposes attending the state National Council for Teachers of Mathematics affiliate conference, for she notices that a number of sessions target the new state assessment and at least a couple of them seem to address the teachers' questions about ways that might help them improve their teaching of these mathematical ideas and hence their students' learning.

Several elements of powerful professional education are evident in this example. The teachers are bent on improving students' performance and they construct a way for themselves to investigate mathematics, assessment, learning, and teaching using their need to look more closely at the test to understand it. The material for their investigation is their own students' last year's tests. The immediacy of the situation is a pressing incentive to participate—using a real task of practice as the context for their work. Their investigation of what was causing students to do so poorly on the test gave them an opportunity to deepen their own understandings of mathematics, as well as of students' thinking and interpretation, and of the structure and worth of tasks. Although any one of them could have done this investigation alone, working together greatly enhanced what was possible to consider and to learn: Across the group, their ideas differed about the mathematics, the tasks, and particular students. Their discussions broadened what any one person could do. Together they began to develop shared ideas and standards that could guide their collective efforts.

Adapted from Deborah Ball and David Cohen, "Developing Practice, Developing Practitioners: Toward a Practice-Based Theory of Professional Education" (paper prepared for the National Commission on Teaching & America's Future, 1995).

The question is: What should they learn and how much do they need to know? And how can schools support this learning?

For standards to be meaningful, they must be accompanied by benchmarks of performance—from "acceptable" to "highly accomplished"—so that students and teachers know how to direct their efforts toward greater excellence. Clear examples of the kind and quality of work expected can motivate students and help teachers to organize their work together. They can build upon the work of their predecessors and colleagues and develop reinforcing opportunities for students to practice and develop their skills. With high-quality assessments that measure important abilities, teachers can teach more purposefully and make greater demands that students and parents can better understand and respond to. Parents can reinforce students' learning at home. And schools can better organize specific academic supports and extra study time after school, on weekends, or in the summer for students who need additional help to develop the levels of competence they need to meet.

Expectations for student achievement should shape discussions of teaching and problem solving in schools. Teachers should work collectively on curriculum that supports the standards, assess how individuals and groups of students are learning, evaluate what kinds of learning experiences they have had, and make changes in what they do. This work is a key professional activity that connects standards of learning to the building of shared standards for teaching. Evidence already exists that where school faculties are working together to translate standards into courses of study, learning tasks, and assessments, they are becoming more expert and more collective in their practice, and students are learning more.[95]

Elements of Systemic Reform

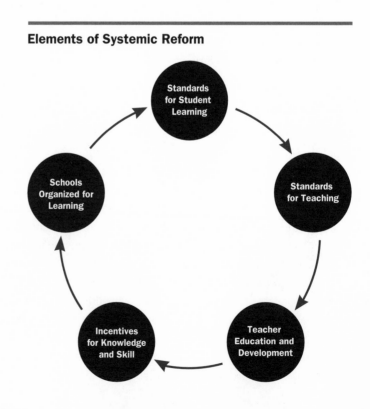

Many have voiced fears that standards and assessments will turn out to be elitist—that they will simply sort out more easily the haves from the have-nots. The Commission's vision is very different. We see standards as a starting point—not an ending point—for change. We understand that standard-setting in and of itself will not produce the changes in teaching and schooling needed to raise achievement. However, standards can create a foundation for other reforms that build the capacity of schools to help all students learn to higher levels. Ultimately, to be productive, student standards must undergird shared standards of practice that allow teachers to work more effectively together and to set expectations for themselves.

Standards for Teaching

Standards for teaching are the linchpin for transforming current systems of preparation, licensing, certification, and ongoing development so that they better support student learning. They can bring clarity and focus to a set of activities that are currently poorly connected and often badly organized. New standards and new opportunities for teacher education must be reinforced by incentives that encourage teachers to acquire ever greater knowledge and skill. These incentives can then, in turn, support the redesign of schools so that they organize themselves more effectively for student and teacher learning.

Clearly, if students are to achieve high standards, we can expect no less from their teachers and from other educators. Of greatest priority is reaching agreement on what teachers should know and be able to do in order to teach to high standards. This standard-setting task was left unaddressed for many decades,

A Professional Continuum for Teacher Development

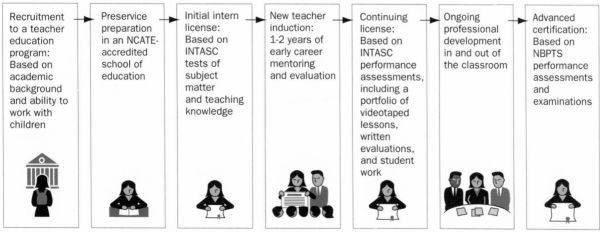

| Recruitment to a teacher education program: Based on academic background and ability to work with children | Preservice preparation in an NCATE-accredited school of education | Initial intern license: Based on INTASC tests of subject matter and teaching knowledge | New teacher induction: 1-2 years of early career mentoring and evaluation | Continuing license: Based on INTASC performance assessments, including a portfolio of videotaped lessons, written evaluations, and student work | Ongoing professional development in and out of the classroom | Advanced certification: Based on NBPTS performance assessments and examinations |

NCATE=National Council for Accreditation of Teacher Education, INTASC=Interstate New Teacher Assessment and Support Consortium, NBPTS=National Board for Professional Teaching Standards

but it has recently been accomplished by the efforts of three professional bodies that have closely aligned their work to produce standards outlining a continuum of teacher development derived directly from the expectations posed by new student standards.

The new standards of the National Council for Accreditation of Teacher Education (NCATE), most recently revised in 1995, reflect the evolution of a much stronger knowledge base for teaching and require schools of education to demonstrate how they are incorporating new knowledge about the effective teaching of subject matter, various approaches to learning, and student diversity in their preparation of teachers.

NCATE's standards are connected to a set of newly developed standards for beginning teacher licensing developed by a consortium of more 30 states and professional organizations—the Interstate New Teacher Assessment and Support Consortium (INTASC)—which has tackled the question of what entering teachers must know and be able to do to teach in the ways student standards demand. The standards outline how teachers should demonstrate their knowledge of subject matter, child development and learning, classroom communication and management, planning, instruction, and assessment, and the ability to work well with parents and colleagues as a basis for gaining a license to teach. INTASC's licensing standards are the basis for tests of subject matter and teaching knowledge for an initial license and for a performance assessment that examines teaching skills during the first year or two of supervised teaching. These tests, currently being piloted by states that belong to the consortium, will become the basis for granting a continuing professional license.

Finally, for experienced teachers, the standards for accomplished practice developed by the new National Board for Professional Teaching Standards—which are compatible with those developed by NCATE and INTASC—provide guidance for ongoing professional development. Teachers that undertake the National Board's challenging performance assessments can receive certification of accomplished practice that recognizes the high levels of expertise they have developed.

Although the work of these organizations may sound unglamorous, they offer the most powerful tools we have for reaching and rejuvenating the soul of the profession. Their standards and assessments examine and insist upon the attributes of effective teachers: subject matter expertise coupled with an understanding of how children learn and develop; skill in using a range of teaching strategies and technologies; sensitivity and effectiveness in working with students from diverse backgrounds; the ability to work well with parents and other teachers; and assessment expertise capable of discerning how well children are doing, what they are learning, and what needs to be done next to move them along. The standards reflect a teaching role in which the teacher is an instructional leader who orchestrates learning experiences in response to curriculum goals and student needs and who coaches students to high levels of independent performance.

These standards offer a cogent vision of teaching that helps to create new classroom realities. As teacher Ann Sayas noted of her experience in working for National Board Certification:

Nothing, I repeat, nothing has forced me to examine my teaching practices as the National Board Certification process did. Nothing else has offered me a vision of what education could be like and opportunities to make the vision a reality. . . . The result is amazing to me: I am more excited about teaching than I have ever been. I no longer dream of moving up the ladder away from daily contact with my students. Not enough time exists to try all the possible ideas that examination of my own classroom has produced.[96]

In the Commission's judgment, these standards represent the new basics for accomplished practice; they include the essentials of effective teaching and focus attention on student learning. They may seem to be a tall order, but many excellent teachers are already teaching as they suggest, and some schools of education are preparing new cohorts of teachers so that they learn to do so. In the last ten years, since issues regarding the status of teaching were first brought to the public's attention,[97] a great deal of headway has been made in developing new standards for teaching, piloting and refining new assessments of teaching, and creating programs that serve as proof that substantially better education for students and teachers is possible. However, if these are to take hold and survive longer than in past eras of reform, policymakers must incorporate them into the policies that govern teaching and schooling.

To make expert teaching the rule rather than the exception, state and local policies should create a continuum of professional learning for teachers based on standards that guide teacher preparation and licensing, early induction, ongoing professional development, and advanced certification. To accomplish this, we recommend that states and local districts take the following steps:

- **Establish professional standards boards in every state.**

Developing coherent standards for teacher education, licensing, professional development, and practice requires a governing partnership between the public and the profession that is not vulnerable to constantly changing politics and priorities. Twelve states have already created boards for teaching like those that govern standard setting in other professions on the conviction that these boards are the best way to maintain rigorous standards and protect the public interest. Such boards are the conscience of each profession; they develop and enforce ethical codes as well as technical standards of practice. They should include accomplished teachers—ultimately, those who are National Board Certified—as well as teacher educators, administrators, and representatives of the public. In other professions, a national confederation of state boards develops common standards, high-quality assessments, and reciprocity agreements. Such a confederation in teaching should help develop common licensing assessments with professionally recommended cut-off scores, so that teachers command comparable skills and can move more easily from state to state.

How would a standards board help solve current problems? First, it would bring greater expertise to bear on the process of setting teaching standards and would do so in a more focused and steady fashion, as standards must be continually updated and reevaluated in light of growing professional knowledge. Second, it would allow the creation of a more coherent set of standards across teacher education, licensing, and ongoing professional development, since they would all be considered by the same body. Finally, it would create a firewall between the political system and the standard-setting process, allowing higher standards that are more connected to the professional knowledge base to be set and maintained. States with standards boards have shown that they enact and maintain more rigorous, professionally current standards than they had been able to do before the standards board was in place.

• Insist on accreditation for all schools of education.

States can most effectively ensure quality control over teacher education in partnership with the National Council for the Accreditation of Teacher Education, whose standards are aligned with emerging new standards for student learning as well as with those of the National Board and INTASC. NCATE's quality standards, recently revised and strengthened, are demanding, but not beyond the reach of any school of education genuinely committed to preparing excellent teachers for the classrooms of a new century. Schools that are serious about preparing teachers should take the necessary steps to become accredited. Those that are not willing and able to develop a critical mass of intellectual resources for training teachers should turn their attention to doing other things well.

Although teacher associations and states are increasingly willing to insist on accreditation for schools of education, the unfortunate truth is that some colleges are alarmed at the prospect of mandatory accreditation, fearing that what is in the public interest may not always coincide with institutional self-interest. It is time for states and higher education to stop playing shell games with ineffective program approval procedures and support professional accreditation by the turn of the century.

• Close inadequate schools of education.

The other side of the accreditation coin is that weak teacher preparation programs should be shut down. As everyone in higher education understands, accreditation amounts to a stamp of approval that a professional school is capable of delivering what it promises the public. After an initial visit, accrediting agencies provide institutions of higher education with ample time, technical assistance, and opportunity to correct shortcomings and shore up weaknesses. If schools, colleges, or departments of education are unable to do so, they should be closed to protect the public's interest in providing well-prepared teachers for all children. To those concerned about the American future, it is painful to hear that some training programs are so weak that their students belittle them, and school systems feel they must start all over again training their graduates. What is more painful is that the situation is tolerated. It should be no longer.

Achieving NCATE Accreditation: The Price and the Prize

When the National Council for Accreditation of Teacher Education (NCATE) strengthened its standards in 1988, nearly half of the schools reviewed could not pass the "knowledge base" standard, which requires a school to be able to describe and enact a coherent knowledge base undergirding its programs. NCATE's evolving standards do not represent a comfortable status quo. They reflect serious program reform. To meet the standards, schools must

- Offer a coherent program of studies that will prepare effective teachers rather than a collection of courses based on what professors prefer to teach;

- Provide a full foundation in the liberal arts and teaching disciplines;

- Prepare candidates to teach children so they can achieve the student standards of professional associations like the National Council of Teachers of Mathematics;

- Prepare teachers who can work with diverse learners and with new technologies; and

- Ensure that candidates gain knowledge of effective learning and teaching strategies and demonstrate their skills in working with students.

About one in five schools of education are denied accreditation on their first attempt. Many have made sweeping changes to revamp courses, secure new resources, and strengthen teaching and are successful in their second attempt. Their experiences illustrate the power of accreditation to create a floor of quality for professional education.

John Carrier, vice president of Concord College in West Virginia, describes how accreditation made a difference in his institution:

The words stung like an ominous medical prognosis: "accreditation denied." It was May 1989, and Concord College had just been notified that we were no longer accredited under the aegis of NCATE, to which we had belonged since 1954. To Concord, questions about the value of accreditation are serious. The question was framed clearly by a youthful reporter, who when later informed of our achievement in regaining accreditation, asked forcefully, "So why is it important? What have you gained as a college?" We responded that we had secured the future of the program under the state board mandate, improved the program under the national reform agenda for teacher education, and enhanced Concord degrees within and outside the state. We believe we will be producing a better teacher through the reforms initiated in our drive for accreditation. These results, the prize, if you will, were, in our judgment, worth the price we paid.

Our reforms were based on: (1) New leadership, including intensive involvement by the president and dean and a new director of teacher education; (2) External review, including the best advice from the literature on teacher education reform and critiques of our program by outside professionals; (3) Comprehensive involvement by the faculty to achieve the coherence and collaboration NCATE demanded; (4) Self-reliance in program reform—though important to us, we would not rely on past NCATE expectations, the state's standards for approval, our own higher education board's support, or appreciation of our situational difficulties by outside visitors from NCATE; and (5) Nationally competitive program elements. Our program had to measure up well when compared with programs in other states.

By the time of the second review, the curriculum content, sequence, and delivery system reflected a model of the "Informed and Thoughtful Decision-Maker." It was intellectually defensible; well understood by students, faculty, and personnel in collaborating public schools; and an integrated statement of what we believe makes a good teacher. We developed reasonable and credible workloads for the faculty and their record for professional activities had increased to nationally competitive levels. The clinical program was revamped, and we added a Beginning Teacher Assistance Program. Multicultural dimensions missing previously were integrated into the programs. The result was recommended passage of all standards.

How did we meet the price for the prize in this instance? Reallocation of institutional resources was critical. Earlier neglect [of teacher education] was replaced by preferential budgetary treatment. Tomorrow's teachers cannot be prepared "on the cheap," or we will get, tragically, what we pay for. The prize is worth the price, a reachable goal, the problems solvable, and the challenge to leadership exciting. Like the journey of Columbus a half-millennium ago, the professionalization of teaching requires maximum commitment with few assurances about the outcome but a definite sense that something important is at stake and we dare not, cannot turn back.

Adapted from John P. Carrier, "Achieving NCATE Accreditation: The Price and the Prize," *Quality Teaching* 1, issue 3 (Spring 1992). Copyright © 1992 by the National Council for Accreditation of Teacher Education. Reprinted with permission.

- **License teachers based on demonstrated performance, including tests of subject matter knowledge, teaching knowledge, and teaching skill.**

An important change in the standards we recommend is that they describe what teachers should know and be able to do rather than listing courses that teachers should take. Performance-based licensing is the norm in other professions. Rather than dictating the curriculum of professional schools, they require rigorous tests to be sure professionals have the skills they need to serve their clients well, and they allow schools to organize courses in any way that achieves the desired outcomes.

In a performance-based licensing system for teaching, all candidates should pass tests of subject matter knowledge and knowledge about teaching and learning *before* they receive an initial license and are hired. They should then pass a performance assessment of teaching skills during their first year or two of supervised practice as the basis for a continuing license. We further recommend that states use common assessments with common, professionally set cut-off scores. This will give them the benefit of reciprocity with one another, thus greatly expanding the pool of teachers upon which they can readily draw.

State partners associated with the Interstate New Teacher Assessment and Support Consortium (INTASC) are already developing high-quality performance assessments of teaching knowledge and skill that, along with improvements in existing subject matter tests, constitute the foundations of an effective licensing system. The INTASC assessments require teachers to demonstrate that they understand the fundamentals of learning and teaching and that they can teach in the way that new student standards demand. With professional accreditation in place, states should reallocate scarce resources from program approval, which is redundant with accreditation, to the administration of high-quality licensing tests that measure actual ability to teach.

In a performance-based system, teacher education programs should be accountable for enabling their graduates to meet the standards. Alternate routes to teaching, such as postgraduate programs for midcareer recruits, should meet the same standards as traditional programs: Their candidates should pass the same assessments before they enter teaching, and programs should show that they prepare candidates to do so successfully. This will allow greater innovation and diversity in teacher training without jeopardizing the welfare of students. A single standard that assesses genuine readiness to teach rather than regulating the content of courses would mean that states could stop issuing substandard teaching licenses that sanction deficiencies in preparation, and parents and students would be assured that anyone who has earned the title "teacher" has the essential skills to teach.

- **Use National Board standards as the benchmark for accomplished teaching.**

It has always been difficult to recognize and reward good teachers in ways that are credible and objective. The merit pay plans of the 1980s (like those of

The Interstate New Teacher Assessment and Support Consortium (INTASC): Linking Student Standards to Teaching Standards

The INTASC standards for teacher licensing are organized around ten principles that reflect the core knowledge, skills, and dispositions teachers should develop in order to teach in the ways that new standards for students demand. These include:

- Knowledge of subject matter and how to make it accessible to students;

- Understanding of how to foster learning and development;

- Ability to create learning experiences adapted to the needs of diverse learners;

- Use of teaching strategies that foster critical thinking, problem solving, and high levels of performance;

- Ability to create a positive, purposeful learning environment;

- Knowledge of how to foster effective communication and collaboration in the classroom;

- Ability to plan instruction based on subject matter, students, curriculum goals, and the community context;

- Understanding and skilled use of a wide array of assessment strategies;

- Ability to reflect on, evaluate, and improve teaching and learning;

- Ability to collaborate with colleagues and parents to support student learning.

INTASC's new performance assessments draw upon these standards and the student standards in each subject matter field to evaluate the extent to which beginning teachers can teach effectively. In mathematics, for example, the tasks teachers undertake for their INTASC performance assessment directly reflect the curriculum standards of the National Council of Teachers of Mathematics (NCTM), which focus on math as problem solving, communication, reasoning, and connections. Teachers must be able to foster mathematical insight in students and help them to apply sophisticated mathematical reasoning to problems, rather than teaching largely by rote. In the current pilot assessments, teachers show how they can do these things by completing the following tasks for their portfolio:

TASK 1: PLAN AN INSTRUCTIONAL UNIT with an emphasis on how problem solving, reasoning, communication, and connections form the structure of the unit. Show how you use tools including manipulatives and technology. Reflect on and revise the instruction.

TASK 2: TEACH A LESSON TO A CLASS that addresses a particular concept or procedure. Teacher-student discourse should be highlighted in a video from the lesson. Evaluate the nature of mathematical discourse and give evidence of the kinds of learning that took place.

TASK 3: ASSESS LEARNING for the purposes of diagnosis, instructional feedback, and grading. The different methods should address mathematics processes as well as products.

TASK 4: CONDUCT AND ANALYZE A SMALL GROUP LESSON in which students work in small groups and use manipulatives for problem solving or reasoning. Student-student discourse should be highlighted in a video from the lesson.

TASK 5: ASSESS MATHEMATICAL POWER as demonstrated in students' work in problem solving, reasoning, mathematical communication, mathematical understanding, and mathematical dispositions. Plan instruction based on your findings and your knowledge of the students.

TASK 6: DEVELOP AS A PROFESSIONAL by describing how you collaborated with other professionals, analyzed your own teaching, and contributed to the professional mathematics community. Establish professional goals and develop a plan for continued development.

This kind of assessment promises to create a licensing process that both identifies competence and shapes preparation and practice in ways that will ultimately support student learning more powerfully.

Adapted from Interstate New Teacher Assessment and Support Consortium (INTASC), *Model Standards for Beginning Teacher Licensing and Development: A Resource for State Dialogue, Working Draft* (Washington, D.C.: Council of Chief State School Officers, 1992); and Interstate New Teacher Assessment and Support Consortium (INTASC), *Model Standards in Mathematics for Beginning Teacher Licensing & Development: A Resource for State Dialogue, Working Draft* (Washington, D.C.: Council of Chief State School Officers, 1994).

the 1950s and 1920s) have already disappeared because local evaluators did not have useful standards, or the time or expertise, to make reliable judgments about teacher competence. Many such plans created distrust and competition among teachers rather than supporting better practice.[98] In contrast, the careful process of National Board Certification—based on evaluation by experts according to well-developed standards and a collaborative process—provides an alternative that teachers find credible, helpful, and an extraordinary learning experience.

Analogous to the process of board certification in medicine, the National Board's standards represent a widely shared consensus about state-of-the-art practice. They are the basis for sophisticated performance assessments that allow veteran teachers to demonstrate their expertise by submitting videotapes of their teaching, lesson plans, and other samples of their own and their students' work. In assessment centers, teachers evaluate texts and teaching materials, analyze teaching situations, assess student learning and needs, and defend teaching decisions based on their knowledge of subjects, students, curriculum, and pedagogy. Teachers who have experienced the board's assessments believe the process captures good teaching and say it provides an extraordinary learning experience because it focuses all of their attention on how their decisions affect students. As states and districts begin to recognize certification as an indicator of high-level competence for purposes of hiring, evaluation, compensation, and advancement, the standards will have increasing practical effect and reach.

National Board standards should become a cornerstone for teacher development and evaluation. Some states have already decided to accept National Board Certification as fully meeting state licensing requirements for veteran teachers who cross state lines, for renewal of a license, or the award of an advanced license. Some states and districts, like Georgia, Kentucky, North Carolina, and Ohio, are acknowledging certification through financial incentives or salary bonuses; others are proposing to use certification as an indicator of qualification for roles such as mentor teacher, principal, or cooperating teacher educator. Districts like Rochester, New York, and Palo Alto, California, have incorporated National Board standards and processes, including teacher portfolios and peer coaching, as part of their teacher evaluation systems. All these strategies help to create a coherent continuum of professional learning based on common professional standards.

Standards are valuable not only in the context of formal certification systems. They can inform professional development efforts ranging from graduate school courses to local seminars and videotape groups that allow teachers to see the standards in action and reflect on their own practice. Graduate schools can organize advanced master's degree programs around the National Board standards. Within schools, vivid descriptions of good teaching can help teachers improve what they do in their daily work. It is when standards are regularly used in this way, as well as to stimulate better preparation and ongoing professional development, that they will come alive in classrooms across the nation.

The National Board's Standards

National Board Certification lets people see what teaching can be. I think that good teaching is an ability to take subject matter expertise, which is one vital component of teaching, and actually transform that into the classroom with the students you have—to make that bridge between your subject and the students' own backgrounds. And that's no easy trick.

— *Brady Kelso, English teacher*

Brady Kelso, an English teacher at Scripps Ranch High School in San Diego, California, was one of the first teachers certified by the National Board for Professional Teaching Standards. A 13-year veteran, Kelso found that the process of assembling a portfolio of his teaching and students' learning "gave me an opportunity to rethink. . . . Looking carefully at my plans and then doing the case studies to follow the kids was good. . . . For me it was a validation of the work that I'd done."

Rick Wormeli, an English teacher at Herndon Middle School in Virginia, agrees. He credits the process of Board Certification with encouraging him to integrate other subjects into his lessons, rethink the organization of reading discussion groups, and use vocabulary words from his students' work in lieu of a book listing words out of context. Even after he'd finished the assessment, he continued to experiment with changes. "I can't turn it off," he noted.

The National Board's standards and assessments help teachers reflect on and learn from their practice. They are based on five major propositions that teachers and researchers agree are essential to accomplished teaching:

1. Teachers are committed to students and their learning. National Board-Certified teachers are dedicated to making knowledge accessible to all students. They adjust their practice based on students' interests, abilities, skills, and backgrounds. They understand how students develop and learn.

2. Teachers know the subjects they teach and how to teach those subjects to students. National Board-Certified teachers have a rich understanding of the subject(s) they teach, and they know how to reveal subject matter to students. They are aware of the knowledge and preconceptions that students typically bring. They create multiple paths to knowledge, and they can teach students how to pose and solve their own problems.

3. Teachers are responsible for managing and monitoring student learning. National Board-Certified teachers create settings that sustain the interest of their students. They command a range of instructional techniques and know when each is appropriate. They know how to motivate and engage groups of students. They use multiple methods for measuring student growth and can clearly explain student performance to parents.

4. Teachers think systematically about their practice and learn from experience. National Board-Certified teachers critically examine their practice, seek the advice of others, and draw on educational research to deepen their knowledge, sharpen their judgment, and adapt their teaching to new findings and ideas.

5. Teachers are members of learning communities. National Board-Certified teachers work collaboratively with other professionals. They use school and community resources for their students' benefit. They work creatively and collaboratively with parents, engaging them in the work of the school.

Shirley Bzdewka, a teacher at Dayton School in Dayton, New Jersey, sums up the effect of her Board Certification experience this way:

I'm a very different teacher now. I know I was a good teacher. But I also know that every teacher always has a responsibility to be better tomorrow than they were today, and I am a much more deliberate teacher now. I am much more focused. I can never, ever do anything again with my kids and not ask myself, "Why? Why am I doing this? What are the effects on my kids? What are the benefits to my kids?" It's not that I didn't care about those things before, but it's on such a conscious level now.

Sources: Adapted from Ann Bradley, "Pioneers in Professionalism," *Education Week* 13 (April 20, 1994): 18-21; "What Price Success?" *Education Week* 15 (November 22, 1995): 1. Copyright © 1994, 1995. Excerpts reprinted with the permission of *Education Week*. The National Board for Professional Teaching Standards (NBPTS), *What Teachers Should Know and Be Able to Do* (Detroit, Mich.: NBPTS, 1994).

II. Reinvent teacher preparation and professional development.

WE RECOMMEND: *that colleges and schools work with states to redesign teacher education so that the two million teachers to be hired in the next decade are adequately prepared and all teachers have access to continuous high-quality learning opportunities.*

More new teachers will be hired in the next decade than in any previous decade in our history. If they are adequately prepared at the beginning of their careers, most of the band-aids and stop-gap efforts now required should prove to be irrelevant in the future. In addition, if teachers have continuous access to the latest knowledge about teaching and learning, they will be better able to respond to the toughest learning problems and the challenge of meeting ever higher standards. For this to occur, several changes are essential.

- **Organize teacher education and professional development programs around standards for students and teachers.**

If teachers are to be prepared to help their students meet the new standards that are now being set for them, teacher preparation and professional development programs must consciously examine the expectations embodied in new curriculum frameworks and assessments and understand what they imply for teaching and for learning to teach.

Among other things, teaching to the new standards will require

1. **Stronger disciplinary preparation** that incorporates an understanding of a discipline's core concepts, structure, and tools of inquiry as a foundation for subject matter pedagogy;

2. **Greater focus on learning and development,** including strategies for responding to different stages and pathways for learning;

3. **More knowledge about curriculum and assessment design** as a basis for analyzing and responding to student learning;

4. **Greater understanding of how to help special-needs students** and address learning differences and disabilities;

5. **Multicultural competence** for working in a range of settings with diverse learners;

6. **Preparation for collaboration** with colleagues and parents;

7. **Technological skills** for supporting student learning and professional learning in the Information Age; and

8. **Strong emphasis on reflection and inquiry** as means to continually evaluate and improve teaching.

Schools of education and other sources of professional development need to model how to teach for understanding in a multicultural context, how to continually assess and respond to student learning, and how to use new technologies in doing so. They need to organize their work to promote the attainment of student standards through the use of teaching standards that are grounded in contemporary knowledge about learning and teaching. To accomplish this we recommend that colleges:

- **Develop extended teacher preparation programs that provide a yearlong internship in a professional development school.**

Over the past decade, many schools of education have incorporated new knowledge about teaching and learning in their programs for prospective teachers. Structuring the experience of learning to teach so that it is actually effective has required a number of changes from traditional practice.[99]

First, successful teacher preparation programs aim to develop a foundation for continual learning about teaching—the capacity to analyze learning and examine the effects of contexts and teaching strategies on students' motivation, interest, and achievement—rather than aiming only to transmit techniques for managing daily classroom activities. This requires building a strong foundation of knowledge about learning, development, motivation, and behavior, including their cognitive, social, and cultural bases. It also requires creating cases and other inquiries that allow students to use this knowledge in applied contexts—to gather information, analyze and learn from their knowledge, and use what they have learned to assess situations and improve instruction. This kind of preparation is essential if teachers are to work productively with diverse learners.

Second, greater attention is paid to developing high-quality clinical learning opportunities in schools that are closely connected to the teacher preparation curriculum. A coherent program of mentoring and instruction by school and university faculty is essential if teacher education is to be a powerful intervention in the experience of prospective teachers. In the long run, universities should focus as much on building strong clinical training and induction programs—including preparing and supporting cooperating teachers and mentors so that they become excellent teachers of teachers and partners in the teacher education process—as they do on the direct instruction of new teachers in courses.

Third, teacher educators serve as bridges between disciplinary and pedagogical coursework so that a solid platform for content pedagogy can be built. More integrated approaches combine attention to learning the disciplines and teaching the disciplines. These should increasingly take into account the changing conceptions of curriculum and assessment embodied in new standards.

Finally, coursework and clinical experiences continually exhibit 21st-century ways of working. They feature technology and teamwork in all that they do, including partnerships with parents as well as work with colleagues.

One of the major structural innovations supporting these improvements in teacher education has been the development of extended programs that add a year (and occasionally two) of graduate-level preparation beyond the traditional four-year undergraduate degree. Graduate-level teacher education has been adopted in many other countries over the last decade and has begun to spread in the United States through the efforts of the Holmes Group of education deans, the National Network for Educational Renewal, and the American Association for Colleges of Teacher Education.

Extended programs allow beginning teachers to complete a bachelor's degree in their subject *and* acquire a firmer grounding in teaching skills, including the knowledge of learning and students' special needs that are growing increasingly important for teaching success. Some are five-year models that allow an extended program of postbaccalaureate preparation for undergraduates interested in teaching. Others are one- to two-year graduate programs serving either recent graduates or midcareer recruits.

In either case, because the fifth year allows students to devote their energies exclusively to teacher preparation for at least a year, these programs allow for extended practice teaching in schools tightly tied to relevant coursework. Such internships permit integration of theoretical and practical learning, providing a much more compelling context for developing skilled and thoughtful practice. Although a very few four-year teacher education programs have been able to create conditions for more extensive student teaching in which coursework is tightly tied to practice, most do not have sufficient control over a large enough segment of their students' overall curriculum to ensure that candidates encounter important knowledge for teaching in ways that make it useful and well used.[100]

Recent studies show that graduates of these extended teacher education programs are rated by principals and teaching colleagues as much better prepared and more effective than graduates of four-year programs, and they are as confident and effective in their teaching as more senior colleagues. They also are significantly more likely to enter teaching and remain in the profession after several years. Studies have found that extended program graduates enter teaching at rates consistently above 90% as compared with 60% to 80% for four-year graduates, and they remain in teaching after several years at rates typically over 80% as compared with 50% to 70% for four-year graduates.[101]

Earlier concerns about the costs of graduate-level programs should now be reevaluated in light of evidence that they appear to produce a much higher yield on their investments. These findings suggest that funds for teacher education could be more productively concentrated on high-quality preparation for serious candidates in professional schools, rather than diluted across many less certain and committed recruits who also are more weakly prepared and less likely to remain in the profession.

Early concerns that such programs would be inaccessible to prospective teachers of color seem not to have materialized. Overall, the enrollments of most graduate-level teacher education programs are noticeably more diverse than those of undergraduate programs.[102] This is partly because master's degree programs have been aggressive about recruitment and also because many recruit from pools that include recent graduates, midcareer entrants, and military and business retirees. They often tailor their offerings in more flexible ways that

Teacher Education for the 21st Century: Teaching for Understanding Using New Technologies

Since 1990, Magdalene Lampert and Deborah Ball have combined their teaching of mathematics in third- and fifth-grade elementary school classrooms with their work as teacher educators. Using hypermedia technology, they have begun closing the gap between theory and practice by bringing the classroom into the university. Their work at Michigan State University and the University of Michigan in the Mathematics and Teaching through Hypermedia (MATH) project has allowed new and in-service teachers to look at what it means to teach toward new student standards by engaging in sustained investigations of practice using video and computer technology.

Lampert's and Ball's elementary school teaching is explicitly focused on helping students to understand and use mathematics in the ways suggested by the new NCTM standards—focusing on reasoning and problem solving rather than the rote work that characterizes most mathematics classrooms. They have videotaped their teaching over the course of a year and have entered these tapes along with other classroom data—lesson plans, students' work, assignments, curriculum materials, and

assessments—into a hypermedia platform. This makes it possible for users of the MATH project to see and study examples of actual teaching in its natural context over time. Together, students can examine a case of teaching, analyze what is happening, ask questions, and seek answers. These investigations of teaching help teacher candidates conduct their own research, look carefully at student learning in relation to teaching decisions, and examine curriculum and assessments firsthand rather than in the abstract.

"By using videos of real-time teaching," explain Lampert and Ball, "we seek to represent the complexities involved in the moment-by-moment problems of practice. We hope to affect users' assumptions about what teachers need to know to teach elementary school mathematics [and] to support investigations of teachers—work that adequately reflect the messiness of practice in the classroom. . . . Technology makes it possible to manipulate such materials of practice in constructively imaginative ways: a child's presence in September can be arrayed for comparison next to her stance in May; patterns of teacher-student dia-

logue can be analyzed across time."

Users can stop and replay the tape to look at events closely, connect what is happening in the lesson with teachers' and students' writing about what they were doing, look at student performance, and keep track of their own ongoing interpretations. In this way, hypermedia supports in-depth analysis of teaching decisions that are often difficult to capture when discussed out of context. Looking at the patterns of classrooms—tone and timing, the expressions of children, a teacher's style—is crucial in learning to teach, because so much of teaching entails hearing and seeing as well as interpreting such information. Access to rich data about the work of teachers *and* the learning of students makes it possible for prospective teachers to build their own detailed knowledge of how to teach diverse learners in ways that lead to greater understanding.

Sources: Magdalene Lampert and Deborah K. Ball, "Using Hypermedia to Investigate and Construct Knowledge about Mathematics Teaching and Learning," in *Mathematics And Teaching through Hypermedia* (Ann Arbor, Mich.: The MATH Project, 1995); and "Aligning Teacher Education with Contemporary K-12 Reform Visions" (paper prepared for the National Commission on Teaching & America's Future, October 1995).

acknowledge previous education and experience.

In tandem with these new program initiatives, more than 200 (out of 1,200) schools of education have created "professional development schools" that, like teaching hospitals in medicine, provide new recruits with sites for intensively supervised internships where they can experience state-of-the-art practice that is linked to their coursework. They also provide sites for research by school- and university-based faculty, creating more powerful knowledge for teaching by putting research into practice and practice into research.[103]

Furthermore, professional development schools create new ways for colleges and school systems to work together around instructional reform, creating greater common ground and leveraging improvements in both settings. In Cincinnati, Ohio; Louisville, Kentucky; San Antonio, Texas; and many other cities, a growing number of new teachers are prepared in professional development schools associated with local universities, thus providing direct pathways from training to hiring for well-prepared entrants and creating a cadre of new teachers who are prepared to undertake immediately the kinds of teaching the district is seeking to encourage. The power of professional development schools for leveraging reform is that they sit at the intersection of universities and schools and of preservice and in-service development for teachers. Thus, they provide the means by which schools and colleges of education can simultaneously redesign their work.

The nation needs many more professional development schools, because these partnerships between higher education and local schools, by harnessing theory to practice, improve both. As with teaching hospitals in medicine, government support will be needed to create enough professional development schools to support high-quality training for all entering teachers.

States should encourage the creation of innovative programs consistent with the recommendations throughout this report. There is an urgent need to accelerate changes in teacher education so that new models of exemplary practice are visible across the country. One approach to this goal is for governors, state boards of education, deans, faculty, and university presidents to designate selected institutions as charter colleges of education. Such colleges would be free of selected regulations and procedures so they could make the curricular, staffing, and other changes necessary to demonstrate best practice in all aspects of their work. As these are evaluated, changes that prove successful should inform statewide policy for teacher education.

- **Create and fund mentoring programs for beginning teachers, along with evaluation of teaching skills.**

Even with more extensive preservice teacher preparation, the beginning year of teaching presents new challenges and problems for all teachers that pose a steep learning curve. Like doctors in their medical residency, teachers who have the support of a more senior colleague and opportunities for continuing their learning become more skilled more quickly. Research shows that beginning teachers who have had the continuous support of a skilled mentor are much more likely to stay in the profession and much more likely to get beyond classroom management concerns to focus on student learning.[104] All beginning teachers should be assigned a skilled mentor. Effective mentors should be selected for their outstanding teaching ability and be given the necessary training and released time to work productively with their new colleagues.

Ideally, the first year or two of teaching should be structured much like a residency in medicine, with teachers continually consulting a seasoned veteran in their teaching field about the decisions they are making and receiving ongoing advice and evaluation. In the quality control system we propose, teachers will have completed the first stage of licensing tests—examinations of subject matter and basic teaching knowledge—and will be ready to undertake the sec-

Trinity University: A Case of Teacher Education Reform

"We've fiddled with the curriculum, we've fiddled with testing, and we've fiddled with finance, but we haven't done anything to get better teachers in American classrooms," observes John Moore, chair of the education department at Trinity University in San Antonio, Texas.

Acting on the belief that teacher quality is the key to educational improvement, Trinity replaced its traditional, four-year education major with five years of preparation nearly ten years ago. The new program integrates more arts and sciences courses with educational coursework to ensure solid disciplinary grounding and attention to content pedagogy. Students receive a bachelor's degree in their academic discipline before they go on to complete a Master of Arts in Teaching. The program also adds a full-year teaching internship for student teachers, which takes place in professional development schools where expert, veteran teachers join with university faculty to provide a supportive, realistic initial teaching experience.

Four schools in the San Antonio area have joined with Trinity in the Alliance for Better Schools. As professional development schools, they are places where theory-based practices are researched and developed, interns receive preparation for teaching, and professional development activities for surrounding schools are held. Sixty classroom teachers from these schools are appointed as clinical faculty at Trinity. They help provide clinical experiences for Trinity students in each of the five years of the program, beginning with classroom observations and culminating with the full fifth-year internship.

Teachers who serve as mentors to student teachers receive an extra planning period each day to work with the beginners and to collaborate with college faculty in designing new curriculum and restructuring school practices. At Nathaniel Hawthorne, for example, an inner-city school once plagued by high student transfer rates and low achievement, elementary teachers in the Trinity program devised a program called the "collaborative," in which students would progress through the grades as a single group and teachers would use common methods based on their analysis of the latest education research. Within a few years, the student mobility rate in the collaborative has declined to 2% as com-

pared with a 59% annual mobility rate for the school overall, and test scores have gone up. The other professional development schools show similar measurable progress toward reform and renewal.

Outcomes of Trinity's program are impressive. Candidates rate the program extremely highly, as do employers. Graduates are eagerly sought out, and 100% are placed in teaching positions, most in San Antonio. As a group, they are extraordinarily successful, winning numerous awards for their teaching from their very first years in the classroom. "In terms of recruiting, training, and renewing teachers, Trinity is one of the most impressive efforts in the nation," Ernest Boyer, the late president of the Carnegie Foundation for the Advancement of Teaching, observed. Trinity's efforts demonstrate how a strong teacher education program can yield important benefits for the community as a whole.

Sources: John H. Moore, "Teacher Education at Trinity University: Program Conceptualization and Development" (March 23, 1995); Gary Putka, "Making the Grade: Teacher Quality Rises With Improved Pay, Concern for Schools," *The Wall Street Journal* (December 5, 1991).

ond stage—an examination of teaching skills conducted through a structured performance assessment that they work on in their first year.

Connecticut's mentoring and performance assessment program (described later) is a prototype for this approach. It provides mentors for all beginning teachers and seminars organized around the state's performance assessments for receiving a continuing professional license. In Minnesota, where professional development schools are among the sites for first-year teaching residencies, the plan is for all beginning teachers to teach 80% of the time under the supervision of mentor teachers and to engage in professional development the remaining 20% of the time. During their first year, they will be evaluated for a continuing teaching license.

Another highly successful model can be seen in school districts that have followed Toledo, Ohio's lead in developing thoughtful, comprehensive programs for supporting beginning teachers. The Toledo model—now used in Cincinnati and Columbus, Ohio; Rochester, New York; and Seattle, Washington—funds expert veteran teachers to work intensively with beginners in their fields and to contribute to serious tenure decisions. In several of these cities, many beginning teachers have completed a yearlong internship in a professional development school before they are hired; then they are assigned a consulting teacher mentor in their first year of teaching. These approaches represent the beginning of a real professional development track for teaching—one that has great potential for creating world-class teachers from the beginning of their careers.

In all of these cases, the programs serve two functions: New teachers receive sustained assistance, and those who do not become competent are counseled out before they receive a continuing license or tenure. This allows systems to invest in useful professional development after tenure, rather than wasting funds on annual evaluations to check for basic competence. Whatever the model, the evidence is clear: Supports for new teachers help them continue their learning during a critical period, one which makes a tremendous difference in the kind of teacher they eventually become and the kind of experience their students have.

- ## Create stable, high-quality sources of professional development.

Ultimately, the quality of teaching depends not only on the qualifications of individuals who enter teaching, but also on how schools structure teaching work and teachers' learning opportunities. Teachers who feel they are enabled to succeed with students are more committed and effective than those who feel unsupported in their learning and in their practice.[105] Those who have access to new knowledge, enriched professional roles, and ongoing collegial work feel more efficacious in gaining the knowledge they need to teach their students well and more positive about staying in the profession.

The critical importance of career-long professional development is finally being recognized. A comprehensive report outlining the components of a professional development system, *Teachers Take Charge of Their Learning*, has recently been released by the National Foundation for the Improvement of Education (NFIE), and we endorse its major findings and recommendations.[106] The report details how high-quality professional development for teachers directly influences student learning, and it recommends a series of steps to make such professional development widespread, including school-based professional development that attends to the needs and achievement of students and the attainment of professional teaching standards; teacher engagement in peer assistance and review as well as other expanded roles; the integral use of information technologies in teaching and teacher development; and more flexible scheduling along with an extended school year for teachers to provide time for professional development.

NFIE defines high-quality professional development as that which

- Has the goal of improving student learning at the heart of every school endeavor;

- Fosters a deepening of subject matter knowledge, a greater understanding of learning, and a greater appreciation of students' needs;

- Helps teachers and other staff meet the needs of students who learn in different ways and who come from diverse cultural, linguistic, and socioeconomic backgrounds;

- Provides adequate time for inquiry, reflection, and mentoring, and is an important part of the normal working day;

- Is rigorous, sustained, and adequate to the long-term change of practice;

- Is directed toward teachers' intellectual development and leadership;

- Is teacher designed and directed, incorporates the best principles of adult learning, and involves shared decisions designed to improve the school;

- Balances individual priorities with school and district needs;

- Makes best use of new technologies; and

- Is site-based and supportive of a clearly articulated vision for students.

These features are rare in professional development today. Most professional dollars are spent either reimbursing teachers for courses that may not be directly related to school needs or their classroom responsibilities or for district-determined workshops with even less connections to teachers' own practice. As traditionally organized, in-service education—usually conducted as mass-produced hit-and-run workshops—is not well suited to helping teachers with the most pressing challenges they face in deepening their subject matter knowledge, responding to student diversity, or teaching more effectively.

There is a mismatch between the kind of teaching and learning teachers are now expected to pursue with their students and the teaching they experience in their own professional education. Teachers are urged to engage their students in actively building their understanding of new ideas; to provide opportunities for practice and feedback as well as for inquiry, problem solving, collaboration, and critical reflection; to connect knowledge to students' developmental stages and personal experiences; and to carefully assess student learning over time. These desirable characteristics of teaching are usually absent in the learning afforded to teachers. There are few parallels between how teachers are expected to teach and how they are encouraged to learn.

Although most teachers experience very few useful, relevant learning opportunities, school systems spend substantial amounts of money on professional development every year, much of it unplanned, a lot of it unnoticed, practically all of it uncoordinated. Central offices manage a professional development fund. Hidden in federal, state, and district programs, large and small, are other pots of money for professional development. By offering salary credit to teachers for practically any coursework they take, districts provide huge subsidies for professional development, whether or not the courses move the mission of the school forward.

A district examination of professional development funding in Flint, Michigan, recently revealed that the nominal district allocation of about $300,000 ballooned to $13 million annually, about 6% of the district budget, when every source of support direct and indirect spending was itemized.[107] Another study in Los Angeles estimated that 22% of teacher salaries, or $253 million, could be attributed to salary point credits earned by taking courses.[108] Paraphrasing the late Senator Everett Dirksen: A couple of million here, a couple of million there, and pretty soon you're talking about real money.

These funds need to be organized around a coherent scheme of professional development that works to improve teaching. New resources should be invested in vehicles that offer relevant, sustained learning for teachers. To accomplish this, states and districts need to do the following:

- **Allocate at least 1% of state and local education funding** to be consistently devoted to high-quality professional development organized around standards for student learning and for accomplished teaching practice. States should also provide matching funds for districts to increase their investments in professional development to 3% of total expenditures.

- **Organize new sources of professional development** such as teacher academies, school-university partnerships, professional development schools, and networks for learning across schools.

A Better Way: Professional Development That Improves Teaching

"Staff training is terribly important for reform to work," notes Pat Rice, principal of Withrow High School in Cincinnati, Ohio. "Look at medicine. Doctors are learning new surgical techniques all the time. If you're going to have a gallstone removed, wouldn't you rather they zap it with a laser than cut you open with a knife?"

Teacher Academies

"The old paradigm of teaching was that you prepared a lesson, you taught it the best way you could, and you covered the curriculum," Rice observes. Now, good teaching is judged by how much learning occurs, she explains. This means staff must keep abreast of new developments, a task made easier by Cincinnati's Mayerson Academy, a staff development center endowed by the business community and run by a local board of teachers and administrators.

"One thing we know about professional development is that it's not worth anything if there isn't ongoing follow-up and support all the time. It can't be inconsistent and it can't be one-shot programs," says Michael Rutherford, Mayerson's executive director. Therefore, Mayerson offers six-week courses dealing with the latest learning about curriculum, instruction, and classroom management, followed up by "action labs" that address specific topics like cooperative learning strategies, cultural diversity, and school improvement. Study groups and school teams meet at the academy, and teachers can use state-of-the-art technologies to see master teachers at work in their classrooms.

One kindergarten teacher notes, "I've come every summer. I've been teaching 21 years, but you can always learn something new. Most teachers come out at least once a year. And sometimes you can come as a whole school." Another teacher remarked, "We get teachers together. There's a whole lot of talk that goes on in the hall—it starts in there and it continues out here."

Teacher Networks

When Linda Starkweather applied to participate in the North Carolina Capital Area Writing Project Summer Institute in 1994, she had no idea what the outcome would be. Based on the philosophy that teachers can best teach teachers, local chapters of the National Writing Project offer monthlong summer institutes at 160 sites. Teachers of all grade levels and subjects come together to demonstrate successful practices, respond to one another's work, discuss current research, and practice their own writing.

Linda was so inspired by this experience that when she returned to her school in the fall, she demonstrated one of the lessons she'd seen and asked her colleagues to make presentations of lessons they had developed for their students. The teachers responded with enthusiasm: At the next professional development day, 15 teachers, and parents offered nine workshops to their colleagues. Teachers who were used to working in isolation were so enlivened by the process that "the walls came tumbling down" as they published their ideas in the staff newsletter and began sharing resources. Notes Linda, "All of a sudden, people were talking about learning. Instead of becoming burned out, we were becoming more creative. What happened was more than just intellectual renewal. The whole spirit of the school changed. It became a joyful place where the adults are excited about learning, and that excitement spreads to the students."

School-University Partnerships

The Southern Maine Partnership links three local colleges with 27 public school districts and three private schools. Shaped by the needs and interests of its participants the partnership is like a neighborhood in which university and school people are constantly in touch with each other about practices, ideas, and issues that affect students' learning.

Activities include mini-grants to teachers to develop and share new assessments of student learning; "Dine and Discuss" evenings at which university and school faculty gather around dinner to discuss texts that inform their work; "Tool Box Sessions" at which teachers share successful teaching practices and materials; and visits to classrooms to look at teaching. In addition, the University of Southern Maine places its student teachers in professional development schools in nine districts, working closely with experienced cooperating teachers in delivering coursework at the school site.

As a result of this work, 50 schools and six districts have improved their assessment and accountability systems. Many have improved their curricula in literacy, math, and science as teachers work with engineers, scientists, and university faculty. Fourteen high schools have restructured schedules to extend student time for learning. Five small districts have formed an alliance to pool resources to improve learning opportunities for students and teachers. College-level courses are made available to high school students, and high school students have started a Student Congress. The students recently submitted a position paper they wrote on high schools to the governor and state legislature, demonstrating that in Maine, collaboration on school reform is for everyone.

- **Make ongoing professional development part of teachers' daily work** through joint planning, research, curriculum and assessment work, study groups, and peer coaching.

Districts and schools should use a major portion of their professional development funds to engage teachers in productive approaches to professional development that involve teachers in professional communities beyond their classrooms.[109] These communities can be organized across subject matter lines, like the National Writing Project; around significant pedagogical issues, like the Performance Assessment Collaboratives in Education; or in support of particular approaches to school reform, like the School Development Program or the Coalition of Essential Schools. They may be departments or teams within schools or networks and school-university partnerships that allow teachers to work together across schools. In any case, they provide opportunities for teachers and other educators to share ideas about teaching and school change, to learn from one another as well as from experts, and lend support to the risk taking that is part of the process of any significant change.[110]

In addition, states and districts should consider establishing teacher academies to support professional development focused on instructional change and schoolwide reform. Successful examples include the Gheens Academy in Louisville, Kentucky, and the Mayerson Academy in Cincinnati, Ohio. Both were established with external corporate or foundation grants; provide a special facility and staff for high-quality, sustained professional development activities; draw on the expertise of local teachers and principals as well as university faculty; and pursue an agenda focused on school reform priorities worked out jointly by teachers and the district. Statewide academies, like the North Carolina Teacher Academy, also provide intensive institutes aimed at skill building and problem solving for school teams as well as the development of teacher leaders to work with other teachers. These institutions have shown how systemwide goals for change can be connected to teachers' desires for continuous professional development that moves beyond "flavor-of-the-month" workshops to support transformations in practice.

Districts should treat professional development as the core function of management, designing a dense network of peer relationships within and across schools that are used to expand knowledge. Problems should be tackled by a combination of practitioners working together across classroom and school boundaries, visiting and observing one another in successful settings, modeling instruction and working with one another as consultants, talking about common instructional problems, and using analyses of student work and new standards as the center of professional discourse.[111]

As we describe later, teachers' time for learning, as well as ongoing collaboration and joint planning, should be supported by redesigned school schedules, structures, and staffing so that teachers can work smarter and students can consistently encounter high-quality instruction.

The East Carolina University Peer Coaching Project

Both of us found it helpful to imagine new approaches to familiar teaching situations and to have another teacher with whom we could stretch out our thinking. When two heads get together, one thought leads to another in exciting ways. Margaret told me that the support and collaboration was very valuable to her because, even though she was a veteran teacher, she realized that she needed new methods with this particular group of students. And the students benefited tremendously, because they themselves were so involved in the process of refining Margaret's teaching philosophies and practices.

— NOELA WOODALL, PEER COACHING PARTICIPANT, BENSON ELEMENTARY SCHOOL, NORTH CAROLINA

The East Carolina University Peer Coaching Project Consortium was formed as an alternative to North Carolina's state-mandated checklist for teacher evaluation. Diane Houlihan began in 1991 working with six pairs of teachers in the Johnston County School System to share ideas, watch each other teaching, and conduct classroom research. Each of these 12 teachers coached another teacher the following year. By 1995, 245 teachers in three country districts were working together in peer coaching partnerships.

The peer coaching process puts teachers in charge of their own learning. When Noela Woodall, a third-grade teacher, began coaching Margaret Adams, also a third-grade teacher at the same school, they began by discussing Margaret's goals for the year. Margaret's short-term goal was to help her students learn to move more smoothly between activities. Her long-term goal was to teach her students to participate in par-

ent-teacher conferences by talking about the work they had compiled in their portfolios. She wrote strategies, a timeline, criteria for measuring success, and a list of the resources she would need to meet her goals, and gave them to her principal.

Before Noela came to observe the class, she asked Margaret questions like, "What can I do to help? How can I get a picture of what you have in mind? How do you want your students to move between activities?" Margaret wasn't entirely sure she could describe the change she sought. So Noela suggested that they videotape these "in between" moments so that Margaret could show the tape to her students and involve them in analyzing their own behavior. When they viewed the tape, Margaret's students volunteered thoughts about the distractions they were causing each other during the transition times. Margaret asked, "How do you think we can improve this?" and the children offered strategies for reducing the chatter. They asked for periodic designated "talk times" during the day. Meanwhile, Noela asked Margaret to notice what happened when she signaled that it was time for the students to get back to work. From the tape, Margaret saw for herself that they quickly returned to their learning tasks and that all of their conversation became "work talk." Since the tape showed that the students were engaging in their work, Margaret realized she could worry less about transitions and direct more of her efforts into guiding their learning.

Toward her second goal, Noela helped Margaret locate useful information about student-led conferences, and together they showed the students how they could meet with their parents and teachers to

talk about their own work. Margaret allowed the children to role-play the process of discussing their portfolios with her and a "parent" played by another student. Noela videotaped these role-plays and asked Margaret questions about what she saw. By the end of the year, a number of Margaret's students had explained their own work to their parents at parent-teacher conferences.

During the year, Margaret and Noela went through four cycles of observations with pre- and postconferences. Sometimes Noela worked with the class while Margaret observed another class, held a conference with parents, or attended a training session. As always in such relationships, the partnership held rewards for them both, as they deepened their understanding of teaching by looking at problems of practice together.

III. Fix teacher recruitment and put qualified teachers in every classroom.

WE RECOMMEND: *that states and districts pursue aggressive policies to put qualified teachers in every classroom by providing financial incentives to correct shortages, streamlining hiring procedures, and reducing barriers to teacher mobility.*

Can we afford to raise standards for teachers and staff classrooms, too? The question is key to America's future, and we answer it in the affirmative. The goal of access to qualified teachers for every student is well within reach if states and districts follow these five principles:

- **Increase the ability of low-wealth districts to pay for qualified teachers and insist that districts hire only qualified teachers.**

All schools must be adequately funded and staffed by first-rate teachers. To continue compromising this goal, especially in poor urban and rural schools, inevitably means the end of the American dream of equal opportunity. To ignore this imperative is to allow the nation to skate dangerously close to irreparably harming its public education system and its single best hope for preserving American democracy. Without adequate education, many children will be unable to contribute productively to society, an outcome that is incompatible with the continuation of healthy democratic life.

There are alternatives to perpetuating inequality. States can ensure that districts have both the capacity and the incentive to hire qualified teachers by equalizing district ability to pay for well-prepared teachers while they raise standards. When Connecticut pursued this strategy in 1986, distributing state funds in an equalizing fashion to enable districts to reach minimum beginning salaries, the state significantly raised standards for teacher education and licensing while eliminating shortages of teachers within three years. It also ensured that these new state funds would be spent on hiring more qualified teachers rather than on any number of other competing agendas that likely would have had less influence on student achievement.

In tandem, states should insist that districts hire only qualified teachers and that they assign teachers only in the fields for which they are approved and licensed. Incentives could include those used in Missouri and Delaware, which approve salary reimbursements only for licensed teachers, as well as sanctions such as disapproval of accreditation for districts that continually flout licensing laws.

- **Redesign and streamline district hiring.**

School districts routinely shoot themselves in the foot with cumbersome, inefficient hiring processes, late hiring, and tolerance for a revolving door of

Putting It All Together: The Quest for Teacher Quality in Connecticut

Like the bunny battery that never stops, Connecticut keeps honing its commitment to quality teaching. Teacher excellence was the heart of Connecticut's 1986 Education Enhancement Act, which committed more than $300 million to

- Raise standards for teacher education and licensing, including a system to support and assess beginning teachers;

- Make teachers' salaries competitive with other occupations requiring similar professional preparation; and

- Equalize district capacity to pay for salaries to reduce inequality among the state's school districts.

The state provided funds on an equalizing basis to school districts, which brought beginning teacher salaries up to a minimum level. This helped to equalize funding for schools while directing the new funds to the place they could have the greatest effect on learning: the hiring of more qualified teachers. Meanwhile the state required entering teachers to meet more rigorous standards for licensing, including a performance assessment coupled with mentoring during the first year of teaching and a master's degree within a few years of entry. As a result of these initiatives, the state experienced a dramatic boost in teacher quality and in the quality of preparation programs, while shortages were eliminated within three years of the bill's enactment.

Since then, the vision for a quality teaching force has remained, while specific components have evolved to reflect ever higher standards. Today, teachers in Connecticut are among the best prepared in the nation. As a result of the state's reforms, the proportion of teachers teaching with both a degree in their field and a license is one of the highest in the country. New teachers must complete a preparation program that includes a four- or five-year degree in their field and a rigorous set of education courses. Teachers can be hired only after passing tests of basic skills and subject matter knowledge. They then enter a two-year induction program that combines mentoring and performance-based assessment as the basis, along with a master's degree, for a continuing professional license.

During the first year of teaching, novices receive help from a school-based mentor or mentor team. Beginning teacher clinics are offered to help them prepare for the assessment of essential teaching competencies, which is conducted by state-trained assessors through observation or videotape. This process, which evaluates basic teaching skills, has been in operation for eight years.

The new component will evaluate first- and second-year teachers' abilities to teach challenging content for understanding and to adapt teaching to the needs of diverse learners. Based on the INTASC standards, teachers develop portfolios of their work, which include videotapes of specific lessons that reflect the teaching expected by new student standards, analysis of student work, and written descriptions of ways in which they adapt instruction to the needs of individual learners.

The 200 teachers who participated in last year's assessments found them extremely worthwhile. Tony Romano, a seventh-grade math teacher in Stamford, found the process of reflecting on his lessons each day during the six-week period he documented for his portfolio "work intensive" but "enlightening." "Although I was the reflective type anyway, it made me go a step further. I think it had more impact on my teaching than just one lesson in which you state what you're going to do. . . . The process makes you think about your teaching, and I think that's necessary to become an effective teacher."

Source: Connecticut State Department of Education/Division of Research, Evaluation, and Assessment, *Research Bulletin,* School Year 1990-91, no. 1 (Hartford, Conn.: Bureau of Research and Teacher Assessment, 1991).

beginning teachers, one that spins all the faster because seniority provisions in many local contracts practically guarantee that inexperienced teachers will be assigned to the most difficult teaching situations. Districts need to

- **Streamline and decentralize hiring procedures using technology.** School districts should create a central electronic hiring hall that lists relevant data for all qualified candidates and provides data on vacancies to candidates. They should then delegate selection and hiring decisions to schools. This will support responsible decentralization by ensuring that only qualified teachers are considered, while allowing schools to move ahead expeditiously in hiring candidates who fit their needs.

- **Focus on competitive early hiring of new teachers.** Districts should establish direct pathways from teacher preparation programs to the classroom through cooperative agreements with universities. They should also develop incentives to encourage veteran teachers interested in transferring or retiring to provide early notification of their intentions so that vacancies can be posted and filled much earlier.

- **Eliminate barriers to teacher mobility.**

Teacher shortages are made all the worse because, in an age of mobility, qualified teachers frequently find themselves unable to transfer their license to their new state, and teachers who could be persuaded to move to districts or states with shortages face the loss of seniority, salary credit, and vested pensions. Most of these roadblocks to mobility were long ago removed for college faculty members; they should be removed for public school teachers as well. Districts need to

- **Insist that their states participate in the INTASC assessment system,** which will allow reciprocal licensing agreements among states.

- **Work with states to create portable pension systems** (similar to the TIAA-CREF system established for college faculty early in this century) and/or to ensure that teachers can remain vested in their original districts.

- Develop policies for ensuring that **incoming veterans receive full salary credit** for their experience.

Recruiting the Best

In his 1983 study, *High School,* Ernest Boyer of the Carnegie Foundation for the Advancement of Teaching observed:

We cannot adequately prepare the coming generation if the least able students enter the profession. Teaching must become a top priority and gifted students must be recruited. . . . The process should begin in high school. We recommend that every high school establish a "cadet" teacher program . . . to identify gifted students and make opportunities for them to present information to classmates, tutor students needing special help, and meet with outstanding school and college teachers. For a young person to be told by a respected adult that he or she could be a great teacher may well have the profound impact on the career choice of that student.

Taking its inspiration from this recommendation, the **South Carolina Teacher Cadet Program** was launched in 1986. Today it involves more than 130 high schools and 19 partner colleges serving nearly 2,100 academically able high school juniors and seniors. The cadets enroll in a yearlong course on teaching in which they study learning, child development, education history, and pedagogy. They engage in seminars, group projects, and discussions with educators. They observe classrooms, teach practice lessons, and tutor other students. In 1993, about one-fourth of the cadets who were high school seniors in 1988 were certified to teach in South Carolina, many of them in high-need rural areas and in critical shortage fields. They were much more diverse as a group and much more likely to report they plan to remain in teaching than other beginning teachers. Cadets say their experience helped them "better prepare themselves for college and for teaching." Nearly 60% of current cadets claim that as a result of the program they are more likely to become a teacher.

Another highly successful recruitment model is the **North Carolina Teaching Fellows Program,** which has thus far recruited 3,600 high-ability high school graduates to teaching, including significant numbers of young men and people of color. The students agree to teach for four years in the state's public schools in exchange for a $20,000 four-year college scholarship, which underwrites their preparation. Fourteen colleges and universities in the state participate in providing intensive year-round learning experiences that extend beyond regular teacher education courses. North Carolina principals report that the Fellows far exceed other new teachers in their performance, and the Fellows themselves give high marks to the preparation they received in instructional methods and teaching diverse students. Notes one Fellow, "The ample observations and early field experience at my university gave me the opportunity to watch many different teachers and many different styles. This exposure really helped prepare me for the 'real world' of a first-year teacher." Another observed that "the best thing the [program] did to prepare me was to make me aware that I would be teaching a diverse group of students. As a first-year teacher, I knew about at-risk students and different learning styles. I knew how to use cooperative learning in my subject area." The collegial emphasis of the program led another to be grateful that her experience "provided me a network of professionals that I can confide in and strategize with." Today, Teaching Fellows are working in some of the most challenging settings in the state.

The **Golden Apple Scholars of Illinois** was initiated by Chicago area teachers who had received Golden Apple Awards for their excellent teaching. They decided to recruit promising young people into the profession by selecting them during their junior year of high school then mentoring them through the rest of high school, their college years, and five years of actual teaching. For four consecutive summers the students attend intensive six-week residential institutes, teaching in Chicago classrooms for three hours each day and attending classes designed for them dealing with leading-edge education ideas. The 60 Golden Apple Scholars each year are now supported with state and city funds and have their Stafford loans repaid if they stay in teaching. Half are from Chicago, and 68% are minority and/or low-income. The program has a 90% retention rate, is now statewide, and involves 22 private and public campuses. The first cohorts of new teachers are now in schools, many of them teaching and succeeding in challenging assignments in Chicago.

- **Aggressively recruit high-need teachers and provide incentives for teaching in shortage areas.**

If student learning is our major concern, we can no longer permit bureaucratic convenience to push aside standards of quality. Teacher shortages are much more rare in states and districts with proactive teacher recruitment policies than in those that have treated teaching in a laissez-faire manner. To assure an adequate supply of top-flight teachers,

- States and the federal government should support **scholarships linked to several years of teaching service for able candidates who prepare to teach,** targeting a major share to those who make a commitment to shortage fields and hard-to-staff locations.

- States should work with schools and colleges to **expand the pools of teachers of color and from diverse linguistic backgrounds through targeted recruitment programs** and financial supports for preparation. These efforts should include supports for programs that encourage middle and high school students to consider a teaching career.

- Districts should **provide additional pay for teachers with licenses in two or more subject areas and consider stipends and other incentives for teachers with licenses in shortage areas** determined by an objective labor market analysis each year.

- **Develop high-quality pathways to teaching for a wide range of recruits.**

The Commission is deeply concerned about back-door and off-the-street hiring that puts unqualified persons in classrooms. At the same time, we applaud the growing number of teacher education institutions that have developed alternative routes to teaching. It is critically important that the pool of persons interested in teaching be expanded and that different approaches to preparation be developed. Every college should create and support programs that build high-quality pathways into teaching, particularly in high-need areas, for recent graduates, midcareer entrants, military and government retirees, and paraprofessionals already in the classroom.

While schools seek qualified teachers, all over the United States young college graduates complain that despite their expensive education they cannot find work. At the same time, displaced midcareer professionals and military and government retirees often spend years seeking employment that uses their expertise. Access to teaching for these groups was historically limited by the fact that teacher education existed only in undergraduate programs in most states, and state approval processes restricted licensing only to those programs. Those who had already graduated from college had few options but to start college over again. Those who began in community colleges had few pathways to continue

Midcareer Recruitment Efforts: Alternatives with Promise

I earned a degree from Purdue in Mechanical Engineering, then went to work as a hydrologist. I really enjoyed my work a lot. . . . But I always knew I wanted to teach.

— A MIDCAREER RECRUIT TO TEACHING
AT INDIANA UNIVERSITY

I've had all the status I need in my naval career. I don't have big demands for money; I don't have a need for status. . . . By virtue of my experience, maybe I can do a little bit better job [for the education system].

— A GRADUATE OF GEORGE WASHINGTON
UNIVERSITY'S MIDCAREER PROGRAM

While public schools are often desperate for trained math and science teachers, many industries and the military are downsizing and letting go of employees with years of experience in these fields. Making the match between these skills and needs, the **California Mathematics and Science Teacher Corps Program at California State University, Dominguez Hills,** was created with help from businesses that provided stipends for retiring employees to prepare to teach. IBM, TRW, McDonnell-Douglas, and Hughes were among the first companies to participate. Among the initial recruits, most already had master's degrees and had worked as engineers. During their year in the program, candidates observe, tutor, and student-teach in schools while taking courses in teaching methods, motivation, learning, classroom management, and multicultural perspectives. This training, they affirm, is essential to their later success.

The Crystal City Secondary Teacher Education Program at George Washington University has prepared retiring military personnel and other technically trained professionals for teaching since 1985. Recruits completing this nine-month program come from all of the armed forces. Between 1986 and 1993, the 200 graduates were 89% male with an average age of 44. Most entered with professional degrees, having been military officers or managers. These sophisticated consumers of education rate their training program highly, especially after they enter teaching and realize how much they use the coursework and student-teaching they experienced. Their school systems rate them highly as well.

The Teacher As Decision Maker Program at Indiana University focuses on midcareer changers of all ages who come from careers including law, business, medicine, scientific research, nursing, engineering, and journalism. The 14-month program is tailored to suit each person's previous experience and professional goals. Students with recent degrees may need less academic work in their disciplines than those who received their degrees years ago. Those with a strong academic major and minor may work toward a license in two teaching fields. Fellows engage in peer mentoring, analyze their teaching on videotape each week, observe exemplary teachers, and participate in an ongoing seminar during their 15 weeks of student teaching, which gradually increases to a full teaching load working closely with an expert mentor.

Colorado State University's Project Promise recruits prospective teachers from fields as diverse as law, geology, chemistry, stock trading, and medicine. The ten-month program emphasizes problem solving, cultural awareness, and student needs as well as subject matter and pedagogical preparation. Candidates cycle through four or five intensively supervised teaching practicums in very different settings for up to nine weeks each. They also engage in regular peer coaching. Evaluation is based on demonstrated performance, not credit hours or seat time. Faculty mentor graduates in their first and second year of teaching, bridging the infamous gap between preparation and induction. Outcome data show that recruits feel exceptionally well prepared to teach, and they enter and stay in teaching at levels far exceeding the average for traditional teacher education students. More than 90% enter and 80% stay over a five-year period. It is no wonder that districts from across the country try to recruit Project Promise teachers.

The nation's nearly 500,000 paraeducators represent another significant source of prospective teachers who are representative of and rooted in the communities in which they serve. **The Navajo Nation Ford Teacher Education Program** is a joint effort of the Navajo Nation and the Ford Foundation to recruit and prepare Navajo teachers through a consortium of six colleges and universities. Participants receive scholarships and stipends amounting to nearly $12,000 to complete their college degrees and education training with academic advisement and support. Most of the more than 200 participants in the program are Navajo-speaking teacher aides, and the program has produced 38 new Navajo teachers so far.

their education in a teaching program. However, more than 200 accredited universities have created successful models that provide high-quality alternative routes into teaching at the postbaccalaureate level as well as articulated pathways for paraprofessionals moving into teacher education from community colleges. These deserve emulation and support.

These kinds of programs have been successful because of the investments in scholarships, loans, and other program supports made by some states and foundations. Evidence suggests that such investments ultimately pay handsome dividends for the schools that hire these recruits. Yet these programs flourish in some communities, while other communities with equally great needs have few avenues for interested candidates to become well prepared for teaching. A well-planned set of incentives that provide financial aid for candidates along with supports for more high-quality programs could make an enormous difference in our capacity to teach all students in all subjects in all communities well.

IV. Encourage and reward knowledge and skills.

WE RECOMMEND: *that districts, states, unions, and professional associations cooperate to make teaching a true profession with a career continuum that places teaching at the top and rewards teachers for their knowledge and skills.*

For generations, teachers have wanted to be considered professionals. Now the confluence of two developments puts that goal within reach. The first is the evolution of a coherent set of high-quality teaching standards; the second, the courageous work of a number of states and local school districts to embody these standards in new systems of teacher evaluation, compensation, and professional development that provide the scaffolding for a true profession—one that is grounded in an unyielding commitment to students, a body of shared knowledge, and willingness to set, enforce, and transmit standards of practice. Creating a profession requires three kinds of actions:

- **Develop a career continuum for teaching linked to assessments and compensation systems that reward knowledge and skill.**

Existing career tracks and compensation systems in teaching create a career pathway that places classroom teaching at the bottom, provides teachers with little influence in making key education decisions, and requires teachers to leave the classroom if they want greater responsibility or substantially higher pay. The message is clear: Those who work with children have the lowest status; those who do not, the highest.

We need a different career continuum, one that places teaching at the top and creates a career progression that supports teachers as they become increasingly expert. Like the path from assistant professor to associate and full professor on campuses—or junior associate to partner in law firms—the new pathway should recognize skill and accomplishment, anticipate that professionals will continue to do what they are trained to do while taking on other roles that allow them to share their knowledge, and promote continued skills development related to clear standards.

Without abandoning the important objectives of the current salary schedule—equitable treatment, incentives for further education, and objective means for determining pay—we believe compensation systems should provide salary incentives for demonstrated knowledge, skill, and expertise that move the mission of the school forward and reward excellent teachers for continuing to teach. High-performance businesses have increasingly found that knowledge- and skill-based pay can support efforts to reorganize work in ways that involve employees in greater decision making and continual learning.[112] Rewarding teachers for deep knowledge of subjects, additional knowledge in meeting special kinds of student and school needs, and high levels of performance measured against professional teaching standards should encourage teachers to continue to learn needed skills and enhance the expertise available within schools.

We start with the presumption that teachers will be hired only after completing a high-quality preparation program and passing tests of subject matter knowledge and teaching knowledge to receive an initial license. We then recommend that compensation schedules build in additional pay for at least three types of demonstrated knowledge and skill:

1. **Successful completion of performance assessments for a full continuing license** as demonstrated by passing INTASC examinations of teaching skill in the first years of teaching.

2. **Licensing in more than one subject area.**

3. **Advanced certification** as demonstrated by successful completion of assessments offered by the National Board for Professional Teaching Standards.

The first and last areas define a career pathway that some districts have already begun to develop—one that ties evaluations to pay increments at several junctures as teachers move from their *initial license*, through a period as a *resident teacher* under the supervision of a mentor, to designation as *professional teacher* after successfully passing an assessment of teaching skills. *Tenure* is a major step tied to a serious decision made after rigorous evaluation of performance in the first several years of teaching, incorporating administrator and peer review by expert colleagues. *Advanced certification* from the National Board for Professional Teaching Standards may qualify teachers for another salary step and/or for qualification to serve as a *lead teacher*—attained by further evaluations of skills and competence and authorizing stipends for a wide range of professional responsibilities.

Increased pay for teachers holding additional licenses would acknowledge the value of being able to teach expertly in two or more subject areas and to provide needed services, such as special education or counseling expertise, within a teaching team or school. Teachers in many European countries gain multiple areas of expertise as part of their basic teacher preparation. In the United States, this kind of strategic pay would address two current major problems: (1) the high levels of out-of-field teaching that occur in most schools; and (2) the underpreparation of most teachers to work effectively with students with special needs. Rewarding teachers for their willingness to gain knowledge to meet these needs is likely to improve learning for many students substantially while deepening the expertise of the teaching force overall.

The public desire to link teacher compensation to evidence that teachers are effective in engendering student learning is one that has been problematic in the past. This is partly because crude measures like average student test scores do not take into account the different backgrounds and prior performances of students, the fact that students are not randomly distributed across schools and classrooms, the shortcomings in the kinds of learning measured by current standardized tests, and the difficulty in sorting out which influences among many—the home, the community, the student him- or herself, and multiple teachers—are at play.[113] Attempts to link student test scores to rewards for teachers and schools have led to counterproductive incentives for keeping out or pushing out low-achieving students, retaining them in a grade so their scores look higher, or assigning them to special education where their scores don't count, rather than teaching them more effectively.[114]

The Commission's proposals connect teacher compensation to student learning and effective practice in a more careful way than has previously been possible. The new assessments of the National Board and INTASC are based on evidence of effective practice, and they evaluate how specific teaching practices contribute to the learning of particular students over time. The evidence in these assessments allows experts to analyze how teachers support student learning through their curriculum decisions, instruction, and assessment; and to track how selected students actually progress in their learning. Only teachers who exhibit high-quality teaching and whose students show evidence of learning can pass these assessments.[115]

One other feature of a new compensation system is key. The central importance of teaching to the mission of schools should be acknowledged by a system in which the highest paid professional in a school system is an experienced National Board-Certified teacher, who should be able to earn as much by teaching as by becoming an administrator. In addition, as in other professions, the distinctions between teaching and administrative roles should be much less visible than they are today, allowing many ways for individuals to use their talents and expertise for the enhanced performance of the team without abandoning the core work of the profession.

In a new career continuum, teachers (and administrators) should have options for multiple professional roles while remaining in teaching.[116] School districts should create more fluid and varied roles for educators throughout their

New Teaching Careers in Cincinnati and Rochester

The Career-in-Teaching programs in Rochester, New York, and Cincinnati, Ohio, aim to provide incentives to attract and retain quality teachers in the profession, improve teachers' professional growth opportunities and give teachers broader roles and responsibilities that will improve student achievement and provide better schools. The career steps—intern, resident, career teacher, and lead teacher—provide supports for learning, evaluation based on professional standards, and salary incentives. Teachers advance in their career as they gain and demonstrate growing expertise.

In both cities, new teachers begin as interns. In Cincinnati, a growing number of beginners have already practiced under supervision in professional development schools as part of the University of Cincinnati's five-year teacher education program. New teachers receive close mentoring from an expert consulting teacher, who also evaluates them for continuation and advancement to the residency level. A less than satisfactory rating leads either to a second year of assistance or to termination. A satisfactory evaluation is needed to move up on the salary schedule. Since the program began, overall attrition of beginning teachers has decreased and beginners become much more competent sooner. In Rochester, for example, retention of beginning interns is 90%, as compared with only 60% before the program was put in place. In both cities, a greater number of probationary teachers than before are asked to leave if they have not met the standards—roughly 8% in Rochester. The foundations for professional accountability are laid early in the career.

Over the next three to four years, resident teachers develop their teaching skills and become active in professional decision making. In Cincinnati, a formal evaluation by the principal is required at the third and fifth years when the teacher applies for career status and tenure. Salary steps for experience at these junctures—and at years 17 and 22—are contingent on evaluation. Advancement to career teacher status carries an additional $1,000 salary increment. Altogether, there are at least six points at which salary advancement is linked to performance. In Rochester, annual salary advancement is linked to satisfactory performance. Teachers who do not meet professional standards do not receive salary increases and are candidates for an intervention process.

Those who wish to can apply for lead teacher status after seven or more years. Lead teachers are not only excellent teachers, they also know how to mentor adults and facilitate school change. They serve as consulting teachers for beginners and veteran teachers who are having difficulty, curriculum developers, clinical faculty in the districts' teacher education partnerships with local schools of education, and leaders for school-based initiatives while continuing their own teaching.

To become a lead teacher in Rochester, candidates must provide confidential recommendations from five colleagues, including teachers and principals. Specific positions as mentors, curriculum designers, and project facilitators come with stipends ranging from 5 to 15% of total salaries—a range of about $3,000 to $9,000. About 32 of Rochester's teachers are currently lead teachers.

In Cincinnati, salary increments for lead teachers range from $4,500 to $5,000. About 300 of Cincinnati's 3,000 teachers have passed the rigorous evaluation process to attain lead teacher status—four to six classroom observations by expert teachers, interviews of colleagues about the applicant, and an extensive application that reveals the candidate's philosophy and experience. Obtaining National Board Certification is another means of becoming credentialed as a lead teacher. Both cities already have more than their share of Board-Certified teachers due to the strong support for participation provided by the teacher associations and local boards.

The chance to contribute gives lead teachers a new lease on their own professional lives while their work improves teaching quality throughout the district. The result is a career in teaching that recruits and retains talented teachers while increasing professionwide knowledge and skill. As Cincinnati lead teacher Helen Buswinka notes:

Participating [as a lead teacher in a professional development school] has given me an occasion to think grandly about what it means to "educate a teacher." In the process, my own vision of teaching has been nourished. As a member of both worlds, I am able to participate in the shaping of the next generation of teachers, to be part of the evolution of my profession.

careers so that knowledge and talent can be more widely shared. They should structure time and responsibility so that teachers can be involved in peer coaching and mentoring, curriculum and assessment development, teacher education, and school leadership. In schools of the future, the roles of teacher, consultant, supervisor, principal, curriculum developer, researcher, mentor, and professor should not be mutually exclusive. Instead they should be frequently hyphenated to allow many kinds of learning and leadership that advance better teaching and schooling.

• Remove incompetent teachers.

A career continuum based on standards of professional practice must also address the need to make judgments about the competence of teachers and to counsel individuals out of the profession when they do not, after receiving assistance, meet professional standards. In some school districts, new career pathways incorporate peer review and assistance from lead teachers who provide intensive support for beginning teachers and for veterans who are having difficulty. Those who do not improve are counseled out of teaching. These systems—collaborations between unions and school boards—have proven more effective than traditional evaluation systems at both improving and dismissing teachers, demonstrating that teachers can be professionally accountable.

Systems that incorporate peer assistance and review have several advantages over traditional systems of teacher evaluation. Typically, school principals are asked to evaluate and support all the teachers in their building, despite the other pressing demands of the principalship, the large numbers of teachers in many schools, and the vast range of subject areas and grade levels. With inadequate time and expertise to assess teaching in-depth, judgments of teacher competence must typically be made in a single quick visit to the classroom with a simple checklist in hand. This approach provides little opportunity for specific feedback that is helpful in the context of a particular classroom and teaching area. Most teachers find it unhelpful to them in improving their practice.[117] Where problems are found, few principals have the time and expertise to provide the intensive assistance needed to help teachers improve or to complete the extensive documentation needed to try to have them removed.

Peer assistance and review programs apply greater time and expertise to the processes of support and evaluation as expert consulting teachers who have released time for this purpose help their colleagues. Where teaching problems are found, they can be worked on in depth over time. Where improvement does not occur, teacher associations do not block dismissal when they have been involved in designing and implementing an approach that provides due process protections throughout.

In a comprehensive system of professional accountability, safeguards against incompetence should occur at several junctures:

- When prospective teachers pass demanding assessments before they receive an initial provisional license;

Promoting Improvement and Removing Incompetent Teachers through Peer Assistance and Review

I think [there was] a generation of people who didn't have anyone there to help them when they walked in the door. . . . They went into their room and shut the door. And every year some kids would come through, and however they [taught], that was what was done. . . . The bottom line is children come first. We are here for the children. We're professional educators and here to teach children. That is a driving factor of the Peer Assistance and Evaluation Program.
— CAROLYN NELLON, PEER REVIEW PANEL, DIRECTOR OF HUMAN RESOURCES, CINCINNATI PUBLIC SCHOOLS

Although many claim it is impossible to truly evaluate teachers or get rid of those who are incompetent, a growing number of districts are transforming old, nonfunctional systems of teacher evaluation into peer review systems that improve teaching performance and counsel out those who should not be in the profession. Peer review and assistance programs initiated by AFT and NEA locals in Toledo, Cincinnati, and Columbus, Ohio; Rochester, New York; and Seattle, Washington, have been successful in helping beginners learn to teach and in helping veterans who are having difficulty to improve their teaching or leave the classroom without union grievances or delays.

Each program was established through collective bargaining and is governed by a panel of 7 to 10 teachers and administrators. The governing panel selects consulting teachers through a rigorous evaluation process that examines teaching skills and mentoring abilities. The panel also approves assignments of tenured teachers to intervention status (through self-referral or referral made by principals) and oversees appraisals of intern and intervention teachers.

In each case, standards for gaining tenure and remaining in teaching have been significantly raised by the Peer Assistance Program. Part of their success is the development of more useful measures to replace what Rochester's Tom Gillett calls "drive-by observation-based checklists." In Rochester, all teachers must participate in a review every third year, choosing colleagues or administrators to examine data on their performance, including information about student learning as well as practice.

Another success factor is the intensive assistance provided by consulting teachers who are freed up to focus on this job. This ensures that adequate help and documentation will occur over the course of the year. A third reason is the expertise of the consulting teacher, who is selected for teaching excellence and who generally is matched by subject area and grade level with the teacher being helped. This increases the value of the advice offered and the credibility of the judgment rendered.

In each city, more teachers have been given help and have made major improvements in their teaching *and* more teachers have been dismissed than ever had occurred under the old systems of administrative review. In Toledo and Cincinnati, roughly one-third of the teachers referred to intervention each year have left teaching by the end of the year through resignation, retirement, or dismissal. In Columbus, about 144 teachers (approximately 2% of the teaching force) were assigned to intervention over an eight-year period. Of those, about 20% retired or resigned. The others have improved substantially: During the first five years in Cincinnati, 61% of teacher dismissals for performance reasons resulted from peer review, as compared with 39% from evaluation by administrators. Five percent of beginning teachers under peer review were dismissed, as compared with 1.6% of those evaluated by principals. Of 60 Rochester teachers assigned to the Intervention Program since 1988, about 10% determined through their work with lead teacher mentors that they should leave the profession. Rochester teachers may voluntarily request the assistance of a lead teacher mentor through the Professional Support Program, which has served about 100 teachers each year since 1991.

When teachers take on the task of professional accountability, it not only improves instruction but it profoundly changes the roles of teachers' unions.

"We can't legitimately protect teachers who are not performing," says Denise Hewitt, director of Cincinnati's Peer Review Panel. At the same time, the improvements in teaching can sometimes be striking. According to Cincinnati consulting teacher Jim Byerly: "We had a teacher who was in intervention ten years ago, who . . . had considerable skills and experience but she had gotten lazy. . . . She needed to start planning the lessons and stick to them and do the hands-on stuff that was needed. . . . Her final appraisal was strong, better than average. I think she felt empowered by the outcome. She went on to be a lead teacher."

- When peer evaluation and review are used during the first years of teaching to support learning and counsel inadequate teachers out of the profession prior to tenure;

- When a continuing professional license is granted only after the passage of performance assessments;

- When districts refuse to hire unlicensed teachers or to allow teaching out of license; and

- When provisions are negotiated in staff agreements for ongoing professional peer review and intervention leading to dismissal where necessary.

The problem of teacher incompetence represents a tiny fraction of the overall teaching force, but in each case where it is left unaddressed, it undermines public confidence and harms hundreds of students. A growing number of districts have demonstrated, with the support of teacher associations, that it *is* possible to remove incompetent teachers and that with systematic supports and interventions in place, the problem grows smaller with each passing year. With these kinds of safeguards, parents can be assured that their children will be taught only by qualified, competent teachers who are continually refining and enhancing their skills.

- **Set goals and enact incentives for National Board Certification in every state and district. Aim to certify 105,000 teachers in this decade, one for every school in the United States.**

The great promise of the National Board is that it clearly delineates standards for accomplished teaching and creates the prospect for a career continuum from entry to expert practice. Having just begun its work, however, the National Board has certified only about 400 teachers thus far. Professional certification in teaching must be helped to grow as it has in medicine, where Board Certification began on a tiny scale in 1916 but has since created the most powerful lever since the founding of the teaching hospital for advancing knowledge in medical education and practice.

In the next ten years, National Board standards must influence every school and school of education and become a part of the professional development plan for virtually all teachers. If by the year 2006 we can point to a Board-Certified teacher in every school, we will have created a situation in which every teacher in the United States has access to a teacher leader who embodies and can promote accomplished practice.

Such a phenomenal increase in the numbers of Board-Certified teachers will not be wished into being. We will achieve it only if the National Board works with individual states and districts to lay out discrete, quantifiable goals, year by year, ascertaining how many teachers—by state and district—can be persuaded to complete the challenging assessments involved in securing Board Certification, teaching's highest accolade. Part of meeting this challenge is making professional standards and assessments a part of every step along the career pathway for teachers.

V. Create schools that are genuine learning organizations.

WE RECOMMEND: *that schools be restructured to become genuine learning organizations for both students and teachers— organizations that respect learning, honor teaching, and teach for understanding.*

Many analysts have noted that there is very little relationship between the organization of the typical American school and the demands of serious teaching and learning. Nothing more clearly reveals this problem than how we allocate schools' major resources of time, money, and people. Our schools are cumbersome bureaucratic inheritances from the 19th century, not the kinds of learning organizations required for the 21st. Far too many people sit in offices at the sidelines of the core work, managing routines rather than promoting innovation aimed at improved quality. A bureaucratic school spends substantial resources on controlling its staff; a thoughtful school invests in knowledge and supports that liberate staff members to do their jobs well. A traditional school administers rules and procedures; a learning organization develops shared goals and talents. Our inherited school anticipates the worst from students and teachers; the school of the future expects and enables the best. As David Kearns, former chief executive officer of Xerox Corporation, explains:

> Lockstep, myopic management is still the norm in American education today, just as it was in American business. . . . Our entire way of thinking needs to be replaced. Today's high-tech firm is lean: It has stripped away middle management. It is decentralized, relying on the know-how and professionalism of workers close to the problem. It is innovative in the deployment of personnel, no longer relying on limiting job classifications. It spends heavily on employee education and training. It invests heavily in research.[118]

Just as businesses have had to restructure to obtain significantly better results, changing school performance will require reallocating funds, restructuring staffing patterns, and redesigning teaching and the use of time. These steps are needed not only to be able to afford more time for teacher learning and collaboration, but also to be able to create settings within which teachers can use their expertise more effectively and work much more productively with students toward more challenging learning goals.

Our schools need to be redesigned so that they honor teaching, respect learning, and teach for understanding. To be able to direct their energies around a common purpose, schools need to adopt shared standards for student learning that become the basis for common efforts of teachers, parents, and the community. Then, schools must structure their work so that teachers can work more intensively with students and with each other and can have greater influence over the design of the learning experiences their students encounter. Schools must be freed of the tyrannies of time and tradition to enable more powerful student and teacher learning. To that end, we recommend that they

- **Restructure time and staffing** so that teachers have regular time to work with one another and shared responsibility for groups of students over time.

- **Rethink schedules** so that students and teachers have more extended time together over the course of the day, week, and years.

- **Reduce barriers** to the involvement of parents so that families and schools can work together toward shared goals.

Learning in America is a prisoner of time, according to the 1994 report of the National Commission on Education Time and Learning.[119] Short, fragmented time periods and rigid expectations for the use of time reduce the amount of learning that can occur for many students. Lack of coordinated time and shared responsibility among teachers reduces accountability for the overall learning experience. We need to create structures that help students undertake more in-depth learning clearly aimed at the new standards they need to reach and that help teachers to be more successful at supporting student learning. Keeping teachers, or teams of teachers, together with the same groups of students over several years is one possibility; longer class periods for students and teachers together within the school day are another. These and other possibilities need to be seriously considered as we work to release schools, students, and teachers from the constraints that impede teaching and learning.

We also need to create time during the school day and year for teacher learning, breaking down the isolation of egg-crate classroom structures and the inefficiencies of fragmented teaching schedules. Restructured schools are finding time by devoting more of their staff energy directly to classroom teaching, rather than to administration, pullout programs, or management of special services. By rethinking time and staffing assignments, they can reduce student loads while giving teachers regular periods each week to work with and learn from each other. In addition, a longer school year for teachers and administrators opens the possibilities for additional time devoted entirely to professional development. Our goal should be at least ten hours per week for collegial work and learning within the school and at least ten days per year of additional professional development time, supported by reallocations of staff and the redesign of responsibilities.

Within this time and the purviews of restructured roles, teachers need opportunities to work in partnership with parents and community members to coordinate their work on behalf of more effective learning and teaching. In schools like Zavala Elementary School in Austin, Texas, major changes in practice and better outcomes for children have proved possible as parents have been involved in school renewal and problem solving, and as the school has

Community Engagement and Teacher Development at Zavala Elementary School

Five years ago, Zavala Elementary School's 486 students—most from two housing projects near the school—were failing badly. Only 34% of its third-graders passed the reading, writing, and math sections of the Texas Assessment of Academic Skills (TAAS), placing it 63rd among Austin's 64 elementary schools. Student attendance was poor, annual staff turnover was 50 percent, and PTA meetings were sparsely attended.

Then Alejandro Mindiz-Melton became Zavala's principal and began cultivating relationships with parents and community leaders, including Austin Interfaith, a coalition of religious organizations. At community meetings, parents asked teachers to work more closely with them to raise their children's academic achievement. Mindiz-Melton and the teachers organized Saturday Community Walks to students' homes, not to address discipline problems as in the past, but to listen to parents' ideas and suggestions about how to improve the school.

These walks changed the tenor of family-school relationships and created a strong partnership for change. Parents began to volunteer throughout the school, where many of them also attend English classes. Teachers worked together to reorganize their teaching, studying recent research on how children learn, coordinating instruction across grade levels, intro-

ducing new language arts and mathematics curriculums, and grouping children in new ways so that they would learn from each other.

Today, as a Texas Alliance school, Zavala's scores on the TAAS are well above the district average in reading, writing, and math, and teacher attrition has all but stopped. Student attendance soared to 97.9% in 1994-95—the highest in the city. As Zavala teachers became active partners with parents and with each other, they learned in many new ways. Claudia Santamaria, a bilingual fourth-grade teacher, tells the story this way:

When I came to Zavala six years ago, we were all just doing our own thing, isolating ourselves in our own rooms. But we failed to see that our children were really failing the TAAS test, which is a major state standard for our children. We thought, "Well, we're in a poor community, our children are often sick, and attendance is bad." We kept coming up with reasons why the kids just weren't learning.

What changed for me professionally wasn't so much through workshops, because workshops had always been there, and we had always been going to them. When we became an Alliance school, our whole frame of thinking changed—we began to think of the

school as a family. What Austin Interfaith did was to bring us together in conversation with each other. We were able to see that we had a lot of strengths that we had failed to recognize, and that we had a lot to learn from one another. Before, I had goals for my children in fourth grade, and the first-grade teacher had hers and the kindergarten teacher had hers, but we really hadn't pulled our resources together to see where we wanted the school to go—we were all pulling in different directions.

We were working really hard, but now we work smarter because we've pulled our resources together. We sat together and asked ourselves, "What's working, what's not?" In the past, I couldn't have told you what my neighbor was doing—I didn't know. Now we have a schoolwide focus. When we work on TAAS writing, all of us are writing on the same prompts, and the children know—they can go home and talk to their little brothers and sisters. Now, as teachers, we know what we're doing, and we know where we're headed. We're holding ourselves accountable.

Sources: Richard J. Murnane and Frank M. Levy, *Teaching the New Basic Skills: Principles for Education Children to Thrive in a Changing Economy* (New York: Free Press, 1996); Dennis Shirley, *Laboratories of Democracy: Community Organizing for School Reform* (Austin, Texas: University of Texas Press, forthcoming); U.S. Department of Education, "Zavala School in Texas Turned Failure into Success," *Goals 2000: Community Update*, no. 20 (January 1995).

strengthened professional development tied to standards for student learning. Other partnerships, like Illinois's Project Success, have placed schools at the hub of family and community services, creating supports for family engagement and child welfare that spill over into improved learning.

These kinds of approaches can be viable on a broader scale only if systemwide efforts are made to free up resources from the many crevices of bureaucracies where they are now lodged so that they can be applied to the frontline needs of children and teachers. The Commission recommends that states and school districts carefully examine the ways they have organized services and allocated resources to create more effective models of service delivery and more efficient uses of limited funds. We urge that systems take three important steps:

Project Success

It was standing room only the night a Decatur, Illinois, elementary school started its class on computers for parents. "We had to scramble to find places for the more than 40 parents who showed up," says Linda Rowden, coordinator of Project Success in Decatur.

This was a welcome problem. Like many schools enrolling many poor children, those in Decatur's Project Success struggled to find ways of drawing alienated parents into the schools. "We had to break down bad feelings," Rowden recalls, created by what seemed like nothing but negative contacts with schools.

Decatur is one of the original six pilot communities of Illinois's Project Success, launched in 1991 to build service networks around families so that all children are ready for school and have continued support. Now operating in 130 communities and almost 400 elementary schools statewide, the program offers many nonthreatening ways for parents to be drawn into schools.

In Decatur, each school set up a parents' lounge and plans social get-togethers at least monthly. There are parenting classes, literacy and GED classes, and courses like the computer class that parents and children attend together. The project makes sure children have the immunizations and supplies they need to enter school. This simple action starts the school experience on a good foot. "Parents think of this as a nice thing to do," says Rowden of the school supplies initiative, "and that opens up rapport between teachers and parents.

Weekly sessions for parents of very young children "build on the skills they already have," says Rowden, "and create a support group for the parents. . . . They share a lot with each other." Collaboration continues over the summer months with the school and Parks Department working together on activities for children and teachers opening up school libraries several times a week to keep in touch with children.

This unique state-community partner-

ship does not create new programs. Rather, it enables communities to use services more effectively. About a dozen state agencies are represented on the Project Success State Steering Committee, coordinated out of the governor's office. Local governing boards made up of schools, community agencies, parents, and businesses identify problems and plan initiatives to solve them. At both the state and local levels, agencies share staff and resources, grant waivers, and cross program lines to serve critical needs of children and families.

With schools as the hub, teachers can access community services to improve child and family well-being in areas ranging from health, safety, and housing to education and after-school care. Well-supported families help children come to school happy, healthy, and ready to learn, secure in the knowledge that their families and school are working together to help them grow.

- **Flatten hierarchies and reallocate resources to send more dollars to the front lines of schools: Invest more in teachers and technology and less in nonteaching personnel.**

Across the United States, the ratio of school staff to enrolled students is 1:9, according to data from the National Center for Education Statistics.[120] However, actual class sizes average about 24, reaching 35 or more in cities like New York and Los Angeles. Teaching loads for high school teachers generally exceed 100 students per day and reach nearly 200 per day in some cities. This is because more than half of all school system staff are not classroom teachers, including large numbers of specialists, supervisors, and teachers who work in pullout settings as well as nonteaching personnel. Although administrators are actually the smallest numbers of such staff, U.S. schools have more layers of hierarchy than those in most other countries, once state agencies, regional units, school districts, and schools are added together. Within these agencies, administrative support staff who manage reporting requirements have increased along with the proliferation of regulations over the last two decades. Within schools themselves, the number of nonteaching staff such as instructional and mental health specialists, aides, and security personnel has climbed, as has the number of teachers who work in special pullout programs for special education, compensatory education, and English as a Second Language instruction.

These staffing patterns are a vestige of the Taylor model of industrial management from the 1920s, in which jobs are broken up and highly specialized, and some staff are supposed to think, plan, and coordinate work while others are supposed to do it. Yet many schools have proved that it is possible to restructure adult use of time so that more teachers and administrators actually work with students on a daily basis in the classroom, thus reducing class sizes while creating more time for teacher collaboration. They do this by creating teams of teachers who share students, engaging almost all adults in these teaching teams where they can share expertise directly with one another, and reducing pullouts and nonteaching jobs. Within these work groups, planning for students can be more effectively managed and blocks of time can be more productively used. The school's resources are pushed into the core classroom structure where they can be used in the context of extended relationships with students rather than sitting around the periphery of the school to be applied in brief encounters with students or in coordinative rather than teaching roles.

In the examples here we describe how both elementary and secondary schools have redesigned staffing to greatly enhance teaching and teacher collaboration and produce greater success for students. On the next page we show how a typical elementary school of 600 students can reorganize its staff so that average class sizes can be reduced from 25 students to 16 or 17 students, while teachers' planning time is increased from less than 4 hours a week to at least 10 hours. This is accomplished by reducing the number of nonteaching staff and by infusing pullout teachers into teaching teams. While keeping key administrative supports in place—including a principal, secretary, bookkeeper, and social worker—this increases the total number of full-time equivalent classroom teachers from 24 to 43 (from less than 50% of all staff to more than 80%).

In the redesigned school, each team of seven teachers serves 100 students and includes teachers with expertise in the arts, counseling, and the teaching of special-needs students. The teams can draw upon this expertise in curriculum planning, and they can organize their time and efforts to take advantage of different talents in various ways for different activities. The three primary grades teams share a media/computer specialist and a lead teacher, who has half of her time released from teaching to facilitate planning and cover classes while other teachers visit and observe one another. The same supports are available to the three upper-grades teams. The result is more personalized education for students, more collegial learning opportunities for teachers, and a system more capable of taking responsibility for student learning.

We need to rethink school staffing so that all personnel are involved in thinking as well as doing. And we need to revamp spending to invest in the front lines of schools, not the back offices. If most staff in U.S. schools were

600 Students
24 Classroom teachers
26 Other staff
Class size = 25
Teacher time = 3.75 hrs./week

600 Students
43 Teachers (FTE)
7 Other staff (FTE)
Class size = 16
Teacher time = 10 hrs./week

Traditional Elementary School

Principal	Assistant Principal	Dean of Discipline	Secretary	Book-keeper	Office Clerk
Special Program for Under-achievers					Counselor
Bilingual/ ESL Pullout					Counselor
Music Specialist					Counselor
Art Specialist					Social Worker
Media Clerk					Psych-ologist
Media Specialist					Special Education Pullout
Reading Specialist					Speech Pullout
Math Specialist	Science Specialist	2 Title I Aides ($^1/_2$ time)	Title I Pullout	Title I Pullout	Resource Room

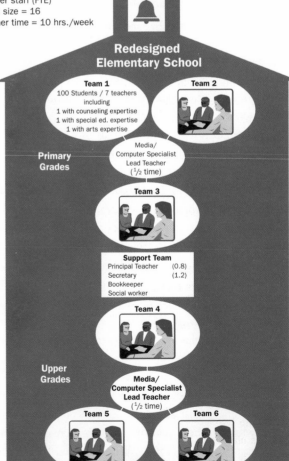

Redesigned Elementary School

Team 1
100 Students / 7 teachers
including
1 with counseling expertise
1 with special ed. expertise
1 with arts expertise

Team 2

Primary Grades

Media/ Computer Specialist Lead Teacher ($^1/_2$ time)

Team 3

Support Team
Principal Teacher   (0.8)
Secretary   (1.2)
Bookkeeper
Social worker

Team 4

Upper Grades

Media/ Computer Specialist Lead Teacher ($^1/_2$ time)

Team 5

Team 6

Restructuring Schools to Support Student and Teacher Learning

Across the country, schools are reorganizing their work to provide more time for student learning, more personalized relationships between teachers and students, and greater opportunity for teachers to work and plan together in teams. Providing teachers with the time they need to work with colleagues and keep up with advances in their profession depends largely on schools' willingness to rethink staffing patterns. A study of the allocation of teachers in the Boston public schools found that even with a pupil-teacher ratio of only 13:1, regular class sizes averaged 23 and went as high as 33, because of the assignment of many staff to pullout and specialist positions.

By combining all of the students into regular classroom groupings rather than using pullouts for Title I and special education, class sizes could drop to about 14 in elementary schools. By rethinking schedules, teachers also can have more time for joint planning. Boston schools like Lyons and O'Hearn elementary schools have recently done just that, sometimes teaming regular and special-education teachers to work together. At Ashley River Elementary in South Carolina, teachers have 80 minutes a day for planning with their grade-level teams, and class sizes were lowered by reducing the number of specialists and counselors; now 75% of staff are classroom teachers. At Hefferan Elementary School in Chicago, teachers teach four full days of academic classes each week and spend the fifth full day planning together

with their multigrade teams while students rotate to "resource" classes in music, fine arts, computer lab, physical education, library science, and science lab. At Quebec Heights Elementary in Cincinnati, Ohio, teachers have found 5.5 hours a week to plan together and have lowered pupil-teacher ratios to 15:1 by creating multi-age clusters of students and teachers, integrating special education teachers into cluster teams, and eliminating separate Title I classes. In all of these cases, evidence shows that students are learning more as teachers develop their expertise.

In high schools, combining subject areas such as English, history, and writing can substantially reduce teaching loads and create time for teachers. This strategy has been used in many of the more than 100 new, small restructured high schools in New York City recently created to replace failing comprehensive high schools. The new schools often create interdisciplinary teams of teachers who share students, and they establish block schedules that reduce teachers' pupil loads while creating more shared planning time. In one model, each teacher teaches two classes (either humanities or math/science) that meet for nearly two hours daily, four times per week. With class sizes of around 20, this results in a total pupil load of 40. Virtually everyone in the school teaches: about 70% to 75% of all staff as compared with the usual 50% to 55%. Teachers have about seven hours a week to plan together in addition to five

hours of individual "prep" time. The co-directors teach some classes and counsel students in advisories—small groups of students who meet weekly with teacher advisers. There are no guidance counselors, attendance officers, assistant principals, supervisors, or department heads, and few security guards are needed because students are so well known. Studies have found that attendance, grades, graduation rates, and college-going rates are all higher in these restructured schools than in the traditional schools they are replacing.

By contrast, teachers in a traditional New York high school of 3,300 have class sizes of 33 and see 167 students per day, although student-adult ratios are only 13:1. Teachers have no joint planning time because the school's person-hours are consumed by the large number of nonteaching staff: 9 assistant principals, 11 guidance counselors, 13 secretaries, 10 school-based services specialists, 17 security guards, 22 nonteaching school aides, 14 paraprofessionals, and 3 librarians. Students and teachers experience the anonymity of the factory model school, which produces far less learning for them both.

Teams that include many kinds of expertise and share groups of students can plan more effectively for students and use time more productively. Resources are better used when they go directly to the classrooms, rather than sitting around the periphery of the school to be applied in brief encounters with students or in coordinative rather than teaching roles.

Sources: Linda Darling-Hammond, "Restructuring Schools for High Performance," in *Rewards and Reform: Creating Educational Incentives that Work*, edited by Susan Fuhrman and Jennifer O'Day (San Francisco, Calif.: Jossey-Bass, 1996); and Karen Hawley Miles, "Freeing Up Resources for Improving Schools: A Case Study of Teacher Allocation in Boston Public Schools," *Educational Evaluation and Policy Analysis* 17 (Winter 1995): 476-493.

	Traditional High School	Restructured High School
Total students	3,380	450
Ratio of student to staff	13:1	10:1
% of Staff who are full-time teachers	58%	73%
Average class size	33	18
Average pupil load	167	36
Joint work time for teachers	45 minutes/week	7.5 hours/week

engaged in teaching, teachers could have both greater time for collaboration and learning *and* smaller class sizes and pupil loads. In the Commission's view, world-class teaching depends on world-class benchmarks. Most nations invest 60% or more of their staff resources in teachers; we should aim for no less.

These investments in teachers should be accompanied by investments in technology that extend the capacity of every teacher and child to connect with an infinite variety of resources and tools for learning. The potential of computers and other technologies to transform teaching remains to be explored in most schools, in part because technology plans have assumed all that was needed were hardware and a few software programs to get them going. Staff development has been largely overlooked, as have communications connections within and beyond the boundaries of the school. Consequently, where computers are available, they are largely tools for word processing or for reinforcing simple skills; rarely are they integrated into the curriculum or used for creating new communication possibilities and sources of information.

Well used, technology can change teaching and learning and improve achievement by encouraging more independent work as well as teamwork and collaborative inquiry; teaching concepts, systems and problem solving as well as basic skills; adapting instruction to student learning needs; presenting more complex material to students who are ready; and allowing teachers to take on the role of coach rather than lecturer.[121] Technologies also can assist teachers in accessing materials for their lessons, tracking student progress, and communicating with parents and colleagues. Teacher training and support can be enhanced with video

Transforming Teaching through Technology

As a teacher at the Saturn School in St. Paul, Minnesota, David Haynes and his students had access to technologies most teachers can only dream about. "I could consult with other teachers and other professions anywhere in the country. I was in contact with other staff in the building for planning and integration. But the most powerful change in me as a teacher is the way in which it forced me to recognize the capacities children have. Technology is very student-centered. It is definitely not teacher-centered," David claims.

Even without all of the Saturn School's resources, technology can transform teaching. Using only his laptop connected to a monitor, science

teacher Damon Moore in Richmond, Indiana, has created a new environment for learning in his classroom. His students use an electronic encyclopedia, follow the human genome project on the Internet, and teach segments of lessons drawn from their research using electronic databases. "Technology gives me an opportunity to level the playing field for all my kids," Damon explains. "Students can explore and build knowledge in lots of different ways. My job becomes one of guide and interpreter."

Technology can also support teacher learning. A group of beginning teachers from Harvard University, connected via electronic network, were able to support one another and consult with their pro-

fessors in their initial years of teaching. Another group of experienced teachers from around the country has worked for several years to develop alternative assessments and new teaching strategies in their classrooms. They share student work, teaching dilemmas, and other experiences on-line as part of the Four Seasons Network—a collaboration of the Coalition of Essential Schools, Foxfire Teacher Outreach Network, Project Zero, and the National Center for Restructuring Education, Schools, and Teaching (NCREST). In all of these cases, teachers' connections to resouces translate into learning opportunities for students.

and telecommunications networks, on-line resources for learning, opportunities to view models of effective teaching, computer and video simulations and cases, and electronic links among student teachers, mentors, and faculty.

To take full advantage of the possibilities of cyberspace, schools need to move from stand-alone computers to connected systems providing on-line access. Teachers and administrators need time and training to envision how new technologies can be used, opportunities to experiment, and just-in-time support for their use. To get schools launched on the information highway, at least one-third of expenditures for computers in schools (an amount that exceeded $2 billion in 1993)[122] should be devoted to professional development to ensure that educators can use these resources well. Of all the things schools could spend money on, teachers and technology are the areas that are likely to offer the greatest payoffs.

- **Provide venture capital in the form of challenge grants to schools for teacher learning linked to school improvement and rewards for team efforts that lead to improved practice and greater learning.**

Schools will not change unless there are incentives that inspire new collective learning and action and rewards that recognize the changes that have occurred. Initiatives like Ohio's Venture Capital Fund, Maine's Innovative Educational Grants, and Iowa's School Improvement Program have been particularly productive in getting faculties to study and undertake major changes in school practices that improve overall school performance. These initiatives all challenge faculties to identify their schools' problems and dilemmas, intensively study alternatives, and put the best ideas into operation. Lasting changes have been triggered by these kinds of high-leverage incentives that reward staff learning aimed at systemic change tied to student learning.[123]

In addition, schools that change their practices to meet professional teaching standards, and that succeed in increasing learning for a wide array of students, should be recognized for their achievements in a way that promotes learning for other schools across the system. To transform systems, incentives must be structured to promote collaboration and knowledge-sharing across organizations, as well as competition among ideas to recognize those that work well. In Ohio, a consortium of business, community, and education organizations—Building Excellent Schools for Today & the 21st Century (BEST)—works together to launch school improvement initiatives in communities across the state and to recognize, reward, and disseminate successful practices. Ohio's BEST Practices Awards provides one model for sharing knowledge about successful strategies. Another model for such awards is IMPACT II, an extremely successful program that provides grants to teachers who have created innovative programs to work with others who receive grants to learn how to use these ideas. Such a program for schools would provide awards to high-performing schools that enable them to extend their work and share it with others.

- ### Select, prepare, and retain principals who understand teaching and learning and who can lead high-performing schools.

If students deserve a qualified teacher as an inalienable right, teachers deserve a highly qualified principal as a right as well. Principals are key leaders and gatekeepers of reform in schools. If schools are to become genuine learning organizations, school leaders must have a deep understanding of teaching and learning for adults as well as children. The job of school leader began as that of a principal teacher, and this conception has become even more relevant as the focus of the school recenters on academic achievement for students. Principals should come from among the ranks of highly skilled teachers, and they should continue to teach at least part of the time, as do most European, Asian, and private school directors. To serve as instructional leaders, they should understand the curriculum and assessment principles that underlie new standards and the learning and development theories that teaching must build upon.

In tomorrow's schools, principals also must know how to lead organizations in which leadership and decision making are shared, and continual learning is fostered for staff and parents as well as students. In a learning organization, the primary job of management is professional development, which is concerned with the basic human resources of the enterprise and people's capacities to do the central job of the organization. For all members of the organization, that job is teaching and learning. To lead the schools of the future, principals will need to appreciate adult learning and development as well as that of children and know how to nurture a collaborative environment that fosters continual self-assessment. They will also need to be able to envision and enact new organizational arrangements in schools so that time, staffing patterns, and relationships between teachers and among teachers, students, and families better serve the goals of serious learning and high-quality teaching.

Standards that should guide the preparation of principals begin with teaching standards—principals of the future should be drawn from among the ranks of National Board-Certified teachers—and continue with licensing standards like those recently developed for school leaders by a consortium of states under the auspices of the Council for Chief State School Officers. Preparation in professionally accredited institutions will also ensure that principals' training reflects the demands of student standards. In a two-year graduate program tied to the authentic activities of educational leadership, candidates would maintain a school-based position while taking ongoing coursework that develops analytic, political, and research skills along with knowledge of curriculum, teaching, assessment, staff development, and policy. Like teachers, principals should complete a yearlong internship during which they assemble a portfolio of evidence about their work as leaders and facilitators of learning and teaching.

As with teachers, initial preparation for the principalship is just the beginning of life-long learning. In fact, principals are often more isolated than teachers and in need of much more collegial support than they generally have available. Principals need the metaphorical jungle gym of learning opportunities that Lynn Stuart describes to anchor them in the same rich environment of change, learning, and reflection that surrounds teachers. Districts must learn how to support them in ongoing professional development and problem solving with other principals as well as teachers, creating opportunities for collaboration and mutual assistance that go well beyond housekeeping chores to the fundamental concerns of learning and teaching.

These investments in teacher and principal learning are among the most critical the nation can make. Strong teachers and principals stand in a place that matters to America's future.

A Better Way: Learning to Teach in the 21st Century

For as long as she could remember, Elena had always wanted to teach. As a little girl, she would sit and read to toddlers, round her friends up to play school, and explain the mysteries of the universe to anyone who would listen. Later, as a peer tutor, she loved the feeling she got whenever her partner learned something new. In high school, she began to look with real interest at the many ways young children learn when she served as a teacher's aide for her community service project. She linked up with other students through an Internet group started by Future Teachers of America. She felt she could spend a lifetime studying children without ever running out of new discoveries.

When she arrived at college Elena knew she would want to prepare to teach, so she began taking courses in developmental and cognitive psychology early in her sophomore year. She chose mathematics as a major and applied in her junior year for the five-year course of study leading to a Master of Arts in Teaching at her university. After a round of interviews and a review of her record thus far, she was admitted into the highly selective teacher education program.

The theories Elena studied in her courses came to life before her eyes as she conducted a case study of John, a seven-year-old boy whom she tutored in a nearby school. She was amazed by John's amazing ability to build things in contrast with his struggles to learn to read. She carried these puzzles back to her seminar and on into her other courses as she tried to understand learning. Over time, she examined other cases, some of them available on a hypermedia computer system that allowed her to see videotapes of children, samples of their work, and documentation from their teachers about their learning strategies, problems, and progress. From these data, Elena and her classmates developed a concrete sense of different learning approaches. In one of these sessions, Elena began to understand how John might be more adept at spatial tasks and less comfortable with verbal ones. She began to think about how she could use his strengths to create productive pathways into other areas of learning.

In her mathematics courses, Elena worked on simulations, modeling, and statistical analyses with students in engineering, architecture, and the social sciences. She deepened her knowledge of mathematics through the study of applications that would be important to her future students as well as herself. These courses were also linked to her work in cognitive psychology. Elena kept a journal of how she herself learned mathematics—what kinds of teaching made the concepts more accessible and what mystified her—and she interviewed fellow students about their experiences, including "math-phobics" who found the field terrifying. In her other courses, she also kept track of which learning experiences helped her and which she found hard to fathom, thus creating an ongoing database for investigating learning.

Elena's education courses gave her the chance to observe and work with students in elementary, middle, and high schools as well as in recreation centers and community sites. Because she was always applying her learning, she never found theory dull or abstract. To the contrary, she found it gave her a powerful set of lenses to bring to bear on the world. In addition, her teachers modeled the kinds of strategies she herself would be using as a teacher: Instead of lecturing from texts, they enabled students to develop and apply knowledge in the context of real teaching situations. These frequently occurred in the professional development school (PDS) where Elena was engaged in a year-long internship guided by a faculty of university- and school-based teacher educators.

In the PDS, Elena was placed with a team of student teachers who worked with a team of expert veteran teachers. Her team included teachers of art, language arts, and science, as well as mathematics. They discussed learning within and across these domains in many of their assignments and constructed interdisciplinary curriculum together. Most of the school- and university-based teacher educators who made up the PDS faculty had been certified as accomplished practitioners by the National Board for Professional Teaching Standards, having completed a set of rigorous performance assessments, including a portfolio of evidence about their teaching. The faculty created courses, internship experiences, and seminars that allowed them to integrate theory and practice, pose fundamental dilemmas of teaching, and address specific aspects of learning to teach.

Located in a port city that served a broad range of racial, ethnic, and economic groups as well as recent immigrants from more than 40 countries, the professional development school enabled new teachers to learn how to support learning for new English-language learners and to examine teaching from many cultural perspectives. In her seminars linked to classroom work as an intern, Elena learned how to identify various learning styles and needs; how to address misconceptions students might hold about specific subject matter concepts; and how to develop teaching strategies for common learning problems like dyslexia. She learned how to construct lessons that would allow entry points for different kinds of learners.

Her work in the PDS included observing and documenting specific children; evaluating lessons that illustrated important concepts and strategies; tutoring and working with small groups; sitting in on family conferences; engaging in school and team planning meetings; visiting homes and community agencies to learn about their resources; planning field trips and curriculum segments; teaching lessons and short units; and ultimately taking major responsibility for the class for a month at the end of the year. This work was supplemented by readings and discussions grounded in cases of teaching.

A team of PDS teachers videotaped all of their classes over the course of the year to serve as the basis of discussions of teaching decisions and outcomes. These teachers' lesson plans, student work, planning journals, and reflections on lessons were also available in a hypermedia database. This allowed student teachers to look at practice from many angles, examine how classroom situations arose from things that had happened in the past, see how lessons turned out and what students learned, and under-

stand the teacher's thinking as she made decisions. Because the PDS was also wired for video and computer communication with the school of education, master teachers could also hold conversations with student teachers by teleconference or e-mail when on-site visits were impossible.

In her classroom work and research, Elena learned how to look at and listen to students so as to understand their experiences, prior knowledge, and learning strengths as well as difficulties. She learned how to create engaging tasks that would stretch and motivate them and how to scaffold the learning process so they could then succeed at challenging work. She began to figure out how to juggle and balance the competing demands of individuals and groups, curriculum goals, and student interests. She learned how to reach out to students who might otherwise slip through the cracks. She learned how to learn from her own teaching and that of her colleagues.

Elena worked to develop authentic learning opportunities for her future students and to evaluate her own teaching. Whereas her students' products were arithmetic problems and puzzles, survey projects, mathematical models, and scientific experiments, Elena's own exhibitions were the lessons and units she designed; the research she conducted about the classroom, school, and community; and her assessments of her students. Some of this work, including case studies of students, curriculum designs, and videotapes of her teaching, was assembled on a videodisc portfolio that would allow the state licensing agency and future employers

to evaluate aspects of her work as a supplement to interviews and licensing examinations.

When Elena finished her rich, exhausting internship year, she was ready to try her hand at what she knew would be a demanding first year of teaching. She submitted her portfolio for review by the state professional standards board and sat for the examinations of subject matter and teaching knowledge that would grant her an initial teaching license. She was both exhilerated and anxious when she received a job offer, but she felt she was ready. She was comforted by the fact that her cohort of fellow graduates and teachers would be available to her throughout the year in an on-line study group as sources of materials and experience.

Elena spent that summer eagerly developing curriculum ideas for her new class. She had the benefit of advice from the district mentor teacher already assigned to work with her in her first year of teaching and an on-line database of teaching materials developed by teachers across the country and organized around the curriculum standards of the National Council of Teachers of Mathematics, of which she had become a member. She could access writers and users of these materials on-line to discuss how they had designed and used particular ideas and to work on how they might be adapted to the needs of her students.

Elena's mentor teacher worked with her and several other new middle school mathematics and science teachers throughout the year, meeting with them individually to examine their teaching and provide support. The mentors and their first-year colleagues also met in groups once a month at the professional development school to discuss specific problems of practice. These meetings kept Elena connected to many of her friends and teachers from the university and to a group of expert veteran teachers across the district who brought with them many different kinds of expertise. With these resources and those of her teaching team at the middle school, Elena never felt as though she was alone in her efforts to tackle the many challenges of beginning teaching.

The most engrossing part of her initiation was the students. Elena was as delighted and intrigued by their interests, energy, and thinking as she had been when she was a student herself. Although she found teaching challenging, she did not feel overwhelmed by classroom management issues as beginning teachers once had. Her internship and ongoing mentoring had prepared her to set up a well-functioning classroom from the start, and she already had experience developing lessons and using a range of teaching strategies.

She met weekly with the other math and science teachers in the school to discuss curriculum plans and share demonstration lessons. This extended lunch meeting occurred while her students were in a Project Adventure/physical education course that taught them teamwork and cooperation skills. She also met with the four other members of her teaching team for three hours each week while their students were at community service placements. The team used this time to discuss cross-disciplinary teaching plans and the progress of the 80 students they shared. In these two

different settings, Elena had access to her colleagues' knowledge about both subject matter and students.

In addition to these built-in opportunities for daily learning, Elena and her colleagues benefited from the study groups they had developed at their school and the professional development offerings at the local university and Teachers Academy. The study groups, created each year based on faculty interests, met during the school's staff development sessions on Friday afternoons while students were in their academic clubs. Each group was led by a faculty member and had funds to purchase books, materials, or consulting help. This year groups were studying strategies for supporting mainstreamed instruction of learning-disabled students; improving the teaching of research skills; implementing the state's new mathematics and science curriculum standards; and understanding language development for new English-language learners. Elena was attending the first of these because she had several children in her classes who were recently mainstreamed and she wanted to know more about how to help them learn mathematics.

At the Teachers Academy, school and university-based faculty taught extended courses in areas ranging from advances in learning theory to teaching methods in fields from elementary science and reading to advanced calculus. These courses usually featured case studies and teaching demonstrations as well as follow-up work in teachers' own classrooms. Multimedia conferencing allowed teachers to "meet" with each other across their schools and to see each others' classroom work.

Teachers could also connect to courses and study groups at the university, including a popular master's degree program that helped teachers prepare for National Board Certification. The Academy provided technologies needed for on-line conferencing and televised classroom observation. It also sponsored meetings for many of the networks that teachers used to create professional learning communities for themselves, such as the National Writing Project, the Urban Mathematics Collaborative, the School Development Program, and the Coalition of Essential Schools.

Elena knew that all of these opportunities would be available to her when she was ready for them. With the strength of a preparation that had helped her put theory and practice together, and with the support of so many colleagues, Elena felt confident that she could succeed at her life's goal: becoming—and as she now understood, always becoming—a teacher.

Next Steps:
Putting It All Together

These, then, are the Commission's core recommendations: Rely on high-quality standards for learning and teaching; reinvent teacher preparation and professional development; recruit qualified teachers for every classroom; encourage and reward knowledge and skill; and re-create schools as learning organizations.

Developing recommendations is easy. Implementing them is hard work. Literally hundreds of education reports of the past decade have issued proclamations and recommendations by the dozens. Many have fallen on deaf ears. Reports do not implement themselves, but must be put into practice by policymakers and the profession. What follows is a road map of next steps to get us from where we are today, in 1996, to where we want to be tomorrow, in the year 2006.

The first step is to recognize that these ideas must be pursued together—as an entire tapestry that is tightly interwoven. Pulling on a single thread will create a tangle rather than tangible progress. The second is to understand that everyone must shoulder his or her share of the burden of transforming American schools. If we think this transformation too difficult to attain, we must again learn the wisdom of the well-known African proverb, "It takes a village to raise a child."

To raise learning in America to new levels, everyone will have to do more, make sacrifices, and work harder with a shared sense of purpose among school, family, and community. Too often today we find avoidance of responsibility and a circle of blame where the failures of education are concerned. The finger-pointing must come to an end—up and down the line from the federal government to the family and student. There is ample work ahead for everyone.

The second step is to build upon the substantial work that has been undertaken over the past decade. Schools have not been standing still while the world changes around them. Since 1986, when a series of reports called for improvements in teaching, many schools of education have met more rigorous standards of quality; more than 300 have created graduate-level programs, many of them featuring professional development school partnerships; thousands of school districts have redesigned schools and have begun to reshape teaching; new programs for teacher induction and evaluation have been invented in a number of places; teacher networks and academies have been established; and a number of states have begun to invest in professional development. New standards and assessments for licensing and certification developed by the National Board and by consortia of states provide levers for transforming preparation and practice on a broad scale.

The issue is how to move from a panoply of individual disconnected efforts to a coherent system of supports for high-quality teaching available to every teacher in every community. There are, as we have noted, important policy steps to be taken. And there are investments to make, although our analysis suggests that major parts of the costs of our recommendations should be managed through reallocations of resources from places where they are currently spent ineffectively—and that sizable benefits and cost savings will result from the individual and collective proposals we have made.

Reallocating Resources

Our proposals call for rethinking school structures and roles and reallocating educational dollars. If teachers assume many of the instructional tasks currently performed by administrative staff (for example, mentoring and supervision), the layers of bureaucratic hierarchy will be reduced. If teachers are more carefully selected and better trained and supported, expenditures for management systems to control incompetence will become unnecessary. If investments are made in the beginning of the teaching career for support and mentoring of entering teachers and for pretenure evaluation, the costs of continually recruiting and hiring new entrants to replace the 30% who leave in the first few years will decline; the costs of band-aid approaches to staff development for those who have not learned to teach effectively will be reduced; and the costs of remediating or seeking to dismiss poor teachers—as well as compensating for the effects of their poor teaching on children—will decrease. Strategic investment in teacher competence should free up resources for innovation and learning.

Rethinking Staffing

In terms of reallocation, we recommend that at least half of the more than $80 billion spent annually on nonteaching costs in public schools be redirected toward investments in a greater number of teaching staff who have much more time scheduled each day for joint work and planning. At current salaries, this would add an additional one million teachers to the teaching rolls, raising the share of teaching staff to nearly 60% of the total, not as high as that in other countries, but substantially better than the current ratio of under 50%.

As others have noted, including the Carnegie Task Force on Learning in the Primary Grades,[124] we must make more effective use of our current investments in education. There are existing sources of funding that could be used for instructional changes to produce much higher achievement for pupils if they were redirected to approaches that have been shown to work. We agree with this analysis. At the same time, we stress that the process of reorganizing districts and schools should proceed incrementally and responsibly. Slashing administrative budgets or reallocating staff without careful planning and analysis can prove disastrous for the operations of systems. Schools' support systems must be redesigned for new staffing patterns to work well.

With thoughtful planning, reallocation of personnel should be accomplished over the coming years in two ways: First, by reducing as much as possible the number of nonteaching staff assigned to programs and functions outside the school. This will require restraint on the part of policymakers in their tendencies to create heavily regulated categorical programs that carry large administrative burdens. It will also require decentralization and redesign of some functions that have been increasingly centralized in school district offices over the past several decades, such as supervision, program administration, and many school support functions, such as maintenance, purchasing, and the like.

These changes rely in part on a shift in management theory from the 1950s' view that centralization always produces greater efficiencies and economies of scale to one that seeks an optimal blend of centralized and decentralized management. It also means an acknowledgment that greater productivity is likely to result from direct investments in teacher and principal competence than from efforts to create accountability through top-heavy inspection and reporting systems that cannot in the long run produce good practice. New York City's Community School District #2 provides a useful example of how funds can be reallocated from central office hierarchy to direct investments in teacher and principal learning and performance review.

Second, the number of classroom teachers can be increased by restructuring the use of staff within schools. As we described in the previous chapter, many schools have increased the proportion of within-school staff who are classroom teachers from the usual 50-55% to 70% or more by assigning regular teaching responsibilities to administrators, specialists, pullout teachers, and counselors who currently sit at the periphery of the teaching/learning enterprise rather than at the center. This has allowed them to both reduce class sizes and pupil loads and to create shared responsibility and planning time for teachers. Creating teaching teams that provide a mix of expertise and take direct, long-term responsibility for children is more effective than placing experts on the side to work with children or teachers in short, disconnected interludes. By redesigning their work, the same staff can be used in much more effective ways.

There are some difficult dilemmas to be confronted in this process. Several studies have found that the share of total resources and teachers devoted to regular education has declined since the 1960s (from 80% to 59% according to one study),[125] and that increases in special education spending (from under 5% to nearly 15%) include large shares for paraprofessionals and nonteaching personnel associated with placement processes rather than instruction. Use of pullout services also contributes to larger classes for regular education teachers and more fragmented service delivery for students. Rethinking the delivery system associated with these critically important special education services seems essential. Greater investments in teaching will require new approaches to identification and placement. Efforts to reduce pullouts will rest both on new organizational and staffing strategies[126] and on growing expertise on the part of all classroom teachers for teaching a wider range of learners.

In addition, as the Carnegie Task Force on Learning in the Primary Grades

Management as Professional Development in New York's District #2

Can school districts make a difference in what schools do and what students learn? This question is raised as school restructuring has often bypassed districts, which have been viewed as either extraneous or hostile to change. Some districts, however, have taken a proactive role in transforming teaching and learning. New York City's Community School District #2—a diverse, multilingual district of 22,000 students—has made professional development the central focus of management and the core strategy for school improvement. The strong belief governing the district's efforts is that student learning will increase as the knowledge of educators grows.

The district's extensive professional development efforts, which are paying off in rapidly rising student achievement, include several vehicles for learning. *The Professional Development Laboratory* allows visiting teachers to spend three weeks in the classrooms of expert resident teachers who are engaged in practices they want to learn. *Instructional consulting services* allow expert teachers and consultants to work with groups of teachers within schools to develop particular strategies, such as literature-based reading instruction. *School visitations and peer networks* are designed to help teachers and principals examine exemplary practices. The district budgets for 300 total days each year so that teachers and principals can visit and observe one another, develop study groups, and work together. *Off-site training* includes intensive summer institutes that focus on core teaching strategies and on learning about new standards, curriculum frameworks, and assessments.

These are always linked to follow-up through consulting services and peer networks to develop practices further. *Oversight and evaluation* of principals focuses on their plans for instructional improvement in each content area, as does evaluation of teachers. There is close, careful scrutiny of teaching from the central office and at the school and continual pressure and support to improve its quality.

A key feature of these strategies is that they have focused intensely for many years on a few strands of content-focused training designed to have cumulative impact over the long term, rather than changing workshop topics every in-service day or picking new themes each year. The district has sponsored eight years of intensive work on teaching strategies for literacy development and four years on mathematics teaching. These efforts are guided by several principles:

1. It's about instruction, and only about instruction. The district conveys the message in everything it does that the work of everyone in the system, from central office administrators to staff in schools, is providing high-quality teaching to students.

2. Instructional change is a long, multi-stage process. Learning begins with awareness of new ideas, followed by opportunities for planning, chances to try them and receive feedback, and time for reflection with others in order to refine practice.

3. Shared expertise drives instructional change. District staff and consultants regularly work with school staff on specific instructional approaches. Principals and teachers engage in regular team meetings on curriculum and teaching, visit other schools and classrooms, and

work together on districtwide staff development issues.

4. Focus on systemwide improvement. The enemy of systemic change, according to District 2 staff, is the "project," which isolates and balkanizes new ideas and makes improvement the responsibility of a select few. To create systemic change, principals and teachers must regularly collaborate with others to examine and develop their practice.

5. Good ideas come from talented people working together. The key to improvement is always people and their knowledge. Recruitment of highly talented professionals and development of their skills is the top priority. Weak principals and teachers are aggressively counseled out. Problems are always addressed by putting people together to learn from one another.

6. Set clear expectations, then decentralize. The district focuses on getting, developing, and keeping good people and clarifying their mission. Then it gets out of the way.

7. Foster collegiality, caring, and respect. Helping people take risks and take on more responsibility for children requires the cultivation of a deep personal and professional respect that is communicated at every level.

Source: Richard F. Elmore, "Staff Development and Instructional Improvement, Community School District 2, New York City" (paper prepared for the National Commission on Teaching & America's Future, 1996).

points out, schools' increased investments over the last two decades in untrained school aides have not always been used as productively as they might. In some cases, aides serve housekeeping rather than instructional functions. In some others, they are given full responsibility for the instruction of special-needs students without adequate training. We recognize that there are necessary and productive arrangements for teaming teachers with paraprofessional staff who provide a very important set of services. We also recognize that if more paraprofessionals were recruited into teaching through high-quality preparation programs, class sizes could be lowered and greater expertise could be brought to bear on the education of students, especially those who most need skilled teaching. Another cost-effective way to add trained personpower to classrooms would be the use of teaching interns from extended teacher preparation programs as teaching assistants.

Redirecting Professional Development Funds

We have noted that while many districts spend relatively little on the direct costs of staff development, such as district-sponsored workshops, large amounts of hidden expenditures in the form of staff time and salaries are spent in ways that are now often less focused and effective than they might be. Of an estimated $19 billion spent annually on the portion of teacher salaries granted for education credits, we recommend that one-half be gradually redirected to restructured compensation systems that incorporate salary steps for performance-based licensing and National Board Certification along with experience and other education.

In addition, we have argued that funds currently spent on ineffective one-shot workshops would be better spent on more useful forms of professional development, including support for teachers' in-school study groups, peer coaching, and other problem-solving efforts as well as teacher-to-teacher networks, teacher academies, and school-university partnerships. Both existing and new funds should be more purposefully targeted on helping teachers learn how to use curriculum and assessments aimed at new standards for student learning. Professional development days sprinkled throughout the year and used for ineffective "one-size-fits-all" staff development should be consolidated and expanded to create a block of at least ten days of time that teachers can spend planning and learning together at the end of the students' school year. At least half the costs of this additional time for teachers is already present in district budgets for professional development time. The remainder should be funded by the new state investments we describe below.

Investing in Strategic Improvements

The estimated additional costs of our key recommendations total just under $5 billion annually, which is less than 1% of the amount expended without fanfare for the federal savings and loan bailout of several years ago. This amount is not too much, we believe, to bail out our schools and to secure America's future.

We believe that the critical new investments should be directed at

1. **Teacher education reforms** aimed at developing extended graduate-level programs that include internships in professional development schools;

2. **Recruitment,** including subsidies that underwrite the preparation of highly able individuals to teach in high-need fields and locations;

3. **Reforms of beginning teacher licensing and induction,** especially the implementation of new performance assessments that develop and test teaching knowledge and skill, and the creation of mentoring supports for beginning teachers; and

4. **More focused and effective professional development** organized around new student standards and standards for accomplished teaching, including the use of new technologies. We urge that states allocate an additional 1% of state and local funds for this purpose, in addition to matching grants to local school districts that increase their investments in professional development.

Type of Investment	Basis of Estimate	Cost per Year
Scholarships for able recruits in high-need fields and areas	25,000 candidates at $20,000 per candidate for a four-year commitment to teaching[1]	$ 500 million
Teacher education including internships in professional development schools	125,000 new teachers annually at $7,000 per candidate[2]	$ 875 million
Mentoring supports and new licensing assessments for all beginning teachers	125,000 new teachers annually at $6,000 per candidate[3]	$ 750 million
New state funds for professional development	1% of total state/local funds for education (plus) matching grants for local school districts	$1.750 billion $1.000 billion
TOTAL		**$4.875 billion**

1. $20,000 should fund a major share of the costs of teacher preparation for three years of an extended program that begins in the junior year of undergraduate school at a state university or one to two years of graduate-level teacher education in an MAT program. A four-year commitment to teaching predicts greater long-term retention in the profession.

2. The estimate of 125,000 new teachers annually is based on current trends that project that half of all newly hired teachers will be newly prepared, while the remainder reenter from the reserve pool of former teachers. Costs are based on estimates for operating professional development schools and creating fifth-year internships within teacher education programs. See Richard L. Clark, "Professional Development Schools: Costs and Finances" (National Network for Educational Renewal, February 1996).

3. Costs are based on district estimates in Cincinnati, Rochester, and Toledo that they spend about $5,000 per teacher for high-quality mentoring programs for beginning teachers, and estimates that initial development costs for new performance assessments for licensing could reach $1,000, some portion of which would be offset by candidate fees and by in-kind subsidies of relicensing credits in lieu of compensation to veteran teachers who serve as assessors.

Whereas states have the primary responsibility for basic school funding and initial teacher licensing, the federal government also has a natural and long-standing role to play in supporting the recruitment and preparation of a capable teaching force. These investments should represent a partnership in the effort to build a strong foundation for the nation's future.

The Commission's charge to the American people is simple—ensure that every student, in every class, is taught by qualified teachers. Instead of cluttering the agendas of everyone involved with multiple actions, the Commission believes the country can close in on that goal if each actor takes responsibility for a major part of the total effort and commits to doing his or her part well.

Time is short. Demographics work against taking too long to make decisions and take action. School enrollments are mushrooming, especially among populations needing the best teaching skills. More important, the opportunities to re-create teaching as a standards-based profession have never been greater. It is not too ambitious to expect the initiatives recommended for each partner to be well under way by the turn of the century and fully functioning by the year 2006.

State Initiatives in Professional Development

In recent years, states have become more active in supporting and targeting professional development.

New allocations are establishing stable sources of funding for professional development. In **Missouri,** the state has created a pool of funds equivalent to 1% of the state's foundation level times the number of students in the state and set it aside for various improvement activities, including regional professional development centers. In addition, Missouri districts are required to set aside 1% of their foundation budgets for school-based staff development, with allocations decided by school-based teams. **Kentucky**'s new funding formula provides each district with an amount per pupil for professional development, allocated at the school level. Schools must develop plans that are reviewed by the state, using established standards. School districts may apply to the state to use up to five instructional days for professional development, above the four days that are required of all districts. In **Kansas,** districts with approved professional development plans are entitled to additional state aid. **South Dakota** provides each district with $225 per teacher to support three days of staff and curriculum development at the start of each school year.

New institutions for providing professional development have been launched in some states, along with challenge grants for stimulating learning and reform. **Oregon** has developed a statewide Professional Development Center together with a fund of competitive school restructuring grants. **Ohio** has created regional professional development centers, along with a ven-

ture capital fund through which schools may obtain additional funding over a five-year period for targeted school improvement activities, and a BEST Practices Award that showcases successful school initiatives. **Maine** supports regional coalitions of school improvement teams, two regional school-university partnerships, and an Innovation Grants Award program for stimulating school-based change. **Iowa** funds school-based inquiry approaches that engage educators in defining and solving their own problems. **North Carolina** established the North Carolina Center for the Advancement of Teaching, a handsomely appointed residential facility that hosts seminars for teachers throughout the state and works directly with districts on reform initiatives. In addition, the Governor's Entrepreneurial School Awards honor innovative schools throughout the state and share their practices. Finally, the state now offers a 4% salary increase for teachers who achieve National Board Certification.

Teacher networks for implementing new curriculum frameworks and assessments have been funded in some states. **California** supports subject-matter collaboratives that provide professional development to teams of teachers around the state's curriculum frameworks. The state has also created networks of trained teacher leaders. **Vermont** supports similar cadres of teacher leaders to work with others on the development, study, and scoring of student portfolios.

Finally, a few states are beginning to use new technologies for professional development. **Nebraska** is using distance technology to provide new learn-

ing for mathematics teachers in rural areas via video presentations of teaching strategies and support materials, and an electronic network. **Kentucky** is creating a statewide electronic network to link teachers and institutions through fiberoptics, computer modems, and satellite dishes. And **Michigan** uses instructional television as a medium through which to present innovative approaches to instruction geared to teachers and the general public.

The Consequences of Action . . . and Inaction

There are two futures at hand. One continues our current course in the face of major demographic and economic changes and expanding expectations of schools. In the year 2006, it looks something like this:

Following a brief and familiar flurry of education reform activity in the 1980s and early 1990s, schools settled back down to business as usual. The education governors had come and gone; educational leaders were relieved to have the waves of commission reports shelved and out of the way. A period of teacher shortages had been addressed by modest salary increases and increased use of emergency and alternative certification. By 1995, teacher salaries had returned to the levels of the early 1970s and then stagnated, remaining 30% below those of competing occupations. As momentum for reform receded, teacher recruitment remained problematic, especially in fields like mathematics and science and in cities and the Sunbelt, where enrollments boomed.

As more than 30% of teachers retired over the 1990s, and many new teachers left shortly after they started, continuous shortages led to larger classes, more out-of-field teaching, and more hiring of untrained people. A growing number of teachers serving poor and minority students had formal pedagogical preparation consisting only of a three-week summer course. They desperately wanted to address the learning needs of their students, but their training in such fundamentals as subject matter, learning and development, and teaching methods was too skimpy to provide them with adequate

ammunition for the job.

Throughout the 1990s, students in the public education system changed, but schools did not. Great waves of immigration boosted the numbers of poor, minority, and non-English-speaking children to nearly 40% of public school enrollments. Some teachers, who had attended restructured schools of education created in the high tide of reform—and who taught in schools redesigned to focus more intensely on learning—were able to teach these and other students successfully. But their successes could not be replicated in other schools where teachers were less well prepared and schools were not designed to support quality teaching.

The public's periodic concern for low student performance was assuaged by the enactment of "stiffer" requirements: more tests, more course requirements, and more recordkeeping procedures. In only a few places were schools staffed by highly skilled teachers able to respond to these mandates. In most cases, they led to disappointing results: More students were held back and dropped out. More watered-down courses were taught by teachers without adequate training in their fields. More add-on special programs were created to "address" student failure. And more bureaucracy evolved to manage all of the above, draining more dollars from classrooms to support the administration of all these mandates.

Because many teachers did not know how to get the results sought, students' learning was increasingly structured by practice tests and worksheets. Scores in basic skills remained static while scores on higher-order

thinking continued to decline. U.S. students continued to rank near the bottom on international tests of more advanced skills.

Earlier enthusiasm for reforms gave way to disillusionment and lower school budgets, as middle-class parents fled to private schools and the general population, made up largely of older citizens without children in schools, voted down tax levies for education. Just as the reforms of the 1960s were replaced in the 1970s by movements to reduce school spending and go "back to the basics," so the reform rhetoric of the 1990s gave way to a backlash against innovation and investment in public education. By the year 2006, public frustration with the schools resurfaced with cries from the business community for employees who could function in an information-based, technological economy. New commissions were born to declare the nation, once again, at risk.

Another future—one that envisions different resolutions of the dilemmas described above—is possible. In this future, teaching continues its progress toward becoming a profession. In the year 2006, a different public education system has emerged. It looks something like this:

Much had changed since the last "crisis" in education during the 1980s. A second wave of reform impelled new coalitions between teachers, administrators, and teacher educators, all of whom began thinking of themselves as members of the same profession with common goals. They developed the first professional definition of teaching knowledge through the National Board for Professional Teaching Standards. This stimulated the creation of state boards that built upon the new vision to create more meaningful standards for teacher preparation and licensing. States worked with colleges to establish internships in professional development schools as part of a master's degree in teaching. Teachers-in-training were coached by expert mentor teachers working in conjunction with university faculty on the reform of schooling and teaching. The new cohort of teachers—more than a million of them—was better prepared than any that had preceded them.

Teacher shortages were met with higher salaries and recruitment incentives. As salaries reached a level comparable with those of other competing occupations, the supply of teachers willing to undergo rigorous preparation programs grew. And as the qualifications of teachers increased, the perceived need to spend large portions of education budgets on massive inspection systems diminished. Long hierarchies that had grown to design, regulate, and monitor teaching flattened out. Teachers took on more professional responsibilities, and schools took on new shapes conducive to professional teaching and intensive learning.

As in other professions, differentiated roles and responsibilities gradually emerged as a means for balancing the requirements of supply and qualifications. Those less extensively trained—such as beginning teaching interns—practiced under the supervision of career professionals, many of

whom were engaged in becoming more expert by pursuing National Board Certification. Practitioners worked in teams that jointly assumed responsibility for groups of students. In settings where several teachers and interns were responsible for a group of students over several years, new possibilities emerged for organizing instruction, for collaborating on teaching plans and decisions, and for developing strategies to meet individual children's needs. These structures promoted consultation and peer review of practice that continually improved teaching and learning.

Educators insisted on selecting and inducting their peers based on professional standards of practice and on shared decision-making so they could pool their wisdom about the best use of resources to meet students' needs. Professional knowledge and effectiveness grew as serious induction, sustained professional development, and collaboration replaced the sink-or-swim, closed-door ethos of an earlier era.

Instructional practices changed too. Schools became more focused on higher standards of performance *and* on the needs of students. As teachers became more skilled, they used more powerful methods of teaching and learning: research projects, experiments, debates, and exhibitions replaced superficial texts and worksheets. Students were encouraged to read great books and engage meaty ideas, to construct and solve intellectual problems, and to demonstrate their learning in challenging performances.

More productive approaches to organizing the school day and the

school year gave individual teachers and students more time together, reducing the pullouts, pass-throughs, start-ups, and wind-downs that had stolen teaching time and decreased teachers' capacity to come to know students well. Schools became smaller and more personalized. Fewer students fell through the cracks.

Incentives to attract the most expert teachers to the profession's greatest needs and challenges also emerged. Lead teachers redesigned inner-city schools as exemplars of professional practice where they coached new teachers, put research into practice—and practice into research—and put state-of-the-art knowledge to work for children. Equity and excellence became joined with professionalism.

By the year 2006, a renaissance had occurred in American education. The best American students performed as well as students anywhere in the world. The vast majority of students graduated with not only minimal basic skills, but with the capacity to write, reason, and think analytically. Complaints from the business community about the quality of graduates subsided for the first time since World War II. And for the first time since the beginning of the 20th century, a decade was launched without a chorus of commission reports crying crisis in the American public schools. The road taken, as it turned out, was the one that finally made a difference.

A Call to Action

The Commission recognizes that achieving the changes we have outlined by the year 2006 is far too late for many, many children. The actual timetable is to make changes as rapidly as possible. Every day of delay is a lost opportunity, gone forever for the children not better served.

We want to speak directly to those with the greatest authority to transform recommendations into policy—governors, legislatures, state boards and departments of education, local school board members, superintendents, school principals, and teacher associations. Even more, we wish to speak to those with the greatest stake in the outcome of these discussions—students, parents, and teachers.

To the nation's governors, we point out that your responsibilities for education are particularly difficult; they spring from two sources. Under the federal and state constitutions you are responsible for education and are required to provide all children with sound basic education on equal terms. Today, such an education requires that all of your state's children have access to competent teaching. We urge you to establish a coordinating effort in your office that brings together all of the parties responsible for improving teaching within your state and direct it toward that goal. Your coordinator should oversee the following marching orders on your authority:

- Propose legislation to create a state professional standards board to develop coherent standards for teacher education, licensing, and professional development.

- Develop an annual public report on the status of teaching in the state in relation to the issues we have raised here.

In addition, nothing is more important today than a national conversation on changing the course of teaching in America. We urge you to work with legislators, state and local education agencies, universities, and parent groups to convene forums and town meetings in local schools across your state to discuss these issues and this report, and to forge a consensus for state and local action.

State legislators have equally challenging tasks—aligning policies, finance, and procedures for licensing, certification, and development of teachers and developing policies that recruit and reward good teachers.

We urge every legislature to enact legislation that sets aside at least 1% of the total state/local budget for education for high-quality, standards-based professional development each year, to set up a framework for funding professional development schools, and to offer venture capital funds for school improvement. We ask you to establish a professional standards board that includes National Board-Certified teachers. We also urge you to work with standards boards and state departments to strengthen teacher preparation through professsional accreditation and close down weak programs, phasing out funding for those that do not improve over a reasonable period of time. We suggest you reallocate funds from redundant program approval activities to high-quality performance examinations for licensing all entrants based on common assessments of subject matter, teaching knowledge, and skills. We also urge you to develop scholarship programs for preparing top-flight candidates for high-need fields and areas, while providing districts with incentives to hire licensed teachers and to reward Board-Certified teachers. Finally, we ask you to conduct an annual audit of your state's policies in all of the areas we have outlined here, to take stock of your state's current commitments to quality teaching, and to organize efforts for sustained and serious reform.

Legislators at the federal level also can help. The federal government has long supported the building of a high-quality medical profession by offering scholarships and forgivable loans to those who train in shortage fields or volunteer to work in shortage areas, and supporting improvements in medical education and the work of teaching hospitals. Similar incentives in teaching were quite successful in the 1970s, and some authorizations have recently been reestablished—though barely funded—to support the training of prospective teachers. We urge Congress to take seriously the nation's need for qualified teachers in all communities, to fully fund the teacher recruitment proposals currently in Title V of the Higher Education Act (authorized at $76 million but funded at only $1 million) and to aggressively pursue initiatives to seed improvements in teacher education and the creation of professional development schools.

To our colleagues in **state boards of education, state education agencies, and professional standards boards,** we insist that you close all loopholes that allow for lowering teaching standards, including emergency and substandard licenses, and work with colleges to create professionally sound alternative routes into the profession. Work with agencies in other states to develop portable pensions and reciprocal licensing. Encourage new approaches to professional development by helping to establish teacher academies, networks, and school-university partnerships, and allocate funds for ten days of professional learning each year focused around new student and teaching standards.

To **college presidents, deans, and professors,** we urge a shared commitment to the goals for higher education articulated for us by Indiana State University president John Moore, who said, "Our challenge is to prepare new teachers and assist practicing teachers so that both can better help diverse learners successfully meet higher learning goals," and by Vanderbilt University chancellor Joe Wyatt, who declared: "Our nation's future depends on a high-quality public education system and a superior force of educators. There is no more important work." We ask that you deepen your commitment to creating high-quality preparation programs based on professional standards for teachers, principals, and other educators; develop extended programs that include intensive internships in public schools; and create professional development school partnerships with local schools for the simultaneous renewal of teaching and teacher education. We also ask that you recognize that preparing teachers is the business of the whole university: It requires high-quality courses in the arts and sciences that model good pedagogy and reveal the fundamental principles of disciplinary inquiry, as well as thoughtful preparation in the school of education itself.

Local school boards and superintendents have a vital role to play. You must

> To those bright young people who want to enter the profession that has been so good to many of us—education—I say "good choice!" My advice to them is not "You're too smart to be a teacher," but rather, "You're too smart *not* to be one." That single affirmation, if made by every educator alive who believes in its truth, could be the greatest impetus ever in our collective move to reform other professions.
>
> — James R. Delisle, teacher, Orchard Middle School, and professor of education, Kent State University, Kent, Ohio

establish environments where hiring and placement policies focus on quality; where exceptional teaching is respected and rewarded; where a diverse, caring, and competent teaching force is sought and supported; and where policies support the professionalism of teachers. We urge you to emphasize quality and streamline hiring procedures; employ only qualified teachers and assign them to the fields in which they are well prepared; allocate more staff and resources to the front lines of teaching; work with teacher associations to develop more effective professional development systems, and redirect portions of existing professional development funds to standards-based work sponsored by teacher networks and academies. We ask you to find time for teachers to work together to learn about new strategies and technologies; and work with unions to develop better systems for teacher evaluation, compensation, and career development that recognize and reward knowledge and skills while keeping good teachers in the profession.

Businesses can make a substantial contribution by sharing expertise and underwriting the installation of new technologies for managing complex personnel systems in schools. You can also make important investments in the professional development of staff by endowing teacher academies, providing management training for shared decision making, and by offering summer positions to teachers in industries where they can update their knowledge and skills.

Principals are challenged as much as any group to fulfill this report's vision. In fact, the vision relies upon school leadership that understands why and how learning and teaching must and can improve. We look to you to help create a learning organization in your school, to re-create the role of principal teacher, and to develop a range of leadership roles by creating new possibilities for shared work and learning among staff as well as parents. Be courageous in examining new strategies for organizing teams, rethinking schedules, and reallocating staff to focus on continuous, well-supported student learning. Encourage research and inquiry inside the school to examine how students are doing and develop strategies for improvement. Work within professional organizations for new standards for principal education and licensing focused on instructional leadership. Use professional standards as a basis for hiring teachers and organizing professional development and evaluation. Continually identify sources of professional learning that support the interests and efforts of the teachers, parents, and administrators with whom you work, as well as your own.

The commitment of **teachers** to the principles in this report and their clear, powerful voices in support of them are absolutely essential. This is an opportunity for teachers to lead their profession. We urge you to take responsibility for making sure policies are adopted locally that give appropriate support to beginning teachers through mentoring and peer review. Embrace and enforce the teaching standards described in this report as a means of improving practice and the profession. Prepare for and fulfill the role of mentor and assessor of beginning teachers in the new performance assessments they undertake. Set National Board Certification as a personal goal and promote Board Certification within your school, district, and state. Look for ways to collaborate with colleagues on work that can improve teaching, curriculum, and school organization in support of student learning. Participate in efforts that encourage promising young people to select teaching as a career.

In addition, work within your associations to meet the challenge of transforming the profession into one that assumes responsibility for meeting the needs of students with a growing base of knowledge, skill, and commitment. Teacher unions, subject matter associations, and other educational groups must join hands to create a union of professionals focused on the job of improving America's schools—first for the students whom they serve and then for those who work within them.

We urge **teacher associations** to promote the preparation and hiring of well-qualified teachers; aid in the recruitment of a diverse teaching force; and work with local school boards, superintendents, and state policymakers to develop better systems for teacher licensing, development, evaluation, and compensation that enhance and recognize knowledge and skills while keeping good teachers in the classroom. These systems should include encouragements for and appropriate use of National Board-Certified teachers.

Aspiring teachers have a major stake in this agenda. Those of you who choose teaching as a career—either initially or in midcareer—must make sure you enter programs with high standards and a commitment to improving teaching and learning. We urge you, first, to find a practicing teacher to guide you in your choices, preferably one who is certified by the National Board and who exhibits the leadership and skills to inspire dedication to quality teaching. Second, we recommend that you select your preparation program carefully. If it is not professionally accredited, do not waste your time. Ideally, it will provide a five-year program of studies extending past the undergraduate degree or a full year or more at the graduate level. It should emphasize professional standards and extensive teaching practice linked to courses. Your search should be diligent, because your reward will be a satisfying lifetime spent teaching to secure the American future.

Finally, we end where we began, speaking directly to the people with the greatest stake in the learning enterprise—students and parents.

If **parents** do not speak for the proposition that their children are entitled to be taught by qualified teachers, we do not know who will. Speak your mind. Seek allies through local parent groups. Examine the qualifications of your schools' teachers and the criteria for hiring, tenuring, and rewarding teachers. Ask that educators publish and display their credentials, so you know how well they are prepared to serve your child. Ask questions about plans for improving teaching quality and making technologies available in the school. In the end, your local schools will be the better for it, and your children will be better prepared for their future.

Students may think they have no role to play in implementing the recommendations of commissions such as these. But students *are* America's future, and it matters greatly that you take your education seriously, understand why higher standards are needed for you to succeed, and think about how you can contribute to your learning and that of others. We urge students of all ages to seek to understand and appreciate what your teachers are trying to accomplish, ask questions about your studies, talk about your own concerns and interests in learning, work with one another as helpers and peer tutors . . . and consider—perhaps—becoming teachers someday yourselves.

It's the sparks. Every time my students get excited about learning something new, I see sparks shooting from their eyes. And though I could fill a book with everything I have to say about the rewards of teaching, the chance to do something meaningful and fulfilling with my life, whenever I'm asked why I became a teacher, that's always the first and best thing that comes to mind. The sparks.

It's not easy work; in fact, I will say that it is the most challenging work I have ever done. I have to be there with my students in body and soul, day in and day out. It can be draining, and it can sometimes seem like a battleground.

But how do I feel at the end of each day? I feel proud of my students. I feel more knowledgeable about living, teaching, and learning. I feel lucky to be a teacher. I feel . . . full of sparks.

— *Irasema Ortega-Crawford,*
teacher, Mesa, Arizona

Endnotes

1. See, for example, *America's Choice: High Skills or Low Wages. The Report of the Commission on the Skills of the American Workforce* (Rochester, N.Y.: National Center on Education and the Economy, 1990); and the reports of the U.S. Secretary of Labor's Commission on Achieving Necessary Skills (SCANS): *Learning for a Living: A Blueprint for High Performance. Executive Summary* (Washington, D.C.: SCANS, U.S. Department of Labor, 1992) and *What Work Requires of Schools* (Washington, D.C.: SCANS, U.S. Department of Labor, 1991).

2. The National Commission on Excellence in Education, *A Nation at Risk: The Imperative of Educational Reform* (Washington, D.C.: U.S. Department of Education, 1983).

3. Department of Commerce, Bureau of the Census, *Current Population Report: Income, Poverty, and Valuation of Non-Cash Benefits, 1993,* Series P-60-188 (Washington, D.C., 1995): table D-5, p. D-17. Also see, U.S. Bureau of the Census, *Current Population Survey, March 1988/March 1995* (Washington D.C., U.S. Bureau of the Census, 1995).

4. The National Education Goals Panel, *National Educational Goals Report: Executive Summary* (Washington, D.C.: U.S. Department of Education, 1995).

5. National Center for Education Statistics, *Report in Brief: National Assessment of Educational Progress (NAEP) 1992 Trends in Academic Progress* (Washington, D.C.: U.S. Department of Education, 1994).

6. Educational Testing Service, *A World of Differences: An International Assessment of Mathematics and Science* (Princeton, N.J.: Educational Testing Service, 1989); National Center for Education Statistics, *The Condition of Education, 1995* (Washington, D.C.: U.S. Department of Education, 1995).

7. Lauren B. Resnick, *Education and Learning to Think* (Washington, D.C.: National Academy Press, 1987); Thomas L. Good and Jere T. Brophy, *Educational Psychology, 3rd Edition* (New York: Longman, 1986); Barbara Bowman, "Early Childhood Education," in *Review of Research in Education, Volume 19,* edited by Linda Darling-Hammond (Washington, D.C.: American Educational Research Association, 1993), 101-134; JoMills H. Braddock and James McPartland, "Education of Early Adolescents," in *Review of Research in Education, Volume 19,* edited by Linda Darling-Hammond (Washington, D.C.: American Educational Research Association, 1993), 135-170; Valerie E. Lee, Anthony Bryk, and Julia B. Smith, "The Organization of Effective Secondary Schools," in *Review of Research in Education, Volume 19,* edited by Linda Darling-Hammond (Washington, D.C.: American Educational Research Association, 1993), 171-267.

8. Lee, Bryk, and Smith, "The Organization of Effective Secondary Schools"; Linda Darling-Hammond, Jacqueline Ancess, and Beverly Falk, *Authentic Assessment in Action: Studies of Schools and Students at Work* (New York: Teachers College Press, 1995).

9. David C. Berliner, "In Pursuit of the Expert Pedagogue," *Educational Researcher* 15 (August/September 1986): 5-13; Linda Darling-Hammond, Arthur E. Wise, and S. R. Pease, "Teacher Evaluation in the Organizational Context: A Review of the Literature," in *Review of Educational Research* 53 (Fall 1983): 285-327; Lee Shulman, "Knowledge and Teaching: Foundations of the New Reform," *Harvard Educational Review* 57 (January 1987): 1-22.

10. See Darling-Hammond, "Teaching and Knowledge," and John Sikula (ed.), *Handbook of Research on Teacher Education,* 2nd edition (New York: Association of Teacher Educators, 1996).

11. Ronald Ferguson, "Paying for Public Education: New Evidence on How and Why Money Matters," *Harvard Journal on Legislation* 28 (Summer 1991): 465-98.

12. Eleanor Armour-Thomas, Camille Clay, Raymond Domanico, K. Bruno, and Barbara Allen, *An Outlier Study of Elementary and Middle Schools in New York City: Final Report* (New York: New York City Board of Education, 1989).

13. Craig B. Howley, "Synthesis of Effects of School and District Size: What Research Says about Achievement in Small Schools and School Districts," *Journal of Rural and*

Small Schools 4 (Fall 1989): 2-12; Craig B. Howley and Gary Huang, *Extracurricular Participation and Achievement: School Size as Possible Mediator of SES Influence among Individual Students* (Washington, D.C.: Resources in Education, January 1992); Emil J. Haller, "Small Schools and Higher-Order Thinking Skills," *Journal of Research in Rural Education* 9 (1993): 66-73.

14. Even *A Nation at Risk*, the landmark education reform document issued in 1983 by the National Commission on Excellence in Education, acknowledged that the average American today is better educated than a generation ago.

15. Peter Drucker, "The Age of Social Transformation," *The Atlantic Monthly* 62 (November 1994): 53-80; and Hudson Institute, *Workforce 2000: Work and Workers for the 21st Century* (Indianapolis, Ind.: Hudson Institute, 1987).

16. Educational Testing Service, *Literacy and Dependency: The Literacy Skills of Welfare Recipients in the United States* (Princeton, N.J.: ETS Policy Information Center, 1995); National Center for Education Statistics, *Literacy Behind Prison Walls: Profiles of the Prison Population from the Adult Literacy Survey* (Washington, D.C.: U.S. Department of Education, 1994).

17. Paul E. Barton and Richard J. Coley, *Captive Students: Education and Training in America's Prisons* (Princeton, N.J.: Educational Testing Service, 1996).

18. Robert J. Gemignani, "Juvenile Correctional Education: A Time for Change. Office of Juvenile Justice and Delinquency Prevention Update on Research," *Juvenile Justice Bulletin* (October 1994).

19. Social Security Administration, *1996 Annual Report of the Board of Trustees of the Federal Old Age and Survivors Insurance and Disability Insurance Trust Funds* (Baltimore, Md.: Social Security Administration, 1996): table II.F19, p.122.

20. National Center for Education Statistics (Washington, D.C.: National Data Resource Center, unpublished tabulations, 1993).

21. For a review, see Linda Darling-Hammond, "Teaching and Knowledge: Policy Issues Posed by Alternative Certification of Teachers," *Peabody Journal of Education* 67 (Spring 1992): 123-154.

22. Emily Feistritzer, *Teacher Supply and Demand Survey, 1988* (Washington, D.C.: National Center for Education Information, 1988); National Center for Education Statistics (Washington, D.C.: National Data Resource Center, unpublished tabulations from the *Schools and Staffing Survey, 1990-91*).

23. Marilyn M. McMillen, Sharon A. Bobbitt, and Hilda F. Lynch, "Teacher Training, Certification, and Assignment in Public Schools: 1990-91" (paper presented at the annual meeting of the American Educational Research Association, New Orleans, Louisiana, April 1994).

24. National Center for Education Statistics, *The Condition of Education, 1995* (Washington, D.C.: U.S. Department of Education, 1995): 415.

25. Richard M. Ingersoll, *Schools and Staffing Survey: Teacher Supply, Teacher Qualifications, and Teacher Turnover, 1990-1991* (Washington, D.C.: U.S. Department of Education, National Center for Education Statistics, 1995), 28.

26. Jeannie Oakes, *Multiplying Inequalities: The Effects of Race, Social Class, and Tracking on Opportunities to Learn Mathematics and Science* (Santa Monica, Calif.: RAND Corporation, 1990).

27. The California Commission on Teaching, *Who Will Teach Our Children?* (Sacramento, Calif.: Author, 1985); Linda Darling-Hammond, "Inequality and Access to Knowledge," edited by James Banks, *Handbook of Research on Multicultural Education* (New York: Macmillan, 1995).

28. National Center for Education Statistics, *Schools and Staffing in the United States: A Statistical Profile, 1990-91* (Washington, D.C.: U.S. Department of Education, 1993).

29. Educational Testing Service, *The State of Inequality* (Princeton, N.J.: Educational Testing Service, 1991); Jonathan Kozol, *Savage Inequalities: Children in America's Schools* (New York: Crown Publishers, 1991).

30. Mary Rollefson, *Teacher Supply in the United States: Sources of Newly Hired Teachers in Public and Private Schools* (Washington, D.C.: U.S. Department of Education, National Center for Education Statistics, 1993), 10.

31. Linda Darling-Hammond, "Instructional Policy into Practice: The Power of the Bottom Over the Top," *Educational Evaluation and Policy Analysis* 12 (Fall 1990): 233-241; Linda Darling-Hammond and Milbrey W. McLaughlin, "Policies That Support Professional Development in an Era of Reform," in *Teacher Learning: New Policies, New Practices,* edited by Milbrey W. McLaughlin and Ida Oberman (New York: Teachers College Press, 1996), 202-235; Linda Darling-Hammond with Eileen Sclan, "Policy and Supervision," in *Supervision in Transition, 1992 Yearbook for the Association for Supervision and Curriculum Development,* edited by Carl D. Glickman (Alexandria, Va.: Association for Supervision and Curriculum Development, 1992), 7-29.

32. National Center for Education Statistics (Washington, D.C.: National Data Resource Center, unpublished tabulations from the *1990-91 Schools and Staffing Survey, 1990-91*).

33. *USA Today,* "USA Today/CNN/Gallup Poll," January 22, 1996, 6D.

34. Jean Johnson and John Immerwahr, *First Things First: What Americans Expect from the Public Schools* (New York: Public Agenda, 1994).

35. Ibid.

36. Linda Darling-Hammond, "The Implications of Testing Policy for Quality and Equality," *Phi Delta Kappan* 73 (November 1991): 220-225; Robert L. Linn, "Accountability: The Comparison of Educational Systems and the Quality of Test Results," *Educational Policy* 1 (1987): 181-198; George Madaus, Mary Maxwell West, Maryellen C. Harmon, Richard G. Lomax, and Katherine A. Viator, *The Influence of Testing on Teaching Math and Science in Grades 4-12* (Chestnut Hill, Mass.: Boston College Center for the Study of Testing, Evaluation, and Educational Policy, 1992); and Resnick, *Education and Learning To Think.*

37. Ibid.

38. For reviews, see Carolyn Evertson, Willis Hawley, and M. Zlotnick, "Making a Difference in Educational Quality through Teacher Education," *Journal of Teacher Education* 36 (May/June 1985): 2-12; Patricia Ashton and Linda Crocker, "Systemic Study of Planned Variation: The Essential Focus of Teacher Education Reform," *Journal of Teacher Education* 38 (May/June 1987): 2-8; and Darling-Hammond, "Teaching and Knowledge."

39. McMillen, Bobbitt, and Lynch, "Teacher Training," table 2.

40. Only three states—Arkansas, North Carolina, and West Virginia—have required accreditation for all schools of education.

41. Studies have found that teacher education programs are funded at lower levels than any other department or professional school on campus. See: Gary Sykes, "Teacher Education in the United States," in *The School and the University,* edited by B. R. Clark (Los Angeles: University of California Press, 1985); and Howard Ebmeier, Susan B. Twombly, and Deborah J. Teeter, "The Comparability and Adequacy of Financial Support for Schools of Education," *Journal of Teacher Education* 42 (May/June 1991): 226-235.

42. For reviews of teacher licensing tests, see Linda Darling-Hammond, "Teaching Knowledge: How Do We Test It?" *American Educator: The Professional Journal of the American Federation of Teachers* 18 (Fall 1986): 18-21, 46; E. H. Haertel, "New Forms of Teacher Assessment," in *Review of Research in Education, Volume 17,* edited by Gerald Grant (Washington, D.C.: American Educational Research Association, 1991); W. Haney, G. Madaus, and A. Kreitzer, "Charms Talismanic: Testing Teachers for the Improvement of American Education," in *Review of Research in Education, Volume 14,* edited by Ernst Z. Rothkopf (Washington, D.C.: American Educational Research Association, 1987); C. J. MacMillan and Shirley Pendlebury, "The Florida Performance Measurement System: A Consideration," *Teachers College Record* 87 (Fall 1985): 67-78; Lee Shulman, "Knowledge and Teaching: Foundations of the New Reform," *Harvard Educational Review* 57 (January 1987): 1-22.

43. John Goodlad, *Teachers for Our Nation's Schools* (San Francisco, Calif.: Jossey-Bass, 1990); Kenneth R. Howey and Nancy L. Zimpher, *Profiles of Preservice Teacher Education* (Albany, N.Y.: State University of New York Press, 1989); The Holmes Group, *Tomorrow's Teachers: A Report of the Holmes Group* (East Lansing, Mich.: Author, 1986); The Holmes Group, *Tomorrow's Schools of Education* (Lansing, Mich.: Author, 1996); Kenneth M. Zeichner, "Traditions of Practice in U.S. Preservice Teacher Education Programs," *Teaching and Teacher Education* 9 (February 1993): 1-13.

44. Mary M. Kennedy, "The Problem of Improving Teacher Quality While Balancing Supply and Demand," in *Teacher Supply, Demand, and Quality: Policy Issues, Models, and Data Base*, edited by Erling E. Boe and Dorothy M. Gilford (Washington, D.C.: National Academy Press, 1992), 93.

45. Abraham Flexner, *The Flexner Report on Medical Education in the United States and Canada* (Washington, D.C.: The Carnegie Foundation for the Advancement of Teaching, 1910).

46. Robert W. Richburg et al., "How Much Does It Cost To Train World-Class Teachers?" *International Journal of Innovative Higher Education* (in press).

47. Gus W. Haggstrom, Linda Darling-Hammond, and David W. Grissmer, *Assessing Teacher Supply and Demand* (Santa Monica, Calif.: RAND Corporation, 1988); David W. Grissmer and Sheila Nataraj Kirby, *Teacher Attrition: The Uphill Climb to Staff the Nation's Schools* (Santa Monica, Calif.: RAND Corporation, 1987); Phillip C. Schlechty and Victor S. Vance, "Recruitment, Selection, and Retention: The Shape of the Teaching Force," *The Elementary School Journal* 83 (March 1983): 469-487.

48. Arthur E. Wise, Linda Darling-Hammond, and Barnett Berry, *Effective Teacher Selection, From Recruitment to Retention* (Santa Monica, Calif.: RAND Corporation, 1987).

49. Elizabeth Arons, personal communication, National Commission on Teaching & America's Future, April 1996.

50. George A. Johanson and Crystal J. Gips, "The Hiring Preferences of Secondary School Principals," *The High School Journal* 76 (October/November 1992): 1-16; Susanna W. Pflaum and Theodore Abramson, "Teacher Assignment, Hiring, and Preparation: Minority Teachers in New York City," *The Urban Review* 22 (March 1990): 17-31; M. Haberman, "Selecting 'Star' Teachers for Children," *Phi Delta Kappan* 76 (June 1995): 777-781; Janice Poda, *1994-95 Annual Report for the South Carolina Center for Teacher Recruitment* (Rock Hill, S.C.: South Carolina Center for Teacher Recruitment, 1995); Beverly A. Browne and Richard J. Rankin, "Predicting Employment in Education: The Relative Efficiency of National Teacher Examinations Scores and Student Teacher Ratings," *Educational and Psychological Measurement* 46 (Spring 1986): 191-197; and Wise, Darling-Hammond, and Berry, *Effective Teacher Selection.*

51. Department of Health, Education, and Welfare, *Health Professions Educational Assistance Act of 1976* (Bethesda, Md.: Health Resources Administration, 1976).

52. McMillen, Bobbitt, and Lynch, "Teacher Training, Certification, and Assignment."

53. Parmalee P. Hawk, Charles R. Coble, and Melvin Swanson, "Certification: It Does Matter," *Journal of Teacher Education* 36 (May/June 1985): 13-15; and C. A. Druva and R. D. Anderson, "Science Teacher Characteristics by Teacher Behavior and by Student Outcome: A Meta-Analysis of Research," *Journal of Research in Science Teaching* 20 (1983): 467-479.

54. C. McKnight, F. J. Crosswhite, J. A. Dossey, E. Kifer, S. O. Swafford, K. J. Travers, and T. J. Cooney, *The Underachieving Curriculum: Assessing U.S. School Mathematics from an International Perspective* (Champaign, Ill.: Stipes Publishing, 1987); Educational Testing Service, *A World of Differences: An International Assessment of Mathematics* (Princeton, N.J.: Educational Testing Service, 1989).

55. National Education Association (NEA), *Status of the American Public School Teacher, 1990-1991* (Washington, D.C.: Research Division, National Education Association, 1992).

56. Kenneth R. Howey and Nancy L. Zimpher, "Patterns in Prospective Teachers: Guides for Designing Preservice Programs," in *The Teacher Educator's Handbook: Building a Knowledge Base for the Preparation of Teachers,* edited by Frank B. Murray (San Francisco, Calif.: Jossey-Bass and the American Association of Colleges for Teacher Education, 1996).

57. Kevin Ryan, "Toward Understanding the Problem: At the Threshold of the Profession," in *Toward Meeting the Needs of Beginning Teachers,* edited by K. Howey and R. Bents (New York: Longman, 1980); Richard Tisher (ed.), *The Induction of Beginning Teachers in Australia* (Melbourne, Australia: Monash University, 1978); Frederick J. McDonald, *Study of Induction Programs for Beginning Teachers. Volume I. The Problems of Beginning Teachers: A Crisis in Training* (Princeton, N.J.: Educational Testing Service, 1980); Leslie Huling-Austin (ed.) et al., *Assisting the Beginning Teacher* (Reston, Va.: Association of Teacher Educators, 1989).

58. Linda Darling-Hammond (ed.), *Professional Development Schools: Schools for Developing a Profession* (New York: Teachers College Press, 1994); Huling-Austin (ed.) et al., *Assisting the Beginning Teacher;* Mark A. Smylie, "Redesigning Teachers' Work: Connections to the Classroom," in *Review of Research in Education, Volume 20,* edited by Linda Darling-Hammond (Alexandria, Va.: Association of Supervision and Curriculum Development, 1994); Linda Darling-Hammond, Tamar Gendler, and Arthur E. Wise, *The Teaching Internship* (Santa Monica, Calif.: RAND Corporation, 1990).

59. David P. Wright, Michael McKibbon, and Priscilla Walton, *The Effectiveness of the Teacher Trainee Program: An Alternate Route into Teaching in California* (Sacramento, Calif.: California Commission on Teacher Credentialing, 1987).

60. Sandra M. Fox and Ted J. Singletary, "Deductions about Supportive Induction," *Journal of Teacher Education* 37 (January/February 1986): 12-15; and Darling-Hammond, Gendler, and Wise, *The Teaching Internship.*

61. Generous estimates that include the costs of staff time for planning and participating in staff development estimate costs at between 1% and 3% of schools' operating budgets. See Barbara Miller, Brian Lord, and Judith Dorney, *Staff Development for Teachers: A Study of Configurations and Costs in Four Districts. Summary Report* (Newton, Mass.: Education Development Center, 1994).

62. David T. Kearns, "An Education Recovery Plan for America," *Phi Delta Kappan* 69 (April 1988); and the National Center for Education and the Economy, *America's Choice: High Skills Or Low Wages,* 64.

63. U.S. Department of Education, *Who's in Charge? Teachers' Views on Control over School Policy and Classroom Practices* (Washington, D.C.: U.S. Department of Education, 1994).

64. Willis D. Hawley, *The Education of Japanese Teachers: Lessons for the United States?* (ERIC Document Reproduction Service No. ED 280 830, 1986); Nancy Sato and Milbrey W. McLaughlin, "Context Matters: Teaching in Japan and in the United States," *Phi Delta Kappan* 73 (January 1992): 359-366; Harold W. Stevenson and James W. Stigler, *The Learning Gap: Why Our Schools Are Failing and What We Can Learn from Japanese and Chinese Education* (New York: Summit Books, 1992); Anne Ratzski, "Creating a School Community: One Model of How It Can Be Done," *American Educator: The Professional Journal of the American Federation of Teachers* 12 (Spring 1988): 38-43.

65. James W. Stigler and Harold W. Stevenson, "How Asian Teachers Polish Each Lesson to Perfection," *American Educator: The Professional Journal of the American Federation of Teachers* 15 (Spring 1991): 12-20, 43-47.

66. Ibid., 46.

67. L. Bailey, *Time Use Among Teachers: Context Paper for Germany* (paper prepared for the U.S. Department of Education, Washington, D.C., 1995); Ratzski, "Creating a School Community."

68. Matthew Miles, foreword to *Professional Development in Education: New Paradigms and Practices,* edited by Thomas R. Guskey and Michael Huberman (New York: Teachers College Press, 1995): vii-ix.

69. Darling-Hammond and McLaughlin, "Policies That Support Professional Development."

70. For reviews see, Anthony S. Bryk, Valerie E. Lee, and Julia B. Smith, "High School Organization and its Effects on Teachers and Students: An Interpretive Summary of the Research," in *Choice and Control in American Education, Volume 1*, edited by William H. Clune and J. F. Witte (New York: Falmer Press, 1990); Linda Darling-Hammond, "Restructuring Schools for Student Success," *Daedalus* 124 (Fall 1995): 153-162; Darling-Hammond, "Teaching and Knowledge"; Valerie E. Lee and Julia B. Smith, *Effects of High School Restructuring and Size on Gains in Achievement and Engagement for Early Secondary School Students* (Madison, Wis.: Center for Education Research, 1995); Fred M. Newmann and Gary G. Wehlage, *Successful School Restructuring: A Report to the Public and Educators by the Center on Organization and Restructuring of Schools* (Madison, Wis.: The Board of Regents of the University of Wisconsin System, 1995). In addition, Emily Feistritzer's analysis of the ten top-scoring states across a number of measures points out that they have greater proportions of small schools and more students taking advanced courses. See C. Emily Feistritzer, *Report Card on American Education: A State-by-State Analysis, 1972-73 to 1992-93* (Washington, D.C.: National Center on Education Information, 1993).

71. Nancy Sato, "Reflections from an Ethnographic Study of Japanese Elementary Schools," (paper presented at the American Association for Higher Education, Fifth National Conference on School/College Collaboration, Washington D.C., November 1994): 12.

72. Ratzski, "Creating a School Community."

73. See reports of the U.S. Department of Education, National Center of Education Statistics: *The Condition of Education, 1994* (Washington, D.C.: 1994) and *Digest of Education Statistics* (Washington, D.C.: 1994); and Lawrence O. Picus and M. Bhimani, "Determinants of Pupil/Teacher Ratios at School Sites: Evidence from the Schools and Staffing Survey" (paper presented at the meeting of the American Statistical Association, Washington, D.C.: National Center for Education Statistics, 1994).

74. National Center for Education Statistics, *The Digest of Education Statistics, 1995* (Washington, D.C.: U.S. Department of Education, 1995): 89.

75. Emily Feistritzer, *Report Card on American Education: A State-by-State Analysis, 1972-73 to 1992-93* (Washington, D.C.: National Center on Education Information, 1993).

76. Department of Labor, *Current Population Survey, 1986-87* (Washington, D.C.: U.S. Department of Labor, unpublished data, 1986).

77. Organization for Economic Cooperation and Development (OECD), *Education at a Glance, OECD Indicators* (Paris: OECD, 1995): 176-177.

78. Linda Darling-Hammond, "Beyond Bureaucracy: Restructuring Schools for 'High Performance,'" in *Rewards and Reform: Creating Educational Incentives That Work*, edited by Susan Fuhrman and Jennifer O'Day (San Francisco, Calif.: Jossey-Bass); Darling-Hammond, Ancess, and Falk, *Authentic Assessment;* The Center for Organizational Restructuring of Schools, *Issues in Restructuring;* Ann Lieberman (ed.), *The Work of Restructuring: Building from the Ground Up* (New York: Teachers College Press, 1995).

79. Peter Senge, *The Fifth Discipline: The Art and Practice of the Learning Organization* (New York: Doubleday, 1990).

80. Louis Harris and Associates, *A Survey of the Perspective of Elementary and Secondary School Teachers on Reform* (prepared for the Ford Foundation, New York: Louis Harris Research, 1993).

81. Ibid.

82. For reviews, see Ashton and Crocker, "Does Teacher Certification Make a Difference?"; Carolyn Evertson, Willis Hawley, and M. Zlotnick, "Making a Difference in Educational Quality through Teacher Education"; Darling-Hammond, "Teaching and Knowledge"; Martin Haberman, *An Evaluation of the Rationale for Required Teacher Education: Beginning Teachers With or Without Preparation* (prepared for the National Commission on Excellence in Teacher Education, Milwaukee, Wis.: University of Wisconsin, September 1984); D. G. Olsen, "The Quality of Prospective Teachers: Education vs. Non-education Graduates," *Journal of Teacher Education* 37 (1985): 56-59.

83. Cynthia A. Druva and Ronald D. Anderson, "Science Teacher Characteristics by Teacher Behavior and by Student Outcome: A Meta-analysis of Research," *Journal of Research in Science Teaching* 20 (May 1983): 467-479; E. G. Begle, *Critical Variables in Mathematics Education: Findings from a Survey of the Empirical Literature* (Washington, D.C.: Mathematical Association of America and National Council of Teachers of Mathematics, 1979); Victor A. Perkes, "Junior High School Science Teacher Preparation, Teaching Behavior, and Student Achievement," *Journal of Research in Science Teaching* 6 (1968): 121-126; Jon J. Denton and Lorna J. Lacina, "Quantity of Professional Education Coursework Linked with Process Measures of Student Teaching, *Teacher Education and Practice* (1984): 39-64; Thomas L. Erekson and Lowell Barr, "Alternative Credentialing: Lessons from Vocational Education," *Journal of Teacher Education* 36 (May/June 1985): 16-19; James D. Greenberg, "The Case for Teacher Education: Open and Shut," *Journal of Teacher Education* 34 (July/August 1983): 2-5; J. B. Hansen, "The Relationship of Skills and Classroom Climate of Trained and Untrained Teachers of Gifted Students" (unpublished dissertation, Purdue University, Indiana, 1988).

84. For a review, see Darling-Hammond, "Teaching and Knowledge."

85. National Center for Education Statistics, *New Teachers in the Job Market, 1991 Update* (Washington, D.C.: U.S. Department of Education, Office of Educational Research and Improvment, 1993).

86. Ibid.

87. Linda Darling-Hammond, Lisa Hudson, and Sheila N. Kirby, *Redesigning Teacher Education: Preparing Nontraditional Recruits for Science and Mathematics Teaching* (Santa Monica, Calif.: RAND Corporation, 1989); Darling-Hammond, "Teaching and Knowledge"; R. J. Coley and M. E. Thorpe, *Responding to the Crisis in Math and Science Teaching: Four Initiatives* (Princeton, N.J.: Educational Testing Service, 1985); Karen Zumwalt, *Alternate Routes to Teaching: Three Alternative Approaches* (New York: Teachers College, Columbia University, 1990).

88. For a review, see Darling-Hammond, "Teaching and Knowledge." See also, Pamela L. Grossman, "Learning to Teach Without Teacher Education," *Teachers College Record* 91 (1989): 191-208; P. O. Copley, "A Study of the Effect of Professional Education Courses on Beginning Teachers," Southwest Missouri State University (Springfield, Mo.: ERIC Document Reproduction Service No. ED 098 147, 1974); J. C. Bledsoe, J. V. Cox, and R. Burnham, *Comparison Between Selected Characteristics and Performance of Provisionally and Professional Certified Beginning Teachers in Georgia* (Washington, D.C.: U.S. Department of Health, Education, and Welfare, 1967); Robert Roth, *Teach for America 1993 Pre-Service Summer Institute: Program Review* (unpublished report, Summer 1993); Michael P. Grady, Paul Collins, and Emily L. Grady, *Teach for America 1991 Summer Institute: Evaluation Report* (unpublished report, October 1991); Linda Darling-Hammond, "Who Will Speak for the Children? How *Teach for America* Hurts Urban Schools and Students," *Phi Delta Kappan* 76 (September 1994): 21-33; J. M. Smith, "School Districts as Teacher Training Institutions in the New Jersey Alternate Route Program," (paper presented at the annual meeting of the Eastern Educational Research Association, Clearwater, Fla., February 1990); Deborah Gomez and Robert P. Grobe, "Three Years of Alternative Certification in Dallas: Where are We?" (paper presented at the annual meeting of the American Educational Research Association, Boston, Mass., April 1990); and National Center for Research on Teacher Learning, *Findings on Learning to Teach* (East Lansing, Mich.: National Center for Research on Teacher Learning, 1992).

89. National Education Association, *Status of the American Public School Teacher: 1990-91* (Washington, D.C.: National Education Association, 1992).

90. Organization for Economic Cooperation and Development (OECD), *Education at a Glance. OECD Indicators* (Paris: OECD, 1995), table P12, p. 168.

91. F. Howard Nelson and T. O'Brien, *How U.S. Teachers Measure Up Internationally: A Comparative Study of Teacher Pay, Training, and Conditions of Service* (Washington, D.C.: American Federation of Teachers, 1993); Shimahara, "Japanese Education"; Ratzki, "Creating a School Community"; Stevenson and Stigler, *The Learning Gap*.

92. National Education Association, *Status of the American Public School Teacher.*

93. Stigler and Stevenson, "Asian Teachers," 45.

94. Charles Kerchner and Douglas Mitchell, "Teaching Reform and Union Reform," *The Elementary School Journal* (March 1986): 449-470; Charles Kercher and Julia Koppich, *A Union of Professionals* (New York: Teachers College Press, 1993); Lorraine M. McDonnell, *Teacher Unions and Educational Reform* (Santa Monica, Calif.: RAND Corporation, 1988); Jerome M. Rosow and Robert Zager, *Allies in Educational Reform: How Teachers, Unions, and Administrators Can Join Forces for Better Schools* (San Francisco, Calif.: Jossey-Bass, 1989).

95. Linda Darling-Hammond, Jacqueline Ancess, and Beverly Falk (eds.), *Authentic Assessment in Action: Studies of Schools and Students at Work* (New York: Teachers College Press, 1995); The Center on Organization and Restructuring of Schools, Ann Lieberman, *The Work of Restructuring Schools;* Fred M. Newmann and Gary G. Wehlage, *Successful School Restructuring: A Report to the Public and Educators by the Center on Organization and Restructuring Schools* (Madison, Wis.: Board of Regents of the University of Wisconsin System, 1995); Judith Warren Little, "Norms of Collegiality and Experimentation: Workplace Conditions of School Success," *American Educational Research Journal* 19 (Fall 1982): 215-340.

96. Ann Sayas, "To Grow a Teacher," *Basic Education* 40 (April 1996): 8-9.

97. In 1986, seminal reports were issued by the Carnegie Forum on Education and the Economy, *A Nation Prepared: Teachers for the 21st Century* (Washington, D.C.: Carnegie Forum on Education and the Economy, 1986); The Holmes Group, *Tomorrow's Teachers;* and the National Governors' Association, *Time for Results: Task Force on Teaching* (Washington, D.C.: National Governors' Association, Center for Policy Research and Analysis, 1986).

98. Richard J. Murnane and David Cohen, "Merit Pay and the Evaluation Problem: Why Most Merit Pay Plans Fail and a Few Survive," *Harvard Educational Review* 56 (February 1986): 1-17; Susan Moore Johnson, "Incentives for Teachers: What Motivates, What Matters?" *Educational Administration Quarterly* 22 (Summer 1986): 54-79; and Allen Odden, "Incentives, School Organization, and Teacher Compensation," in *Rewards and Reform: Creating Educational Incentives That Work,* edited by Susan H. Fuhrman and Jennifer A. O'Day (San Francisco, Calif.: Jossey-Bass, 1996).

99. Willis D. Hawley, "New Goals and Changed Roles: Re-visioning Teacher Education, *Educational Record* 74 (1993): 26-31; Linda Darling-Hammond et al. Background research for the National Commission on Teaching & America's Future, (forthcoming).

100. In a companion study to this report that is forthcoming, the National Commission has investigated notably effective teacher education programs. Of seven programs identified by virtue of reputational surveys and student outcome data, all but one—Alverno College—were graduate-level programs. The remaining programs are located at Bank Street College, Trinity University, the University of California-Berkeley, the University of Southern Maine, the University of Virginia, and Wheelock College.

101. For data on effectiveness and retention see Michael Andrew, "The Differences between Graduates of Four-Year and Five-Year Teacher Preparation Programs," *Journal of Teacher Education* 41 (March/April 1990): 45-51; Thomas Baker, "A Survey of Four-Year and Five-Year Program Graduates and Their Principals," *Southeastern Regional Association of Teacher Educators (SRATE) Journal* 2 (Summer 1993): 28-33; Michael Andrew and Richard L. Schwab, "Has Reform in Teacher Education Influenced Teacher Performance?: An Outcome Assessment of Graduates of Eleven Teacher Education Programs," *Action in Teacher Education* 17 (Fall 1995): 43-53; Jon J. Denton and William H. Peters, "Program Assessment Report: Curriculum Evaluation of a Non-Traditional Program for Certifying Teachers" (Texas A&M University, College Station, Texas, 1988); and Hyun-Seok Shin, "Estimating Future Teacher Supply: An Application of Survival Analysis" (paper presented at the annual meeting of the American Educational Research Association, New Orleans, Louisiana, April 1994).

102. American Association of Colleges for Teacher Education (AACTE), *Teacher Education Pipeline III: Schools, Colleges, and Departments of Education Enrollments by Race, Ethnicity, and Gender* (Washington, D.C.: AACTE, 1994); "Review of Program Enrollment Data" (unpublished data collected by the National Commission on Teaching & America's Future, Teachers College, Columbia University, New York, 1995). See also: Linda Darling-Hammond, Mary E. Dilworth, and Marcella L. Bullmaster, "Educators of Color" (paper prepared for the Invitational Conference on Recruiting, Preparing, and Retaining Persons of Color in the Teaching Profession, Office of Educational Research and Improvement, Washington, D.C., January 1996).

103. For reviews, see Cassandra L. Book, "Professional Development Schools," in *The Handbook of Research on Teacher Education,* second edition, edited by John Sikula (New York: Association of Teacher Educators, 1996), and Darling-Hammond, *Professional Development Schools: Schools for Developing a Profession.*

104. Darling-Hammond, *Professional Development Schools;* Huling-Austin et al., *Assisting the Beginning Teacher;* Mark A. Smylie, "Redesigning Teachers' Work: Connections to the Classroom," in *Review of Research in Education,* edited by Linda Darling-Hammond (Washington, D.C.: American Educational Research Association, 1994).

105. Wise, Darling-Hammond, and Gendler, *The Teaching Internship;* Joan E. Talbert and Milbrey W. McLaughlin, "Understanding Teaching in Context," in *Teaching for Understanding: Challenges for Policy and Practice,* edited by D. K. Cohen, M. W. McLaughlin, and J. E. Talbert (San Francisco, Calif.: Jossey-Bass, 1993); and Susan Rosenholtz, *Teacher's Workplace: The Social Organization of Schools* (New York: Longman, 1989).

106. National Foundation for the Improvement of Education (NFIE), *Teachers Take Charge of Their Learning: Transforming Professional Development for Student Success* (Washington, D.C.: NFIE, 1996).

107. Drew Lindsay, "Money Talks—Reforming Professional Development Programs," *Education Week* 15 (April 17, 1996): 19-24.

108. Randy Ross, *Effective Teacher Development through Salary Incentives* (Santa Monica, Calif.: RAND Corporation, 1994).

109. Ann Lieberman, "Practices That Support Teacher Development: Transforming Conceptions of Professional Learning," *Phi Delta Kappan* 76 (April 1995): 591-596; Linda Darling-Hammond and Milbrey W. McLaughlin, "Policies That Support Professional Development in an Era of Reform," *Phi Delta Kappan* 76 (April 1995): 596-604; and Judith Warren Little, *Teachers Professional Development in a Climate of Educational Reform* (New York: Teachers College, Columbia University, National Center for Restructuring Education, Schools, and Teaching, 1993).

110. Ann Lieberman and Milbrey W. McLaughlin, "Networks for Educational Change: Powerful and Problematic," *Phi Delta Kappan* 73 (1992): 673-677; Judith Warren Little and Milbrey W. McLaughlin, *Urban Math Collaboratives: As Teachers Tell It* (Stanford, Calif.: Center for Research on the Context of Teaching, 1991).

111. Richard F. Elmore, "Staff Development and Instructional Improvement: Community District 2, New York City" (paper prepared for the National Commission on Teaching & America's Future, March 1996).

112. This discussion of compensation for knowledge and skills is informed by Allan Odden and Sharon Conley, "Restructuring Teacher Compensation Systems," in *Rethinking School Finance: An Agenda for the 1990s,* edited by Allan Odden (San Francisco, Calif.: Jossey-Bass, 1992); and Sharon Conley and Allan Odden, "Linking Teacher Compensation to Teacher Career Development," *Educational Evaluation and Policy Analysis* 17 (Summer 1995): 219-237.

113. Linda Darling-Hammond, "The Implications of Testing Policy for Quality and Equality," *Phi Delta Kappan* 73 (November 1991): 220-225.

114. Ibid. See also, Richard L. Allington and Anne McGill-Franzen, "Unintended Effects of Educational Reform in New York," *Educational Policy* 6 (December 1992): 397-

414; Linda Darling-Hammond and Carol Ascher, *Accountability in Big City Schools* (New York: National Center for Restructuring Education, Schools, and Teaching and Institute for Urban and Minority Education, Teachers College, Columbia University, 1991); Lorrie A. Shepard and Mary Lee Smith, "Escalating Academic Demand in Kindergarten: Counterproductive Policies, *Elementary School Journal* 89 (November 1988): 135-145; and Frank Smith et al., *High School Admission and the Improvement of Schooling* (New York: New York City Board of Education, 1986).

115. Teacher evaluation systems in Rochester, New York, and in Oregon also have begun to look at student work in relation to teaching practice as a key aspect of understanding teacher effectiveness. Rochester Teachers Association, *Performance Appraisal Review for Teachers (PART)* (Rochester, N.Y.: Career in Teaching Governing Panel, October 1995); H. Del Schalock, Mark D. Schalock, David Myton, and Jerry Girod, "Focusing on Learning Gains by Pupils Taught: A Central Feature of Oregon's Outcome-Based Approach to the Initial Preparation and Licensure of Teachers," *Journal of Personnel Evaluation in Education* 7 (1993): 135-158.

116. Rochester Teachers Association, Ibid.

117. Arthur E. Wise, Linda Darling-Hammond, Milbrey W. McLaughlin, Harriet T. Bernstein, *Teacher Evaluation: A Study of Effective Practices* (Santa Moncia, Calif.: RAND Corporation, 1984); Darling-Hammond, Wise, and Pease, "Teacher Evaluation in the Organizational Context."

118. David T. Kearns, "An Education Recovery Plan for America," *Phi Delta Kappan* 69 (April 1988): 565-570.

119. National Education Commission on Time and Learning, *Prisoners of Time* (Washington, D.C.: U.S. Department of Education, 1994).

120. National Center for Education Statistics, *Digest of Education Statistics,* 87. "Staff" includes district employees, school administrators, teachers, instructional aides, guidance counselors, librarians, and support staff.

121. J. D. Fletcher, "The Effectiveness and Cost of Interactive Videodisc Instruction," *Machine-Mediated Learning* 3 (1989): 361-385; Jay Sivin-Kachala and Ellen R. Bialo, *Report on the Effectiveness of Technology in Schools, 1995-1996* (Washington, D.C.: Software Publishers Association, 1995).

122. Office of Technology Assessment, *Teachers and Technology: Making the Connection* (Washington, D.C.: U.S. Congress, 1995).

123. Linda Darling-Hammond, "Policy for Restructuring," in *The Work of Restructuring Schools: Building from the Ground Up,* edited by Ann Lieberman (New York: Teachers College Press, 1995); Ohio Department of Education, *Venture Capital in Ohio Schools: Building Commitment and Capacity for School Renewal* (Columbus, Ohio: Ohio Department of Education, 1995); and Ohio Department of Education and Building Excellent Schools for Today and Tomorrow (BEST), "Profiles of 1995 Ohio's BEST Practices" (Columbus, Ohio: Ohio Department of Education, 1995).

124. Carnegie Task Force on Learning in the Primary Grades, *Years of Promise: A Comprehensive Learning Strategy for America's Children* (New York: Carnegie Foundation, in press).

125. Richard Rothstein with Karen Hawley Miles, *Where's the Money Gone? Changes in the Level and Composition of Education Spending* (Washington, D.C.: Economic Policy Institute, 1995).

126. Karen Hawley Miles, "Freeing Resources for Improving Schools: A Case Study of Teacher Allocation in Boston Public Schools," *Educational Evaluation and Policy Analysis* 17 (Winter 1995): 476-493.

Grateful acknowledgment is made to the following for permission to reprint copyrighted material:

John Synder and Michelle Renee Houy quoted in the Milken Family Foundation, *The Impact of the Educator* (Santa Monica, Calif.: Milken Family Foundation, 1995), 16, 102. Material adapted and reprinted with permission. Copyright © 1995 by the Milken Family Foundation.

Lee Shulman quoted in "Autonomy and Obligation," by Lee S. Shulman and Gary Sykes (eds.), *The Handbook of Teaching and Policy* (New York: Longman, 1983), 504.

Robert Fiersen quoted in "Teacher-Quality Issues: A Few More Suggestions," Letters to the Editor, *Education Week* 14 (September 6, 1995): 42. Material adapted and reprinted with permission. Copyright © 1995 by Education Week.

W. Dean Eastman and Verleeta Wooten quoted in *I Am A Teacher: A Tribute to America's Teachers* by David Marshall Marquis and Robin Sachs (New York: Simon and Schuster, 1990), 24, 81.

Cynthia Ellwood quoted in "Preparing Teachers for Education in a Diverse World," *Rethinking Schools: An Agenda for Social Change*, edited by David Levine et al. (New York: The New Press, 1995), 246-247. Material adapted and reprinted with permission from *Rethinking Schools: An Agenda for Change*, Rethinking Schools, 1001 E. Keefe Ave., Milwaukee, WI 53212; 414-964-9646.

Lynne Davis and Dana Richardson from Betsy Golden, *Jewels of the Journey: Twelve High School Seniors' Impressions of Best Teachers and Most Significant Lessons Learned* (Unpublished doctoral dissertation, Teachers College, Columbia University, 1996).

The Holmes Group quoted in *Tomorrow's Schools of Education* (East Lansing, Mich.: The Holmes Group, 1995), 9.

John Goodlad quoted in *Teachers for Our Nation's Schools* (San Francisco, Calif.: Jossey-Bass, 1990), 3-4.

Lou Gerstner quoted in "Education in America," remarks delivered at the National Governors' Association Annual Meeting in Burlington, Vermont, July 30, 1995.

James Delisle quoted in "Too Smart to Be a Teacher: Why Do Those Who Should Know Better Keep Selling the Profession Short?" *Education Week* 15 (September 13, 1995): 32. Material adapted and reprinted with permission. Copyright © 1995 by Education Week.

Irasema Ortega-Crawford quoted in Recruiting New Teachers, Inc., *Careers in Teaching Handbook* (Belmont, Mass.: Recruiting New Teachers, 1993), p. 4-5.

Gary D. Fenstermacher quoted in "The Place of Alternative Certification in the Education of Teachers," in *The Alternative Certification of Teachers,* Teacher Education Monograph No. 14, edited by Willis D. Hawley (Washington, D.C.: ERIC Clearinghouse on Teacher Education, 1992): 182.

Appendix A: Meetings and Forums of the Commission

The Commission held six meetings at which teachers, administrators, researchers, and policymakers from across the country shared and added their expertise. During this two-year period, nine forums were held for additional feedback, at the annual meetings and conventions of the Commission's policy, parent, community, and teacher education advisory groups. Supplementary meetings and focus groups of parents and teachers were also held.

Meetings

November 15, 1994
Cincinnati, Ohio

November 19-20, 1995
New York, New York

June 9-10, 1995
Cullowhee, North Carolina
Asheville, North Carolina

March 12-13, 1995
New York, New York

January 21-22, 1996
New York, New York

May 17-18, 1996
Raleigh, North Carolina

Forums

February 14, 1995

American Association of Colleges for Teacher Education (AACTE)
Annual meeting, Washington, D.C.

July 18, 1995

National Conference of State Legislatures (NCSL)
Annual conference, Milwaukee, Wisconsin

July 28, 1995

American Federation of Teachers (AFT)
QuEST conference, Washington, D.C.

October 7, 1995

American Association of School Personnel Administrators (AASPA)
Annual meeting, New Orleans, Louisiana

October 14, 1995

National Association of State Boards of Education (NASBE)
Annual conference, Pittsburgh, Pennsylvania

October 27, 1995

American Association of Higher Education (AAHE)
School-College Partnership meeting, Washington, D.C.

November 4, 1995

Recruiting New Teachers, Inc. (RNT), Pathways to Teaching
Precollegiate Teacher Recruitment symposium, Pasadena, California

February 24, 1996

National Association of Secondary School Principals (NASSP)
Annual convention, San Francisco, California

July 28, 1996

National Conference of State Legislatures (NCSL)
Annual conference, St. Louis, Missouri

Supplementary Meetings

October 17, 1996
Policy Advisory Group
Alexandria, Virginia

March 22, 1996
Parent-Community Advisory Group
Washington, D.C.

April 22, 1996
Focus groups of parents and teachers
Wilmington, Delaware

Appendix B: Presentations to the Commission

Linnette Aponte
Teacher Intern, PS 87, New York, New York

Deborah Loewenberg Ball
Professor, Michigan State University

J. Michael Brandt
Superintendent of Schools, Cincinnati Public Schools

Sharon Draper
Teacher, Walnut Hills High School, Cincinnati, Ohio

Carol Edwards
Director of Programs
National Foundation for the Improvement of Education

Richard Elmore
Consortium for Policy Research in Education
Graduate School of Education, Harvard University

Jerry Franson
Senior Fellow, North Carolina Center for the Advancement of Teaching, Cullowhee, North Carolina

Jane Hand
Principal, PS 87, New York, New York

Denise Hewitt
Professional Issues Representative
Cincinnati Federation of Teachers

Harry Judge
Professor Emeritus, Oxford University

Rosemarie Kolstad
Professor, East Texas State University

Magdalene Lampert
Professor, The University of Michigan-Ann Arbor

Helen Lee
Teacher, PS 87, New York, New York

Susan Lockwood
Florida Center for Teachers, Tampa, Florida

Phillip Middleton
Teacher, Duplin County, North Carolina

Tom Mooney
President, Cincinnati Federation of Teachers

Scott Muri
Teacher, Avery County Middle School, North Carolina

Allan Odden
Professor and Co-Director, Consortium for Policy Research in Education, University of Wisconsin-Madison

Trudi Orgas
Teacher, PS 87, New York, New York

Sima Rabinowitz
Minnesota Humanities Commission's Teacher Institute
St. Paul, Minnesota

Sharon Porter Robinson
Assistant Secretary for Educational Research and Improvement
U.S. Department of Education

Larry Rowedder
President, Mayerson Academy for Human Resource Development, Cincinnati, Ohio

Nancy Sato
Center for Research on the Context of Secondary School Teaching, School of Education, Stanford University

Frances Schoonmaker
Co-Director, Preservice Preparation Program in Elementary Education, Teachers College, Columbia University

Melisande Schwartzfarb
Teacher, PS 87, New York, New York

Penny Smith
Professor, University of North Carolina-Greensboro

Cooper Snyder
Senator, 14th District, State of Ohio
Chairman, Ohio Senate Education and Retirement Committee

Jean Spruell
Teacher, Oak City, North Carolina

Linda Starkweather
Teacher, Lincoln Heights Elementary School
Fuquay-Varina, North Carolina

Carolyn Toben
Center for the Advancement and Renewal of Educators
San Francisco, California

Mary Jo Utley
Director, North Carolina Center for the Advancement of Teaching, Cullowhee, North Carolina

Robert Yinger
Professor and Director, Cincinnati Initiative for Teacher Education, University of Cincinnati

Appendix C: Policy, Parent, and Community Advisers

Gordon Ambach
Council of Chief State School Officers

Bob Bhaerman
Quality Education Project for Minorities

Julie Bell
National Conference of State Legislatures

Marsha Berger
American Federation of Teachers

Ronald Blackburn-Moreno
ASPIRA Association, Inc.

Charles Bremer
National Black Caucus of State Legislators

Gene Carter
Association of Supervision and
Curriculum Development

Michael Casserly
Council of the Great City Schools

John Cawthorne
National Urban League

Eric Cooper
National Urban Alliance

Jacqueline Danzberger
Institute for Educational Leadership

Sheryl Denbo
National Coalition of Educational
Equity Advocates

Timothy Dyer
National Association of Secondary
School Principals

Ramona Edelin
National Urban Coalition

Marion Wright Edelman
Children's Defense Fund

Harold Fisher
National School Boards Association

Calvin Frazier
Education Commission of the States

Michael Gordon
National Panhellenic Council

Paul Houston
American Association of School
Administrators

David Imig
American Association of Colleges for
Teacher Education

Connie Koprowicz
National Conference of State Legislatures

Ivan Lanier
National Black Caucus of State Legislators

H. Michael Lemmons
National Congress of Black Churches

Kay Luzier
National PTA

Ginny Markell
National PTA

Shirley McBay
Quality Education Project for Minorities

Ann McLaren
National Education Association

Charles Marshall
Association for School, College, and
University Staffing

Jean Miller
Council of Chief State School Officers

Evelyn K. Moore
National Black Child Development
Institute

Frank Newman
Education Commission of the States

Paul Ramsey
Educational Testing Service

Judith Rényi
National Foundation for the Improvement
of Education

Mark Rigdon
National Governors' Association

Virginia Roach
National Association of State Boards of
Education

Herb Salinger
American Association of School Personnel
Administrators

Samuel Sava
National Association of Elementary
School Principals

Thomas Shannon
National School Boards Association

Dennis Sparks
National Staff Development Council

Scott Thomson
National Policy Board for Educational
Administration

Joseph Vaughan (observer)
Office of Educational Research and
Improvement, U.S. Department of
Education

Tony Wagner
Institute for Responsive Education

Victor Young
The Learning Communities Network, Inc.

Appendix D: Contributors to Commission Research

Nabeel Alsalam
National Center for Education Statistics

Jerry D. Bailey
School of Education, University of Kansas

Robert Baldwin
Social Security Administration

Mary Dean Barringer
National Board for Professional Teaching Standards

Sharon Bobbitt
Office of Educational Research and Improvement, U.S. Department of Education

Ann Bradley
Education Week

Richard L. Clark
Center for Educational Renewal, University of Washington

Noreen Connell
Education Priorities Panel

Tom Corcoran
Consortium for Policy Research in Education

Christine E. Deer
University of Technology, Sydney

Betty Duvall
Community College Liaison, U.S. Department of Education

C. Emily Feistritzer
National Center for Education Information

Mary Futrell
George Washington University

Matthew Gandal
American Federation of Teachers

Jewell Gould
American Federation of Teachers

Paul Goren
National Governors' Association

Katie Haycock
American Association for Higher Education

Richard Ingersoll
The University of Georgia

Bill Ingram
National School Boards Association

Jack Jackson
Ohio Department of Education

Joanne Kogan-Krell
National Board for Professional Teaching Standards

Marsha Levine
Professional Development Schools Project, National Council for Accreditation of Teacher Education

Anne C. Lewis
Freelance writer

Dreama Love
National PTA

David H. Monk
Cornell University

John W. Moore
Indiana State University

Michelle Moser
Robert F. Wagner Graduate School of Public Service, New York University

Patrick O'Rourke
Hammond Federation of Teachers, Hammond, Indiana

Ray Pecheone
Connecticut Board of Education

Jon Reischel
National Board for Professional Teaching Standards

Diana W. Rigden
Council for Basic Education

Carl Schmidt
National Data Resource Center

Eileen M. Sclan
Long Island University

Nobuo K. Shimahara
Rutgers University

Hugh Sockett
Institute for Educational Transformation

Carol F. Stoel
American Association for Higher Education

James Stigler
University of California, Los Angeles

Gary Sykes
Michigan State University

Adam Urbanski
Rochester Teachers Association, Rochester, New York

Joe Wyatt
Vanderbilt University

Appendix E: Commissioned Papers

Eight technical papers were commissioned to synthesize research and inform the Commission on issues of teacher learning and professional development; policy issues in teacher development; labor-management issues in school reform; teacher recruitment, selection and retention; teacher education; and teaching for diverse learners. The report draws upon each of these papers. They will be published in a separate volume.

Aligning Teacher Education with Contemporary K-12 Reform Visions
Deborah Loewenberg Ball, Michigan State University
Magdalene Lampert, University of Michigan

Developing Practice, Developing Practitioners: Toward a Practice-Based Theory of Professional Education
Deborah Loewenberg Ball, Michigan State University
David K. Cohen, Michigan State University

Organizing the Other Half of Teaching
Julia E. Koppich, University of California-Berkeley
Charles T. Kerchner, Claremont Graduate School

Organizing Schools for Teacher Learning
Judith Warren Little, University of California-Berkeley

Preparing Teachers for Diversity: Historical Perspectives, Current Trends, and Future Directions
Gloria Ladson-Billings, University of Wisconsin-Madison

The Problem of Enactment
Mary M. Kennedy, Michigan State University

Staff Development and Instructional Improvement: Community District 2, New York City
Richard F. Elmore, Harvard University

Transforming Teacher Recruitment, Selection, and Induction
Barnett Berry, University of South Carolina
David Haselkorn, Recruiting New Teachers, Inc.

Appendix F: State-by-State Report Card, Indicators of Attention to Teaching Quality, July 1996

State		Total Quality Indicators (out of 10)	Investments in Teacher Quality		
			Unqualified Hires[1] (% of new hires who are unlicensed) * = 2% or less	Out-of-Field Teaching[2] (% of math teachers without at least a minor) (*@ less than 20%)	Teachers as a % of Instructional Staff[3] (-/+ % from previous year) (* @ 60% or higher)
Alabama		0	09%	21%	52.5 -
Alaska	★	1	07%	63%	47.6 +
Arizona	★	1	02% *	31%	51.2 +
Arkansas	★★★	3	09%	20%	52.2 +
California	★★★★	4	13%	51%	51.6 +
Colorado	★★	2	04%	35%	53.7 +
Connecticut	★★★	3	00% *	11% *	54.5 -
Delaware	★	1	00% *	—	54.6 -
District of Columbia	★★	2	53%	—	58.2 +
Florida	★	1	17%	39%	48.8 =
Georgia	★★★★	4	07%	35%	48.3 -
Hawaii	★★	2	10%	51%	61.8 + *
Idaho	★	1	04%	25%	59.4 -
Illinois	★	1	08%	28%	54.2 -
Indiana	★★★★	4	02% *	30%	48.1 -
Iowa	★★★★★	5	02% *	18% *	52.5 =
Kansas	★★	2	00% *	13% *	53.8 -
Kentucky	★★★★★★	6	01% *	17% *	47.5 +
Louisiana	★	1	23%	31%	49.5 -
Maine	★★	2	09%	33%	52.6 -
Maryland	★	1	29%	40%	55.0 +
Massachusetts	★	1	11%	37%	55.9 -
Michigan	★★★	3	04%	33%	48.9 +
Minnesota	★★★★★★★	7	00% *	14% *	62.7 = *
Mississippi	★	1	09%	23%	47.5 +
Missouri	★★	2	00% *	15% *	48.4 +
Montana	★	1	05%	14% *	54.6 +
Nebraska	★★	2	08%	26%	53.2 +
Nevada	★★	2	07%	37%	58.1 +
New Hampshire	★	1	05%	—	54.2 -
New Jersey	★★	2	00% *	34%	52.8 =
New Mexico	★	1	08%	47%	49.2 -
New York	★	1	05%	34%	51.1 +
North Carolina	★★★★	4	03%	24%	52.0 -
North Dakota	★★	2	00% *	21%	56.0 -
Ohio	★★★★	4	00% *	17% *	53.5 +
Oklahoma	★★★	3	03%	34%	50.3 -
Oregon	★★★★	4	02% *	33%	52.0 -
Pennsylvania	★★★	3	00% *	14% *	53.2 +
Rhode Island	★★★	3	00% *	—	65.2 + *
South Carolina	★	1	14%	29%	53.2 -
South Dakota	★	1	03%	20%	55.5 -
Tennessee	★★★	3	00% *	28%	49.2 -
Texas		0	12%	30%	52.0 +
Utah	★	1	10%	44%	54.0 =
Vermont	★★	2	00% *	—	49.3 -
Virginia		0	15%	34%	54.7 +
Washington	★★★	3	01% *	46%	51.3 -
West Virginia	★★	2	10%	16% *	54.6 =
Wisconsin	★★★★	4	00% *	17% *	53.5 -
Wyoming	★★	2	03%	25%	51.6 +

Attention to Teacher Education & Induction | Attention to Teaching Standards

Professional Accreditation[4] % of NCATE accredited programs (* @ 80% or more)	Student Teaching[5] # of required weeks (* @ 12 weeks or more)	Student Teaching[6] Experience with diverse learners (* with yes)	New Teacher Induction[7] State-required and funded (* with yes)	Professional Standards Board[8] (* with yes)	Nationally Certified Teachers[9] (*with 20 or more)	Incentives for National Board Certification[10] — Link to Licensing	Support for Professional Development	Financial Rewards (* with at least two types of incentives)
60%	10	no	no		7	no	yes	no
20%	12*	no	no		3	no	no	no
0%	10 e	no	no			yes	no	no
100%*	12*	yes*	no			yes	no	no
18%	15*	yes*	partial	yes *	56*	no	no	no
41%	—	yes*	pending		18	yes	yes	no *
13%	10	no	yes*		11	no	no	no
25%	09	no	proposed			no	no	no
71%	09	yes*	yes*			no	no	no
43%	12*	no	partial		5	no	no	no
53%	10	yes*	yes*	yes *	8	yes	yes	yes *
00%	09	no	no	yes *		no	no	no
83%*	10 e	no	no		2	no	no	no
30%	08	yes*	no		5	no	yes	no
84%*	10	no	yes*	yes *	5	no	no	no
23%	12*	no	no	yes *	10	yes	yes	no *
55%	10	no	piloting		11	no	no	no
42%	12*	no	yes*	yes *	1	yes	no	yes *
60%	06 e	no	yes*		5	no	no	no
23%	15*	yes*	no		2	no	no	no
14%	08 e	no	no			yes	yes	no *
19%	06 e	yes*	no			no	yes	no
48%	08 e	yes*	partial		54*	yes	yes	no *
84%*	08 e	yes*	yes*	yes *	14	no	no	no
67%	00	no	no		4	no	yes	yes *
50%	00	no	partial			no	no	no
38%	10 e	no	proposed			yes	no	no
87%*	14*	no	no		1	no	no	no
100%*	08	no	no	yes *		no	no	no
38%	—	yes*	no			no	no	no
36%	16*	no	no		8	no	no	no
38%	06 e	no	no		22*	yes	no	no
05%	—	no	no		24*	no	no	no
96%*	10	yes*	proposed		65*	yes	yes	yes *
70%	10	no	no	yes *		no	no	no
40%	10	yes*	proposed		6	yes	yes	yes *
81%*	12*	no	no			yes	no	yes *
36%	15*	yes*	no	yes *		no	no	no
20%	12*	no	no		2	no	no	no
25%	10 e	yes*	no		1	yes	no	no
21%	12*	no	no		8	no	no	no
67%	10	yes*	no			no	no	no
46%	15*	yes*	no			no	no	no
18%	10	no	partial		2	no	no	no
83%*	08 e	no	no			no	no	no
08%	12*	no	no			no	no	no
38%	10	no	partial		6	no	yes	no
52%	08	yes*	yes*		7	no	no	no
79%	00	no	partial	yes *		no	no	no
38%	18*	yes*	no			no	no	no
100%*	—	no	no	yes *		no	no	no

Appendix F: State-by-State Report Card Notes

1. **% of New Hires Who Are Unlicensed**—Percentage of newly hired teachers not certified in main assignment field. (Source: U.S. Depatrment of Education, National Center for Education Statistics, *1990-91 Schools and Staffing Survey,* Unpublished tabulations, National Data Resource Center)

2. **% of Math Teachers Without At Least a Subject Matter Minor**—The percentage of public school teachers who taught one or more classes in mathematics without at least a minor in the field. (Source: U.S. Department of Education, National Center for Education Statistics, *1990-91 Schools and Staffing Survey;* Richard P. Ingersoll, *Schools and Staffing Survey: Teacher Supply, Teacher Qualifications, and Teacher Turnover, 1990*)

3. **Teachers as a Percent of Staff**—Percentage of instructional and administrative staff who are teachers, fall 1994. NOTE: Other support staff—e.g., bus drivers, maintenance, and food service—are **not** included. (Source: U.S. Department of Education, National Center for Education Statistics, *Statistics in Brief— Public School Student, Staff, and Graduate Counts by State, School Year 1994-95,* May 1996)

4. **Professional Accreditation**—The percentage of teacher education institutions that are accredited by NCATE (National Council for the Accreditation of Teacher Education). (Source: National Council for the Accreditation of Teacher Education, June 1996)

5. **Required Number of Weeks of Full-Time Student Teaching**—Number of weeks of student teaching required by the state. An (e) indicates an estimate based on required clock or college semester credit hours. May vary by grade level. (Source: National Association of State Directors of Teacher Education and Certification: Manual on Certification and Preparation of Educational Personnel in the United States and Canada, 1996-97)

6. **Student Teaching Experience Includes Teaching Special Needs Students in Diverse Settings**—Whether or not a state requires that the student teaching experience include work with diverse learners who are either special/exceptional students or in a multicultural setting. (Source: National Association of State Directors of Teacher Education and Certification, *Manual on Certification and Preparation of Educational Personnel in the United States and Canada, 1996-97*)

7. **New Teacher Induction or Mentoring Programs**—Indicates whether or not a state requires that new teachers participate in a formal induction or mentoring program that is state-funded with state or district training for mentors. (Developed from current survey of state-by-state professional development policies and practices. The Consortium for Policy Research in Education, University of Pennsylvania - July 1996)

8. **Professional Standards Boards**—Whether or not a state has established an independent professional teacher standards boards to set standards for teacher education and licensing. (Source: National Council for Accreditation of Teacher Education, 1995)

9. **Nationally Certified Teachers**—Number of National Board-Certified teachers by state. (Source: National Board for Professional Teaching Standards, Detroit, Michigan, July 1996)

10. **Incentives for NBPTS Certification**—Whether or not state policy has been established to (1) link National Board Certification to licensing (e.g., portability, license renewal, or advanced certification status); (2) support participation in National Board assessments as a prominent form of professional development; and (3) financially reward National Board-Certified teachers. (Source: National Board for Professional Teaching Standards, Detroit, Michigan, July 1996)

Appendix F: Percentage of Newly Hired Unlicensed Teachers, by State, 1991-92

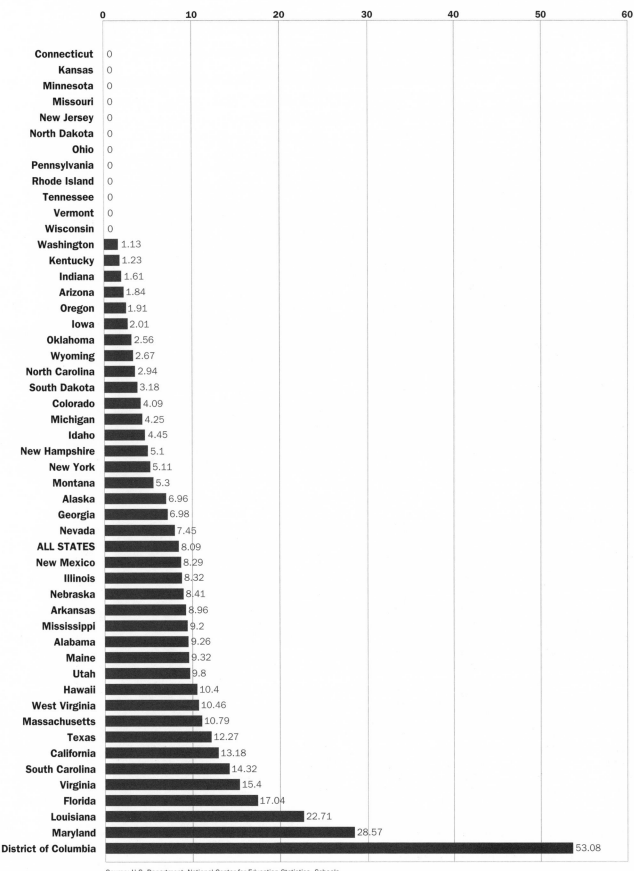

State	Percentage
Connecticut	0
Kansas	0
Minnesota	0
Missouri	0
New Jersey	0
North Dakota	0
Ohio	0
Pennsylvania	0
Rhode Island	0
Tennessee	0
Vermont	0
Wisconsin	0
Washington	1.13
Kentucky	1.23
Indiana	1.61
Arizona	1.84
Oregon	1.91
Iowa	2.01
Oklahoma	2.56
Wyoming	2.67
North Carolina	2.94
South Dakota	3.18
Colorado	4.09
Michigan	4.25
Idaho	4.45
New Hampshire	5.1
New York	5.11
Montana	5.3
Alaska	6.96
Georgia	6.98
Nevada	7.45
ALL STATES	8.09
New Mexico	8.29
Illinois	8.32
Nebraska	8.41
Arkansas	8.96
Mississippi	9.2
Alabama	9.26
Maine	9.32
Utah	9.8
Hawaii	10.4
West Virginia	10.46
Massachusetts	10.79
Texas	12.27
California	13.18
South Carolina	14.32
Virginia	15.4
Florida	17.04
Louisiana	22.71
Maryland	28.57
District of Columbia	53.08

Source: U.S. Department, National Center for Education Statistics, Schools and Staffing Survey, 1991-92.

Appendix F: Percentage of Public High School Teachers Who Taught One or More Classes in a Field Without at Least a Minor in that Field, by Field and State: 1990-91

	Math	Science	Social Studies	English	Foreign Lang.	Voc. Ed.	Art/Music	Phys. Ed.
Total Public	30.5	16.9	16.9	21.9	15.4	19.0	15.4	14.6
Alabama	21.2	18.6	22.2	22.6	—	20.1	22.1	7.2
Alaska	63.3	22.3	34.9	27.7	—	38.1	—	48.5
Arizona	30.7	17.8	21.0	21.2	—	14.9	26.2	21.5
Arkansas	20.2	14.6	25.3	21.9	—	11.6	6.6	8.9
California	51.0	18.2	16.2	29.0	22.5	27.5	20.1	33.3
Colorado	35.1	18.4	21.6	20.8	13.2	15.8	14.2	10.3
Connecticut	11.1	4.6	14.7	13.0	0.0	27.4	—	—
Delaware	—	—	—	—	—	—	—	—
District of Columbia	—	—	—	—	—	—	—	—
Florida	38.8	29.6	20.7	16.6	—	30.7	26.5	10.9
Georgia	35.0	21.7	19.6	21.4	22.0	22.3	—	22.6
Hawaii	50.6	—	—	—	—	—	—	—
Idaho	24.5	9.7	18.3	19.1	—	14.3	26.2	11.7
Illinois	27.5	16.8	20.1	26.0	8.0	16.2	8.5	5.9
Indiana	29.7	15.3	5.5	12.9	24.0	13.1	9.4	8.3
Iowa	18.0	21.6	8.8	16.5	17.7	6.2	12.7	16.7
Kansas	13.0	17.7	25.6	24.0	—	8.5	6.4	8.3
Kentucky	17.4	19.8	11.2	19.2	—	8.3	15.4	—
Louisiana	30.9	24.2	19.8	23.8	—	12.4	—	17.3
Maine	32.9	19.8	15.2	27.4	—	21.8	24.0	—
Maryland	39.6	22.6	19.0	29.7	—	28.2	—	—
Massachusetts	36.8	16.7	14.3	15.9	10.5	44.2	—	—
Michigan	32.8	22.1	20.0	25.3	—	13.9	16.6	14.6
Minnesota	14.2	8.3	14.1	7.1	9.5	6.9	9.4	9.6
Mississippi	22.8	9.2	12.8	20.4	—	23.9	8.6	15.5
Missouri	14.9	22.9	13.8	19.6	22.3	15.3	15.0	18.9
Montana	13.6	21.7	12.9	15.8	20.7	12.1	16.2	7.1
Nebraska	26.2	10.8	22.3	20.7	—	6.7	14.1	19.1
Nevada	37.3	—	20.9	25.3	—	23.4	—	—
New Hampshire	—	—	—	2.1	—	—	—	—
New Jersey	33.6	19.7	15.3	25.0	9.3	20.6	17.3	8.9
New Mexico	47.1	43.9	19.6	41.0	—	13.7	—	16.7
New York	33.5	12.5	12.9	23.6	8.5	19.9	16.1	3.6
North Carolina	23.7	8.1	18.0	24.2	—	19.2	18.1	10.3
North Dakota	21.2	7.8	13.7	7.6	19.4	7.9	7.0	9.6
Ohio	17.1	9.8	13.3	15.6	—	23.8	8.8	—
Oklahoma	34.2	23.9	24.8	21.7	24.5	5.9	18.2	23.0
Oregon	33.4	11.0	26.9	28.8	—	13.6	24.8	18.5
Pennsylvania	14.4	9.6	11.6	19.8	9.8	18.6	11.5	2.9
Rhode Island	—	—	—	—	—	—	—	—
South Carolina	28.7	22.0	13.5	13.0	—	27.2	11.3	19.7
South Dakota	19.7	13.9	24.6	27.7	15.8	10.8	12.5	20.8
Tennessee	27.8	26.4	26.8	27.0	15.6	24.2	21.0	16.5
Texas	30.4	13.9	16.3	18.2	26.4	23.6	18.1	12.2
Utah	43.7	11.7	22.4	24.8	19.5	16.3	26.3	12.5
Vermont	—	—	—	12.9	—	—	—	—
Virginia	34.0	14.0	13.9	16.7	2.2	11.2	10.1	—
Washington	46.0	24.3	17.6	28.9	9.7	23.2	29.1	33.3
West Virginia	16.0	17.1	32.2	32.9	—	13.0	16.6	6.1
Wisconsin	16.5	16.5	4.9	18.2	—	10.3	7.8	2.4
Wyoming	24.9	8.3	27.8	16.7	—	9.1	20.0	4.5

— Too few cases for reliable estimate

Source: U.S. Department of Education, National Center for Education Statistics, 1990-91 Schools and Staffing Survey (Teacher and School Questionnaires).
From: Richard M. Ingersoll, *Schools and Staffing Survey: Teacher Supply, Teacher Qualifications, and Teacher Turnover, 1990-91* (U.S. Department of Education, Washington, D.C.: National Center for Education Statistics, 1995), p. 28.

Appendix F: Minimum and Average Teacher Salaries, by State: 1993-94

	Minimum (beginning) salary	Average salary
United States	$23,258	$35,813
Alabama	22,500	28,659
Alaska	31,800	47,902
Arizona	21,825	31,825
Arkansas	19,694	28,312
California	25,500	40,636
Colorado	20,091	33,826
Connecticut	28,052	50,389
Delaware	22,795	37,469
District of Columbia	25,825	43,014
Florida	23,171	31,944
Georgia	21,885	29,214
Hawaii	25,100	36,564
Idaho	18,700	27,756
Illinois	25,171	39,416
Indiana	22,021	35,741
Iowa	20,709	30,760
Kansas	22,624	31,700
Kentucky	21,257	31,639
Louisiana	18,195	26,243
Maine	19,840	30,996
Maryland	24,703	39,475
Massachusetts	23,000	38,960
Michigan	24,400	45,218
Minnesota	23,408	36,146
Mississippi	18,833	25,153
Missouri	21,078	30,324
Montana	18,750	28,200
Nebraska	20,804	29,564
Nevada	24,155	37,181
New Hampshire	22,400	34,121
New Jersey	29,346	45,582
New Mexico	22,057	27,922
New York	26,903	45,772
North Carolina	20,002	29,727
North Dakota	17,453	25,506
Ohio	19,553	35,912
Oklahoma	22,181	27,612
Oregon	23,186	37,589
Pennsylvania	28,231	42,411
Rhode Island	23,365	39,261
South Carolina	20,533	29,414
South Dakota	18,935	25,259
Tennessee	19,625	30,514
Texas	21,806	30,519
Utah	18,787	28,056
Vermont	22,982	34,517
Virginia	23,273	33,472
Washington	23,183	35,860
West Virginia	21,450	30,549
Wisconsin	23,677	36,644
Wyoming	20,416	30,954

Source: American Federation of Teachers, *Survey and Analysis of Salary Trends, 1991, 1993 and 1994.*
Published in *Digest of Education Satistics 1995* (Washington, D.C.: National Center for Education Statistics, 1995), Table 78, p. 86.

Production Credits

Edwin Kuo, Inkspot Design
Art Director

Matthew Forrester
Production

para•graphics
Information Graphics